WORDS AND MEANINGS

*Essays presented to David Winton Thomas
on his retirement from the
Regius Professorship of Hebrew in the
University of Cambridge, 1968*

Professor David Winton Thomas

WORDS AND MEANINGS

ESSAYS PRESENTED TO

DAVID WINTON THOMAS

on his retirement from the
Regius Professorship of Hebrew in the
University of Cambridge, 1968

EDITED BY

PETER R. ACKROYD

Samuel Davidson Professor of Old Testament Studies in the
University of London King's College

AND

BARNABAS LINDARS, S.S.F.

Lecturer in Old Testament Studies in the University of Cambridge

CAMBRIDGE

AT THE UNIVERSITY PRESS

1968

Published by the Syndics of the Cambridge University Press
Bentley House, 200 Euston Road, London, N.W.1
American Branch: 32 East 57th Street, New York, N.Y.10022

© Cambridge University Press 1968

Library of Congress Catalogue Card Number: 68–29649

Standard Book Number: 521 07270 0

Printed in Great Britain
at the University Printing House, Cambridge
(Brooke Crutchley, University Printer)

CONTENTS

Contents

FOREWORD

I count it a great privilege to be asked to write a Foreword to this volume of essays in honour of Professor David Winton Thomas.

My own life has been greatly enriched by his friendship over the years. His was a name to conjure with in the Hebrew Room at Merchant Taylors' School—it was a source of encouragement to know that the man who had covered himself with glory at Cambridge had sat where I sat and grappled with Davidson and with Brown, Driver and Briggs. Then he succeeded two of my greatest teachers in the chair of the Regius Professorship of Hebrew at Cambridge, R. H. Kennett and S. A. Cook—a goodly succession, indeed.

Recently, as President of the Society for Old Testament Study in its Jubilee Year, I have been in touch with him again and have been enabled to see how much that learned Society owes to his leadership and inspiration. *Archaeology and Old Testament Study*, which he edited, alone will serve as a reminder of that fact.

My closest association with him was over a period of four years when together we worked on *The Revised Psalter*. It was a small, happy and closely knit team that produced that book, including among its members T. S. Eliot and C. S. Lewis. The man to whom, above all others, we looked for guidance in the realm of Hebrew scholarship was David Winton Thomas. Nor were we ever disappointed. From his store of Semitic scholarship he would draw out things new and old and, weighing them up with a nicely balanced sense of judgement, would ensure a translation which did not do despite to the meaning of the original.

The translation of the Bible into the multitudinous languages of the world is a task which calls for great and varied skills. Translators all over the globe have to rely on experts in the sphere of Semitics to guide them in their work. In the very front

Foreword

rank of experts in *Understanding the Old Testament* (to quote the title of his Ethel M. Wood Lecture, 1967), David Winton Thomas has stood for many years and will stand, we hope, for many more.

We salute him—with gratitude and affection.

DONALD EBOR.

Bishopthorpe
York

PREFACE

The contributors to this volume are a few only of those—
colleagues, pupils and friends—who would wish to share in
offering congratulations and good wishes to David Winton
Thomas on his retirement after a thirty-year tenure of the
Regius Chair of Hebrew in Cambridge. The whole range of
biblical and Hebrew scholarship has been influenced and enriched by his work, and by that meticulous accuracy and
balance of judgement which have characterized it throughout.
His qualities as a teacher have been enjoyed by those fortunate
enough to follow his classes on Hebrew texts. As a colleague to
many, he has brought support and stimulus. As a friend, and
particularly as one who takes much interest in the work of
younger scholars, he has given encouragement and the pleasure
of a companionship born of a real sympathy with other people.
And this has been shown equally in the kindness and hospitality
which has been offered so generously by his wife Marion and
himself over the years.

This volume is offered as a token of affection and respect. We
who have edited it have had the pleasure of warm support from
the contributors; it has been our regret that we could not include all who might have been invited, and that illness and
other unavoidable causes have prevented some who intended
to write for the volume. But we hope that as a modest contribution to an area of study to which D. Winton Thomas has given
so much, it may serve both to honour him and to convey good
wishes for his retirement, and also stimulate further the pursuit
of 'Words and Meanings'.

The Editors wish to express their gratitude to the Cambridge
University Press for undertaking to produce this volume. They
also acknowledge the assistance of Mrs Daphne Hope Brink in
the translation of the article by Professor Fohrer, of Pastor
Eckhard von Rabenau in the translation of the article by
Professor Eissfeldt, and of Mr K. W. Carley in compiling the
index.

P. R. A.
B. L.

ABBREVIATIONS

AJSL	*American Journal of Semitic Languages and Literature* (Chicago).
ANET	*Ancient Near Eastern Texts relating to the Old Testament*, ed. by J. B. Pritchard (2nd ed. Princeton, 1955).
ASTI	*Annual of the Swedish Theological Institute in Jerusalem* (Leiden).
ATD	*Das Alte Testament Deutsch* (Göttingen).
BASOR	*Bulletin of the American Schools of Oriental Research* (New Haven and Baltimore).
BDB	*A Hebrew and English Lexicon of the Old Testament*, by F. Brown, S. R. Driver and C. A. Briggs (Oxford, 1906).
BJRL	*Bulletin of the John Rylands Library* (Manchester).
BK	*Biblischer Kommentar* (Neukirchen).
BSOAS	*Bulletin of the School of Oriental and African Studies* (London).
BWANT	*Beiträge zur Wissenschaft vom Alten und Neuen Testament* (Stuttgart).
BZAW	*Beihefte zur Zeitschrift für die Alttestamentliche Wissenschaft* (Giessen).
CBQ	*Catholic Biblical Quarterly* (Washington).
DOTT	*Documents from Old Testament Times*, ed. by D. Winton Thomas (London, 1958).
EB	*Encyclopaedia Britannica* (London).
ET	*The Expository Times* (Edinburgh).
GK	*Gesenius–Kautzsch Hebrew Grammar*, rev. by A. E. Cowley (Oxford, 1910).
HAT	*Handbuch zum Alte Testament* (Tübingen).
HTR	*Harvard Theological Review* (Cambridge, Mass.).
HUCA	*Hebrew Union College Annual* (Cincinnati).
IB	*The Interpreter's Bible* (New York and Nashville).
ICC	*The International Critical Commentary* (Edinburgh).
JAOS	*Journal of the American Oriental Society* (Boston and New Haven).

Abbreviations

JBL	*Journal of Biblical Literature* (New York, New Haven and Philadelphia).
JC	*Jewish Chronicle* (London).
JJS	*Journal of Jewish Studies* (London).
JPhil	*Journal of Philology* (London and Cambridge).
JPOS	*Journal of the Palestine Oriental Society* (Jerusalem).
JQR	*Jewish Quarterly Review* (Philadelphia).
JSS	*Journal of Semitic Studies* (Manchester).
JTS	*Journal of Theological Studies* (Oxford).
KAI	*Kanaanäische und aramäische Inschriften* (Wiesbaden).
KAT	*Kommentar zum Alten Testament* (Leipzig).
KBL	*Lexicon in Veteris Testamenti Libros*, by L. Koehler and W. Baumgartner (Leiden, 1953).
LSJ	*A Greek–English Lexicon*, by H. G. Liddell and R. Scott, new ed. H. S. Jones (Oxford, 1925–40).
OBL	*Orientalia et Biblica Lovaniensia* (Louvain).
OLZ	*Orientalistische Literaturzeitung* (Leipzig).
PEFQS	*Palestine Exploration Fund Quarterly Statement* (London).
PEQ	*Palestine Exploration Quarterly* (London).
PGL	*Patrologiae Cursus Completus*. Series Graeco–Latina, by J. P. Migne (Paris, 1857–66).
PJB	*Palästinajahrbuch* (Berlin).
PL	*Patrologiae Cursus Completus*. Series Latina, by J. P. Migne (Paris, 1844–55).
Rev. Sém.	*Revue Sémitique* (Paris).
RGG	*Die Religion in Geschichte und Gegenwart* (Tübingen).
TDNT	*Theological Dictionary of the New Testament* (Grand Rapids). English translation of *TWNT*.
TLZ	*Theologische Literaturzeitung* (Leipzig).
TWNT	*Theologisches Wörterbuch zum Neuen Testament*, ed. by G. Kittel and G. Friedrich (Stuttgart). English translation, *TDNT*.
TZ	*Theologische Zeitschrift* (Basle).
VT	*Vetus Testamentum* (Leiden).
VTS	*Supplements to Vetus Testamentum* (Leiden).
WC	*The Westminster Commentaries* (London).
ZAW	*Zeitschrift für die Alttestamentliche Wissenschaft* (Giessen).

Abbreviations

ZDMG	*Zeitschrift der Deutschen Morgenländischen Gesellschaft* (Leipzig).
ZNTW	*Zeitschrift für die Neutestamentliche Wissenschaft* (Giessen).

Aq.	Aquila.
AJV	American Jewish Version.
AV	Authorized Version.
BH	*Biblia Hebraica*, ed. by R. Kittel, third edition (1937).
LXX	Septuagint Version.
MT	Massoretic Text.
NEB	New English Bible.
OL	Old Latin.
Pesh.	Peshiṭta Version.
RSV	Revised Standard Version.
RSV[mg]	Revised Standard Version margin.
RV	Revised Version.
RV[mg]	Revised Version margin.
Sa'ad.	Sa'adyah.
Symm.	Symmachus.
Syrohex.	Syrohexapla.
Targ. O.	Targum of Onkelos.
Targ. Ps.-J.	Targum of Pseudo-Jonathan.
Theod.	Theodotion.
Vulg.	Vulgate Version.

1

MEANING AND EXEGESIS

by Peter R. Ackroyd

I

Ideally the meaning of any word in a given passage should be established in order that the exegesis of the whole passage can be set out without prejudice. In practice, such a counsel of perfection is rarely to be followed consistently. For while it is true that in many biblical passages the sense of an otherwise unknown word may be determined clearly—either by reference to cognate words in the same language or in closely related languages, or by the obvious sense required (and here poetic passages may provide the added assistance of a verbal parallel) —yet it is often the case that the really debatable sentence remains difficult to expound, because the precise shade of meaning cannot be readily determined either by philological research or by an examination of context. In an unpublished paper read to the Society for Old Testament Study at its Jubilee Meeting in York in July 1967, David Winton Thomas reviewed recent work on Isa. 53—work in which he himself has, over the years, played a notable part. The problems of interpretation in this particular chapter are well known, and not to be solved ultimately without full reference to the wider issues of its relationship to the other chapters of Deutero-Isaiah, though not exclusively to those which make use of the much-debated term עבד, so often isolated whether intentionally or unconsciously from their context. In the course of the paper, he expressed again, as on other occasions when discussing the exact connotation of a Hebrew word,[1] the conviction that exegesis must depend upon precise delimitation of meaning; it must not be allowed to determine the particular sense in which a word is used in the passage under discussion in order to provide support for one

---

[1] Cf. e.g. 'Some Observations on the Hebrew Root חדל', *VTS*, IV (1957), 8–16; see p. 16.

particular line of interpretation.[1] Yet, sound though the advice undoubtedly is, the questions remain: What kind of criteria exist for the understanding of the meanings of words, and how far are these criteria adequate to the problems of biblical exegesis?

In recent years, biblical scholars have become sensitive to the dangers of philology, partly as a result of the sometimes rather negative strictures of James Barr.[2] The warning has been properly given that words cannot be used as counters. To establish the root meaning of a word does not establish its meaning in a given passage. In some respects the problem for Hebrew is unlike that for some modern languages. It may be reasonably postulated that a particular word in English is derivable from a particular word in Latin. Sufficient evidence of usage may be available for there to be a tracing of the semantic development of this particular word, and this may show, in some degree, the process by which that one word's meanings have changed; it may be seen that its various modern usages— often apparently very remote from the original Latin—are intelligible in the light of philology. Yet even here, when account is taken not simply of the 'correct' usage of a word— according to some standard which we may profess—but also of its popular use, we may soon observe that shades of meaning are present which are much less readily explicable, and the line between correct and colloquial use is never a completely clear one. (The word 'wild' in its varieties of modern use, both English and American, is a good example.) It is clear too that anyone who ventures to speak in a foreign language, related to one already familiar to him, will make all manner of errors if he supposes that corresponding words have the same or similar meanings. This was the error into which the German-born American immigrant Hyman Kaplan fell when he was describing 'nature' and spoke passionately of 'de trees, de boids, de grass, de bloomers' (*The Education of Hyman Kaplan*, by L. Q. Ross). To

---

[1] A comparison may also be made with the opening of his Ethel M. Wood lecture for 1967, *Understanding the Old Testament* (London, 1967), see pp. 3 ff., and the introduction to *Archaeology and Old Testament Study* (Oxford, 1967), see pp. xxviii–xxx.

[2] *The Semantics of Biblical Language* (Oxford, 1961).

one who knows German and English, Dutch may seem fairly readily intelligible, but there are many snares in the supposition that its finer nuances are appreciated. Even at a simple level, it may be clearly intelligible to the linguist that 'satt' in German should mean 'satisfied with food', and that the same word, though differently spelt, 'zat' in Dutch, should mean 'drunk'; failure to recognize this may cause embarrassment. The stories of the curious errors perpetrated by translation machines only serve to show that, while technical equivalents may be found, there may still be something wanting to the full conveying of meaning for which only a really deep understanding of both the languages involved can possibly be adequate.

A further comment may be added here on the already mentioned use of words as 'counters', interchangeable between different contexts. It has been rightly urged that we have to allow for differences of usage, dictated by context; the fact that a word in one passage bears a particular meaning does not mean that in other passages it can automatically be understood in the same way. A criticism made of the rendering of the Greek New Testament in the New English Bible has been that, for example in Romans, the Greek word δικαιοσύνη is not always rendered by the same English equivalent. (As a result, the NEB has been quite properly found to be of no very great use as a crib for the Greek text.) But the fact is that the shades of meaning expressed by δικαιοσύνη are different in range from those of the most natural English equivalents; if these shades of meaning are to be conveyed, then a choice has to be made, sometimes of one word, sometimes of another, though admittedly as soon as this is done, exegesis enters into the picture, and indeed, except in a very limited degree, translation cannot avoid a certain exegetical element.

But while this is true, there must also be a recognition of overtones in biblical material. Such overtones are present in every language which has a literature whether written or oral; among both the more sophisticated and the more simple, a particular word or phrase may evoke a well-known story. Sensitiveness to such overtones will increase the richness of understanding of the individual concerned. This is likely to be true of the biblical material in a special degree because of its virtually universal religious content and concern, though the limitation of the literature with which we are familiar to a relatively small corpus can inevitably lead us astray into finding allusions which are not there. Later rabbinic discussion often seemed to centre upon what we should regard as the minutiae of the text; lists were made of the occurrences of the same form, and marginal notes added containing such information—the kind of information which the modern reader has available in lexicon and concordance. The fact that the same, slightly unusual, form occurs perhaps three times immediately suggests a link; much discussion in more modern commentaries of literary structure and editing has laid stress upon occurrences of the same word by which it was often thought that dependence of one passage upon another could be demonstrated. This was particularly true if the word was a rare one, perhaps occurring only in the two passages in question. In this kind of discussion far too little allowance was made for the limitations of our material, and for such a phenomenon as that aptly described as 'hibernation' by which in the chances of the material a word may occur once in a very early passage and then be unattested until a relatively late date.[1]

But we must nevertheless allow for the possibility, and indeed the probability, that already in biblical times overtones were discernible by the sensitive reader or hearer which are not immediately apparent to us. Thus the use of the word התיצבו in 2 Chron. 20: 17 may appear to be neutral; it may not seem to need any explanation that the writer chose this word rather than some other.[2] But it is not unreasonable to hear an overtone here from Exod. 14: 13 and to realize that the ancient reader could catch an echo of the great moment of religious experience of the Exodus in this apparently simple word. Our understanding of 2 Chron. 20: 17 is therefore determined not simply by a discussion of the words used and their meanings, but also by this allusion which we may suppose to be present, by which

---

[1] For a comment on this, cf. Winton Thomas, *Understanding the Old Testament*, pp. 13 f.

[2] On the problem of discovering why a biblical writer 'chose' a particular word, cf. also below.

Meaning and exegesis

התיצבו virtually becomes a 'counter', inviting reminiscence of a particularly instructive kind.

If we return now to the question of philology, we may observe that its problems are different in Hebrew, because the 'origin' or 'original meaning' of a word cannot with any certainty be obtained by study of the cognate languages. It is proper to recognize that other Semitic languages, especially Accadian and Arabic with richer vocabularies, are likely to have preserved many roots unfamiliar in biblical Hebrew as it has been traditionally understood. Yet it is not necessarily possible to show a chronological linkage. An Arabic word may suggest the possibility that a corresponding root existed in Hebrew, a root now concealed by reason of the identity of its consonants with some other, much more familiar word. The root ידע, which D. Winton Thomas has shown to be divisible into ידע I and ידע II, is a case in point, and some further comments will be made on this subsequently. But the large number of unaccepted suggestions of this kind which have found their place in learned articles over the past half century—suggestions often made with a proper tentativeness and sometimes subsequently withdrawn by their originators—shows that unless corroborative evidence can be found elsewhere, in the ancient versions for example, there can be no more than conjecture in such proposals. Even where a corresponding root may be traced in Accadian, the problem is not necessarily any less difficult. For while it may appear *prima facie* reasonable to regard as more original a word which occurs in a text more ancient than most biblical passages, it is not necessarily justifiable to assume that the Hebrew is directly derived from the Accadian; possibly both are to be ultimately derived separately from a more ancient, hypothetical proto-semitic form, and the semantic development may be quite different. The definition of the meaning of נביא in relation to Accadian *nabū* is inevitably still debated; the nature of its meaning in Hebrew is more precisely definable only in terms of use. Accadian did not, so far as we know, use this root for the expression of the peculiarly specialized sense of נביא.[1]

---

[1] The nearest point of contact is in the use of *nabū* in the sense 'vocation, called (by a deity)'. I am indebted to D.J.Wiseman for confirming this point.

Even where, as in passages in Ezekiel, the presence of a number of otherwise unknown Hebrew words which may be explained from Accadian suggests the direct influence of the vocabulary of the community in which the prophet was living—and hence this has been used as an argument to defend the traditional location of the prophet in Babylonia[1]—it must be admitted that the argument is too much of a negative kind to be totally persuasive. Relatively so little is known to us of the vocabulary of earlier Hebrew that we cannot be sure that such occurrences are not due merely to the chances of the material we possess. Probability may be shown: certainty cannot be established.

To the linguist who lays emphasis on words and their forms and who treats them as units to be handled independent of context, the search for meaning in contexts only is not entirely satisfying. It may well be that, especially with the limited material at our disposal, we can only hope to say that a given word appears to be used in a given passage in a particular sense—and to relate this tentatively to other uses of the same word either in the same sense or in a readily relatable meaning. Context remains an untrustworthy guide since—especially when some vital theological question is at issue—the uncertainty about the whole will inevitably lead to uncertainty about the parts.

An example may serve to show the kind of problem which appears. The explanation of the name באר שבע depends upon whether the second part of the name is regarded as derivable from the word meaning 'seven' or from the word meaning 'oath, swear'. On a philological basis, a case could be made out for either meaning. On a contextual basis, the same uncertainty is found, for we have two alternative narratives offering different explanations of how the place was named. In the one case (Gen. 21), the reference to שבע כבשת הצאן (verses 28 ff.) provides a pointer to the former interpretation, whereas the following verse 31 explains the place-name as due to the swearing of an oath. In the other (Gen. 26), no reference to

---

[1] Cf. the remarks on Babylonian influence in the language of Ezekiel by G. R. Driver, 'Ezekiel's Inaugural Vision', *VT*, I (1951), 60-2.

'seven' appears in the narrative at all, and the explanation is related solely to the swearing of an oath—שבעה (verse 31). It seems likely enough that there is in fact a further complication in that the narrative in chapter 21 is not all of one piece, and that two alternative traditions concerning the place are here combined.[1] But the fact remains that if we work from context alone, then we have to affirm that either possibility is valid. If it can be shown that the place-name could only have been derived from one or other of the roots proposed,[2] then we shall have to affirm that the other explanation represents a piece of popular, and in this case false, etymology. We should not, however, be any nearer then to understanding the import of the narratives. We cannot say that the story elements which are philologically unsound are necessarily historically untrue, in the sense that the events described cannot be a description of the actual events which led to the naming of the place. (In this particular example, we have in any case two narratives which use the 'oath' theme; and these can hardly both be historical.) If the place is named because there were seven springs, then the oath story is a piece of attached legend; but its attachment has taken place because its narrators believed that the meaning of the name was appropriately given by reference to the swearing of an oath. The alternative tradition which links the name with seven and specifically with seven lambs is equally open to question, even though its philological basis might be regarded as more sound. Context does not here provide an adequate answer. But from the point of view of exegesis, nor does correct linguistic explanation give any sort of final answer. If we are to interpret the material, then we have to take account of the way it was understood by its ancient transmitters. Meaning—in the broader sense—is more significant than mere philology. Popular etymologies may be frowned on by the purist, but they are nevertheless influential in the development of thought. The much-debated naming of שמואל in 1 Sam. 1—explained in such a way, from the root שאל, as to suggest the possibility that in reality the story was originally not connected with Samuel at

---

[1] Cf. e.g. the comments of G. von Rad, *Genesis* (E.T. London, Philadelphia, 1961), pp. 230 ff.   [2] So *KBL*, p. 105, accepts 'seven'.

all but with שאול (Saul)—shows how a question of the nature
and limits of popular etymology may influence the overall
interpretation of the narrative. For if this is really a Saul
narrative, now interwoven with other motifs not connected with
Saul at all, then some light is shed both on the recession of the
Saul traditions behind those of Samuel, and also on the evolu-
tion of the Samuel narratives to give to that now so complex
figure a prominence which it did not necessarily originally
enjoy. But if popular etymology can stretch so far as to see an
equation in שמואל-שאול—and popular etymology is not nice
about spelling but appears to be more influenced by sound and
by general similarity, and does not work according to the neat
rules of vowel and consonant change—then this particular line
of approach to these traditions is precluded.

II

The problem of false—popular—etymology leads on into
another more obviously theological question. This concerns the
influence in theological thinking and formulation of explanations which are subsequently shown to be philologically
erroneous. The debate about typological exegesis in recent
years not improperly begins by recognizing that typology is a
characteristic of some parts of the biblical exegesis of itself.
Thus not only is such exegesis to be found in early Christian
writings, for example, in Paul: it is also demonstrable in such
expository material as Deutero-Isaiah, with its 'Exodus typology'.[1] To understand the biblical material, we have to enter
sympathetically—as גרים, as H. Wheeler Robinson advised—
into the thought world. Otherwise we may dismiss out of hand
a way of approach which is strange. But the further question
is less easy to resolve. How far is typological exegesis still ad-
missible? How far are biblical theological statements determined
by or limited by such a method? How far are conclusions drawn
which may be suspected of being theologically invalid? How

[1] Cf. B. W. Anderson, 'Exodus Typology in Second Isaiah', in *Israel's Prophetic Heritage*, ed. B. W. Anderson and W. Harrelson (Philadelphia and London, 1962), pp. 177–95.

far is an exegetical structure built upon a misunderstanding to be allowed to stand? By what criteria can we test its theological truth? Out of exegesis have arisen conventions of use. Traditionally the words of Gen. 3: 15 have been taken to be a promise of the Christian gospel and termed the *protevangelion*. The passage is read, therefore, as the first in the series of nativity lections. Such an understanding is remote from the original purport of the narrative; but original purport is only part of the meaning, as this material has been read. The later expositions are a legitimate part of the history of the material, and even if they are historically or philologically erroneous, they are part of what we have to handle. By what criteria do we adjudicate between a sound and an unsound development of thought? Much older Christian exegesis has tended to distinguish between 'Judaic' developments, leading on into rabbinic thought, and often believed to be antagonistic to some other development, leading on into Christian thinking and thought to be more true. But such a simplified distinction is very unsatisfactory, especially in view of the proper emphasis on the intimacy of the relationship between the thought of Jesus and the early Christians and their contemporaries in the Jewish community.

That Job 19: 25 ff. presents substantial problems of interpretation is evident. The precise definition of the גאל of verse 25 remains uncertain. While the most natural view appears to be that there is a reference here to God as the 'kinsman' who acts to protect a man's interests, and in particular to preserve his memory (cf. the book of Ruth for a typical delineation), it must be admitted that this is obliquely expressed in such a way as to leave room for doubt. And the accompanying phrases are no easier to interpret, if only because each of them can be interpreted so as to refer to experience within this life, or to experience beyond death, whether that is thought of in terms of the narrower limits of the conception of Sheol, or in terms of a dawning understanding of the nature of a real continuance of relationship with God. But for the modern Christian exegete at least, the influence of centuries of interpretation—with a reference to New Testament events and experience, and with overtones of Handel's *Messiah* 'I know that my redeemer liveth'—inevitably has its repercussions. To dismiss this as mere later construction is no more legitimate than to exclude from our consideration of the biblical text everything which may be remotely described as a gloss, with the intention of operating only with the original wording. Old Testament and New Testament studies have revealed the precariousness of the attempt at getting back to origins—*ipsissima verba* whether of a prophet or of Jesus; at no point can there be absolute separation between a message which was spoken on a specific occasion, sometimes identifiable, more often only to be conjectured, and the way in which that message has been incorporated into the larger presentation to which it now belongs, the subsequent understanding of that message in new contexts of which later Christian history and later Jewish history offer two related but distinct types. The development of Christian exegesis of Job 19 : 25 ff. is one possible development. The recognition of totally erroneous interpretation of a particular word or phrase excludes such interpretation from modern use. But it does not undo the history of exegesis in which the modern interpreter stands at the end of a particular tradition, and from which inevitably he approaches the problems of a particular passage. The very questions which we ask about interpretation are in part conditioned by this tradition. So far as the particular example under discussion is concerned, it may be asked how far the line of interpretation, oversimply presented by Handel, conforms to the emphasis of the book of Job upon the absoluteness of divine action in redemption; and if it does so conform, how far is it not in harmony with that book, though it is clear that it represents a narrowing of the field of choice and a restricting of understanding to one particular development which does not cover all that might have come out of those words?

III

These more general comments may be clarified by a reference to a particular range of problems of meaning and exegesis, linked with various occurrences of the Hebrew root ידע. As is well known, this root has been the subject of prolonged study by D. Winton Thomas over the past thirty years and more, and full details of the discussions of some of its occurrences may be found in the bibliographical list included in this volume. It has been shown, and to many it seems conclusive, that two distinct Hebrew roots are here subsumed under the one form: ידע I with its meaning of 'to know', with a variety of connected senses which include such ideas as 'care for' and denote various kinds of intimacy of relationship, among which the sexual use of the term is presumably to be included; ידע II with the meaning of 'be made submissive, still, quiet, at rest' with a similarly wide range of senses in its diverse usage. Perhaps the most obviously probable of all the occurrences of this second root is to be found in Judg. 16: 9[1] ולא נודע כחו where the new sense of 'be made submissive' is confirmed by the Syriac rendering *'ttzy'* ('be disturbed') and by the comparable statement in 16: 19 in which the word לענותו suggests the idea of 'humiliation' implied in the use of ידע II. Direct support from the ancient versions is in fact hardly available for any of the other occurrences postulated for this root, though there are some indirect indications of such support and of Jewish tradition (in regard to Isa. 53: 3) which suggest a preservation of the alternative sense which ידע II offers. For the most part, almost inevitably, the decision as to which Hebrew root is present depends on a consideration of the sense of the passage—in some measure therefore on exegesis—the suitability or otherwise to the context of a meaning properly derivable from ידע I, that is, one which may be found without the kind of semantic acrobatics in which commentators have sometimes engaged. If on balance it appears that a more natural meaning can be obtained by invoking ידע II, then this is a justifiable procedure.

But can we go further than this? If we concentrate on two theologically very significant passages—Isa. 53: 3 and 11—we have possibilities of interpretation which are of considerable significance in the understanding of this obviously difficult but vital section. The rendering of Isa. 53: 3 וידוע חלי as 'humbled, disciplined by sickness'[2] finds some support in Jewish

[1] Cf. *JTS*, xxxv (1934), 298 ff.
[2] First proposed by G. R. Driver in dependence on D. Winton Thomas in *JTS*, xxxviii (1937), 48 f.

tradition in the recognition that the עבד was 'broken by disease'.[1]
The further occurrence of ידע in 53:11 in the phrase מעמל נפשו
יראה ישבע בדעתו יצדיק צדיק עבדי לרבים introduces a suggestive
understanding of the relationship between the humiliation of
the עבד and the function which he is divinely appointed to
fulfil.

It is not to be wondered at that the Hebrew root ידע II has
been confused with the obviously much more common ידע I.
But this confusion poses a certain problem. For in so far as
evidence is to be found—in the versions and in later Jewish
tradition—that such a second meaning was known, it becomes
to that extent more difficult to understand how, in a passage in
which the idea of humiliation is so entirely appropriate, the
'tradition' should have so largely lost sight of this meaning.
The almost universal testimony of the ancient witnesses that
the meaning here is to be connected with ידע I is impressive
and this has persisted until very recently. Even now, the new
understanding has not penetrated as far as one might have expected.[2]
In the case of Isa. 53:3, this may be understood from
the fact that there is ancient evidence, both in the versions and
from Qumran, for a reading יודע, for which the rendering
'familiar with' is appropriate where it is problematic for ידוע.
The original form here could presumably be read in either way,
and traditional exegesis came down on the side of 'familiar'
rather than observing the occurrence of a rare root. In the case
of 53:11 the problems are more complex, and the interpretation
of the verse depends not merely upon the meaning of single
words, but on questions of textual corruption—is צדיק due to
dittography in MT or is its omission in some manuscripts due
to an equally explicable haplography?—and of metrical division
—does בדעתו belong with what follows (so MT) or with what

---

[1] Cf. D. Winton Thomas in *JTS*, xxxviii (1937), 404 f.
[2] RSV keeps 'acquainted' and 'knowledge', and does not even deign to
notice the alternative in its marginal notes. So too the Jerusalem Bible in
53:3 has 'familiar' and in 53:11 has another variant 'by his sufferings',
following one Hebrew MS. Among modern commentators some (e.g. C. R.
North, *The Second Isaiah* (Oxford, 1964), pp. 232 f., 237 f., 244 f.; C.
Westermann, *Das Buch Jesaja Kap 40–66* (*ATD*, xix, 1966), 20 ff.; J. Muilenburg,
IB, v (1956), 620, 630) accept one of the new possibilities but not
the other.

Meaning and exegesis

precedes? D. Winton Thomas proposes taking the word with what precedes and renders:

> 'When the righteous one[1] shall have drunk deep[2] of his anguish,
> When he shall have received his full measure of humiliation[3]...'

This provides a good poetic parallel and avoids almost all emendation of the text. It commends itself on these grounds, but it is not the only interpretation possible.

The resolving of the broader questions of meaning and exegesis in this passage is beyond both the space available for this article and the competence of its author. But a further comment on the nature of the problem may be ventured, a comment of necessity tentative because it attempts to penetrate further into the mind of the prophet-poet himself. If we ask why he used the root ידע in these two contexts, it is clear that we cannot expect to get a satisfying answer. What considerations of usage, of sound quality, of assonance, of length may not have been influential—consciously or unconsciously—in the selection of ידע rather than such other words as might have been employed? In view of what has often been said about the Hebrew love of play upon words and meanings[4]—and this has been seen particularly in Deutero-Isaiah[5]—may we not wonder if the prophet chose ידע because of its subtle overtones? (If a conscious play upon words was intended, was the use in 53: 3 designed to convey a different sense from that in 53: 11?) In 53: 3, its use could suggest both humiliation and intimacy;[6] the divergent text

---

[1] Reading צדיק from 11b here, though it may be questioned whether this is necessary, and whether the simple omission of this word is not to be preferred. [2] רוה = ראה.
[3] So in the translation circulated at the S.O.T.S. meeting at York, July 1967.
[4] Cf. the article by G. R. Driver in this volume. Play upon meanings may be traced in Amharic poetry (cf. D. N. Levine, *Wax and Gold* (Chicago, 1965), pp. 5 ff. My colleague Michael A. Knibb has drawn my attention to this). It may also be found in Arabic (cf. A. Guillaume, in *Promise and Fulfilment*, ed. F. F. Bruce (Edinburgh, 1963), pp. 110 ff.).
[5] Thus we may observe ראה in one sense in 53: 10 and in another sense (= רוה) in 53: 11. For a critical discussion of this theme, cf. D. F. Payne, 'Characteristic Word-play in "Second Isaiah": a Reappraisal', *JSS*, XII (1967), 207–29.
[6] How far are such overtones also to be heard in the way in which ידע was understood in its sexual connotation?

13

forms could preserve the two alternatives. Subsequent understanding emphasized the latter, but the memory of the former
could not be quite lost. In 53: 11, 'knowledge' in the sense of
'knowledge of God'—that intimacy which a man may enjoy
in contact with the deity—is an appropriate overtone for the
'humiliation' of the עבד. Indeed, in another passage, intimacy
with the Deity is described in such terms: in Mic. 6: 8 the form
הצנע—commonly rendered 'humbly'—has been shown by D.
Winton Thomas himself to have rather the sense of 'proper
respect, due circumspection'.[1] To the pious Hebrew—and perhaps we should say to the religiously inclined of any tradition—
there can hardly be 'knowledge of God' where there is not
a proper circumspection, a proper submissiveness or humility.
When the Old Testament employs the expression דעת אלהים it is
right that we should emphasize that this is not intellectual
knowledge, or not that alone, but rather the intimacy of a
personal relationship. May it not also carry the overtone of
'religion' in the sense in which this term has often been understood, namely, a proper regard for the situation in which a man
finds himself in the presence of his God?

If such an argument appears to be designed to get the best of
all possible exegetical worlds, it must be remembered that the
use of words is a highly sophisticated matter. A man's choice of
words, particularly if he is a poet, is an expression of the depth
of his understanding; to subject his utterances too rigidly to the
formal rules, and to limit his meaning to one straight equivalent,
may be to miss the subtle pictures which he evokes by the use of
this word rather than that, this image rather than some other.[2]

[1] Cf. *JJS*, 1 (1949), 182 ff. Cf. also Bo Reicke, 'The Knowledge of the
Suffering Servant' in *Das Ferne und Nahe Wort* (*Festschrift L. Rost*), ed.
F. Maass (Berlin, 1967), pp. 186–92, who interprets 'knowledge' as
'obedience'.

[2] D. F. Payne, 'Old Testament Exegesis and the Problem of Ambiguity',
ASTI, v (1967), 48–68, appeared too late to be discussed here. It enters
some important cautions in regard to the possibility of ambiguity,
and in particular offers criticism of the linguistic discussions of the
root(s) ידע.

2

ON THE SYNTAX OF
אהיה אשר אהיה IN EXODUS 3: 14

by Bertil Albrektson

I

Most papers on the explanation of the divine name in Exod. 3:
14 seem to begin with a statement that 'the passage has remained
one of the unsolved difficulties for both translators and exegetes'[1]
or words to that effect. The short sentence אהיה אשר אהיה has
been understood and interpreted in an almost endless number
of ways. Indeed the very abundance of explanations—several
of them advanced with impressive learning and admirable in-
genuity—serves to emphasize the ambiguity of the sentence and
could perhaps be taken to support the view that the statement
is an evasive and mystifying answer to Moses's question about the
name of God. In fact Martin Noth, in his well-known commentary on the Book of Exodus, asserts with a certain resigna-
tion that the words allow of several explanations and that it is
hardly possible to settle the question conclusively.[2] Nor is the
purpose of this article primarily to advocate one particular
exegesis of the disputed words, still less to suggest a new interpretation. My intention is simply to discuss a question which must
be studied before we begin to ask how the divine answer should
be expounded, namely, the question of the syntactical structure
and the correct translation of the sentence. And I hope that
here at least, in insisting on the necessity of dealing with the
philological problem before any attempt at interpretation and
exegesis, I may prove a faithful pupil of the eminent hebraist
to whom this discussion is gratefully dedicated and who has
constantly tried to impress this rule of method on his pupils.
I do not intend to investigate either the problem of the original

---

[1] So W. A. Irwin, 'Exod. 3: 14', *AJSL*, LVI (1939), 297.
[2] *Das zweite Buch Mose. Exodus. Übersetzt und erklärt (ATD*, V, 1959), p. 31.
English translation, *Exodus* (London, 1962), p. 44.

significance of the tetragrammaton or the correctness of the explanation which is given in Exod. 3: 14; nor do I wish to consider the theory about an earlier and more original formulation of this explanation which may lie behind the present wording, as suggested by P. Haupt,[1] and accepted by W. F. Albright,[2] and others.[3] I am only concerned with the correct analysis of the syntax of the divine answer to Moses in the Exodus narrative as it has come down to us in the Massoretic text.

The problem of the correct grammatical analysis of אהיה אשר אהיה is as a rule not given much attention by the commentators. Generally they take for granted that the syntax and the translation of the sentence do not involve any difficulties, and they simply accept the traditional translation which is represented —with minor variations without material differences—in most editions of the Bible: 'I am that I am' (AV and RV), 'I am who I am' (RSV), 'I will be that I will be' (RV[mg]), or 'I will be what I will be' (RSV[mg]). As a rule opinions are divided only on the question of the precise import of this statement.

Lately, however, there have been attempts to master the difficult problem of the correct interpretation by contesting the current translation and propounding an analysis of the syntax of the three words resulting in a new translation: 'I am the one who is', which creates also a new basis for the endeavours to reach the real meaning of God's reply to Moses. Recently this new understanding has been maintained by Joh. Lindblom of Lund in an interesting article on the explanation of the divine name in Exod. 3: 14.[4] For the grammatical problem Lindblom also refers to a detailed investigation by E. Schild of Toronto, who reached the same conclusion.[5] Schild's analysis of the syn-

---

[1] 'Der Name Jahwe', *OLZ*, xii (1909), cols. 211 ff.

[2] 'The Name *Yahweh*', *JBL*, xliii (1924), 376.

[3] E.g. D. N. Freedman, 'The Name of the God of Moses', *JBL*, lxxix (1960), 152 ff. (with some modification of Haupt's suggestion), and F. M. Cross, Jr., 'Yahweh and the God of the Patriarchs', *HTR*, lv (1962), 255.

[4] 'Noch einmal die Deutung des Jahwe-Namens in Ex. 3: 14', *ASTI*, iii (1964), 4 ff., esp. pp. 8 f.

[5] 'On Exodus 3: 14—"I am that I am"', *VT*, iv (1954), 296 ff.

tactical problem, especially the understanding of the relative clause, seems to be the most exhaustive so far.[1]

The situation appears to be that the only detailed discussions of the syntax of אהיה אשר אהיה in Exod. 3: 14 have been provided by scholars whose aim is to defend the unusual translation 'I am the one who is', whereas those who retain the traditional rendering 'I am who I am' or some similar translation have not in fact thought it necessary to discuss the syntactical question at all. It seems justified, therefore, to reconsider the subject and to examine in some detail the arguments which have been put forward in favour of the new syntactical analysis. Moreover, the very fact that this new thesis has been defended by so eminent a scholar as Lindblom certainly makes it worthy of serious consideration.

II

It seems appropriate first to present fairly fully the view of the syntactical structure of the sentence which is the basis of the new translation 'I am the one who is', and the arguments for it. As mentioned above, the most detailed investigation is that of Schild, and so I shall in the main follow his exposition.

Schild first gives an account of the traditional interpretations and notes some minor variations between them. He then observes: 'All these interpretations rest on the same syntactical approach to the text of our passage. They must be regarded as highly questionable, however, in view of a point of syntax which seems to have been generally overlooked. On the basis of the syntax of the relative clause in Hebrew, an entirely different translation may be obtained and yield a greatly preferable meaning.'[2] This point of syntax is the rule which in

---

[1] The most detailed recent study of the sentence is otherwise a thesis by M. Reisel, *Observations on* אהיה אשר אהיה, הואהא, *and* שם המפורש (dissertation, Amsterdam, 1957). Reisel's treatment of the question of the correct translation is however not quite clear: on p. 13, for instance, he seems to accept Schild's view, which is said to be 'undoubtedly supported by the facts', but his own final translation on p. 24 runs: 'I *shall* (show to) be, who I *would* (show to) be', which is precisely the type of translation that Schild is arguing against. [2] *VT*, IV (1954), 297.

Cowley's translation of Gesenius–Kautzsch's Hebrew grammar
(*GK*) has been formulated thus (§ 138*d*): 'If the governing substantive forms part of a statement made in the first or second
person, the retrospective pronoun (or the subject of the apposi-
tional clause) is in the same person.' A typical case, quoted in
the grammar, is Gen. 15: 7 אני יהוה אשר הוצאתיך מאור כשדים
'I am Yhwh who brought you out of Ur of the Chaldeans'.
But Schild is not satisfied with the formulation in Gesenius–
Kautzsch as far as the bracketed part is concerned. He points
out that it applies only if 'the governing substantive is the *subject* of the relative clause', and suggests the following wording
of the bracketed part of the rule: 'If the governing substantive
is the subject of a relative clause and is, in the main clause,
equated with, or defined as, a personal pronoun, then the predicate of the relative clause agrees with that personal pronoun.'[1]
He then proceeds to analyse the different ways in which the
governing substantive may be equated with the personal pro-
nouns.[2] There are four such cases. The governing substantive
may be (1) a personal pronoun, as e.g. in 1 Sam. 25: 33 וברוכה
את אשר כלתני 'and blessed be you who restrained me...';
(2) a vocative, i.e. in implicit apposition to the personal pronoun of the second person, as e.g. in Isa. 51: 17 קומי ירושלם אשר
שתית 'arise, O Jerusalem, who have drunk...'; (3) a predicate noun (in the main clause) defining a personal pronoun,
as e.g. in Judg. 13: 11 האתה האיש אשר־דברת אל־האשה 'Are you
the man who spoke to the woman?'; (4) a noun in apposition
to the predicate noun defining a personal pronoun (in the main
clause), as e.g. in Lev. 20: 24 אני יהוה אלהיכם אשר־הבדלתי אתכם
מן־העמים 'I am Yhwh, your God, who have separated you from
the peoples'.

The next step in the argument is to establish that the same
rule applies to the type of sentence called 'independent relative
clause', which is not dependent on a noun but itself expresses
a substantival idea.[3] In such clauses אשר is usually translated
'he who', etc. One of the examples quoted is 1 Chron. 21: 17
אני־הוא אשר־חטאתי והרע הרעותי, which is rendered 'I am the

---

[1] *VT*, IV (1954), 298.   [2] *Ibid.* pp. 298 ff.
[3] In *GK*, § 155*a*, such relative clauses are called 'complete relative clauses'.

On the syntax of אהיה אשר אהיה

one who sinned and did wrong'. This leads up to the main thesis of Schild's paper:

> Here, in my opinion, we have the key to a better understanding of Exod. 3: 14 אֶהְיֶה אֲשֶׁר אֶהְיֶה. Except for the absence of the copula, which is unnecessary because the whole sentence is a verbal one, the construction is identical with that of 1 Chron. 21: 17. אֲשֶׁר אֶהְיֶה is the predicate of the first אֶהְיֶה and the verbal form of היה must therefore agree with the person of the main clause subject, which is contained in the form אֶהְיֶה, i.e. first person. Just as 1 Chron. 21: 17 is translated as 'I am the one who (or: he who; or: one who) sinned', Exod. 3: 14 ought to be translated and interpreted as 'I am the one who is' or 'I am he who is', the 'am' expressing identity and the 'is' expressing existence.[1]

As is pointed out by Lindblom, the problem of the interpretation would become much simpler if this translation could be accepted: the divine answer would then clearly indicate 'dass Jahwe im gewissen Sinne der Seiende wäre'.[2]

Lindblom has also called attention to the fact that the syntactical analysis which he himself adopts, and which has been argued most fully by Schild, in fact had advocates long ago, though they have been few and far between. He mentions August Knobel, who in his commentary on Exodus and Leviticus in 1857 referred to the same rule of grammar and suggested the translation 'I am the one who is'.[3] Both Schild and Lindblom also refer to Edouard Reuss. In his French translation of the Bible in 1879 Reuss gave this rendering of the disputed sentence: 'Je suis celui qui est', with the following comment: 'On remarquera que nous traduisons: Je suis celui qui *est*, et non pas: celui qui *je suis*. Cette dernière traduction provient de ce qu'on méconnait une règle de la syntaxe hébraïque, d'après laquelle la proposition relative se met à la même personne que le sujet.'[4]

---

[1] *VT*, IV (1954), 300 f.   [2] Lindblom, *ASTI*, III (1964), 9.

[3] *Die Bücher Exodus und Leviticus (Kurzgefasstes exegetisches Handbuch zum A.T.*, XII, Leipzig, 1857), p. 28: 'eig. *ich bin, welcher ich bin* d. h. ich bin derjenige, welcher ist, also der Seiende, wirklich Existirende. Nämlich אֲשֶׁר zu den beiden Verbis gehörig ist *is qui* wie Num. 22: 6. 2 Sam. 18: 4. und das zweite אֶהְיֶה für יְהְיֶה gesetzt, indem der Hebräer mit dem Relat., wenn es auf eine erste Person zurückgeht, gern die erste Person verbindet...'

[4] *La Bible. Traduction nouvelle avec introductions et commentaires*, III, 2 (Paris, 1879), 9 n. 3 (the words quoted above are found on p. 10).

Schild gives vent to his surprise that this explanation of the sentence has escaped the notice of later scholars,[1] and Lindblom finds it strange that the grammatical rule in question has not been applied more often to the passage in Exodus.[2]

III

As far as the rule of grammar is concerned there can hardly be any doubt that Schild's detailed discussion of its correct formulation and his distinction between four different subsections is valuable and a definite improvement in comparison with Gesenius–Kautzsch. One could possibly object that his introduction to the series of examples, 'The OT yields the following examples of this rule',[3] is likely to give the impression that what follows is a complete list of all instances found in the Old Testament, which is not correct: several clear cases have not been included. I have for instance noted 1 Kings 13: 14 האתה איש־האלהים אשר־באת מיהודה 'Are you the man of God who came from Judah?' and Neh. 9: 7 אתה־הוא יהוה האלהים אשר בחרת באברם והוצאתו מאור כשדים ושמת שמו אברהם 'Thou art Yhwh, the God who didst choose Abram and bring him out of Ur of the Chaldeans and give him the name Abraham'. Of these instances the first should be included in Schild's subsection (3) and the second in (4).

The assertion that the rule applies also to independent relative clauses is more questionable. From a purely formal point of view the statement seems oddly self-contradictory: an independent relative clause is, by definition, one which has no antecedent, and the rule in question is one which defines how the predicate of the relative clause agrees with the antecedent, so that it would appear intrinsically impossible for the rule to apply to an independent relative clause. And it is in fact doubtful if the two examples which Schild adduces in support of his thesis can be labelled 'independent relative clauses'. The first example is Ps. 71: 20 אשר הראיתנו צרות רבות ורעות תשוב תחיינו, translated by Schild 'Thou, who hast made us see many dangers and disasters, do thou quicken us again'. The verse

[1] *VT*, IV (1954), 302.　　[2] *ASTI*, III (1964), 9.　　[3] *VT*, IV (1954), 299.

seems to be difficult from a text-critical point of view, and many
commentators delete אשר at the beginning of the sentence,[1] but
as the reason for this emendation is not particularly strong:
metri causa, it is not unreasonable of Schild to retain MT. But
one may wonder whether this is at all an *independent* relative
clause: the word אלהים in the vocative (originally probably
יהוה) is found several times in the preceding lines of the psalm
(verses 17, 18, 19), and the words immediately before those
quoted by Schild run: אלהים מי כמוך. It seems much simpler
and more natural to take this vocative אלהים (also represented
by the suffix in כמוך) as the antecedent of the following relative
clause: 'O God, who is like thee, who hast made me see many
and sore troubles...' In that case we have here simply a case
of Schild's subdivision (2), where the governing substantive is
a vocative. It should be noted that Schild himself assigns the
beginning of the preceding verse of the same psalm to this subdivision (2): וצדקתך אלהים עד־מרום אשר־עשית גדלות, translated
'Thy righteousness, O God, extends unto the high heavens, thou,
who hast done great things'. I see no reason why the two relative clauses in verses 19 and 20 should be differently classified;
they seem entirely parallel, and verse 20 should be analysed in
the same way as verse 19.

Schild's second example of an independent relative clause
where the rule of concord applies is also questionable. It is the
sentence from 1 Chron. 21: 17, quoted above in section II:
אני־הוא אשר־חטאתי והרע הרעותי, which Schild renders 'I am
the one who sinned and did wrong'. A still better translation
would perhaps be 'It is I who have sinned and done very
wickedly' (so, e.g., RSV). As was pointed out above, a true
independent relative clause is one which has no antecedent or
governing noun; a clear case is for instance found in Deut. 27: 26
ארור אשר לא־יקים את־דברי התורה־הזאת לעשות אותם 'Cursed be
he who does not keep the words of this law to do them'. It is
hardly satisfactory to regard the clause in 1 Chron. 21: 17 as a
parallel case: obviously the word אני here serves as a kind of

[1] E.g. R. Kittel, *Die Psalmen übersetzt und erklärt* (*KAT*, xiii, Leipzig, 1914),
ad loc.; H. Schmidt, *Die Psalmen* (*HAT*, 1, 15, 1934), *ad loc.*; H.-J. Kraus,
Psalmen (*BK*, xv, 1960), *ad loc.*; cf. also F. Buhl in *BH*.

antecedent which governs the verb of the relative clause. Such cases, where a so-called independent relative clause functions as the predicate of a subject which is then allowed to influence the construction of the relative clause, form the background of Schild's seemingly self-contradictory statement. The current Hebrew grammars as a rule do not mention these cases at all; generally it is only said that an independent relative clause can be the subject of the principal clause, the object of its verb, or dependent on a noun or a preposition in it.[1] V. Baumann, however, in his study of relative clauses in Hebrew, mentions that an independent relative clause may also serve as a predicate.[2] He gives two examples. The first is 2 Sam. 2: 4 אנשי יביש גלעד אשר קברו את־שאול 'It was the men of Jabesh-Gilead who buried Saul'. But this sentence is difficult, and most scholars hold that the word אשר has been accidentally transposed and should stand immediately before the words quoted (cf. 2 Sam. 1: 4).[3] This passage must therefore be regarded as not altogether reliable evidence. Baumann's second example is however safer from a text-critical point of view: Josh. 24: 17 runs כי יהוה אלהינו הוא המעלה אתנו...ואשר עשה לעינינו את־האתות הגדלות האלה 'For it is Yhwh our God who brought us...and who did these great signs in our sight'. The question whether a relative clause of this kind ought really to be regarded as *selbständig*, 'independent', is intricate; at any rate it seems clear that it refers back to a sort of antecedent (a possible influence upon the verb of the relative clause is not, of course, noticeable here, as the antecedent is in the third person), which is by no means the case in the passage Deut. 27: 26 just quoted, where we find an entirely clear case of an independent relative clause.

---

[1] See, e.g., *GK*, §138*e*; H. S. Nyberg, *Hebreisk grammatik* (Uppsala, 1952), §94*h*; C. Brockelmann, *Hebräische Syntax* (Neukirchen, 1956), §151.

[2] *Hebräische Relativsätze* (dissertation, Leipzig, 1894), p. 22.

[3] See, e.g., S. R. Driver, *Notes on the Hebrew Text and the Topography of the Books of Samuel* (2nd ed. Oxford, 1913), *ad loc.*, and cf. *BH*. This transposition is accepted also by H. W. Hertzberg, *Die Samuelbücher* (*ATD*, x, Göttingen, 1956), *ad loc.* English translation, *I and II Samuel* (London, 1964), p. 245.

On the syntax of אהיה אשר אהיה

IV

The question of the classification of this type of relative clause is not, however, of crucial importance, though it is not without interest. More important is the question whether the comparative material which is the basis of Schild's and Lindblom's analysis of the syntax of the sentence אהיה אשר אהיה is relevant and entirely parallel. The vital passage is 1 Chron. 21: 17, quoted by Lindblom and regarded by Schild as the principal support for his solution: it is, in his own words, 'this example which is directly and forcefully relevant to our problem and affords an excellent parallel to it'.[1]

On closer consideration, however, the alleged parallelism turns out to be far from complete. As a matter of fact the two sentences are differently construed on a vital point: in 1 Chron. 21: 17 there is an אני which the relative clause refers back to and which decides the form of the verb, whereas in Exod. 3: 14 no such pronoun is found, only the verbal form אהיה. Or, in other words: the main clause in 1 Chron. 21: 17 is a nominal clause, whereas in Exod. 3: 14 it is a verbal clause. Lindblom does not deal with this difference at all; Schild mentions it in passing without really discussing it seriously. But as I understand it, this difference is a strong argument against the suggested new analysis; it means in fact that no complete parallel to the syntactical construction presupposed in the new translation has been presented. It is not only 1 Chron. 21: 17, the main passage referred to, that is different in this respect: *all* the alleged parallels cited by Lindblom (Gen. 15: 17; 45: 4; Exod. 20: 2 par.; Lev. 20: 24; Num. 22: 30; 1 Kings 13: 14; Isa. 41: 8; 49: 23;[2] 1 Chron. 21: 17), as also all those adduced by Schild (in addition to Lindblom's, also Judg. 13: 11; 1 Sam. 25: 33; 1 Kings 8: 23 f.; Isa. 51: 17; Jer. 5: 22; 32: 17 ff.; Ps. 71: 19; Eccles. 10: 16 f.),[3] as well as other examples of this rule of syntax, have

---

[1] Schild, *VT*, IV (1954), 300.
[2] These two passages from Isaiah do not belong in the same category as the rest and are hardly relevant at all: they are not examples of agreement between the antecedent and the verb in the relative clause but of the use of a retrospective pronoun, the *'ā'id* of the Arab grammarians.
[3] What is said above in n. 2 about Isa. 41: 8 and 49: 23 is true also of Eccles. 10: 16 f.

one thing in common: the antecedent is always an explicit noun or pronoun, *never* as in the suggested analysis of Exod. 3: 14 a pronominal concept implied in a verbal form. Schild, it is true, has suggested the possibility that the governing substantive in Isa. 51: 17 קומי ירושלם אשר שתית 'arise, O Jerusalem, who have drunk...', is the pronoun implied in קומי,[1] but this is neither necessary nor even probable: the governing noun is certainly the vocative 'Jerusalem'. Thus it is at any rate clear that the comparative material adduced is not sufficient to prove the thesis: true parallels to the construction which is said to occur in Exod. 3: 14 still remain to be found.

If it should be objected that the suggested new analysis is not unproved merely because parallels are shown to be lacking, it must be remembered that the only argument advanced by both Schild and Lindblom is the argument by parallels: they explain the construction of the disputed sentence by referring to other Hebrew sentences which are said to be built on an identical pattern. If it is shown that the pattern is in fact not identical, the argument of course breaks down. It may perhaps even be claimed that a grammatical explanation always requires the existence of parallels even if this is not explicitly stated. For a rule of syntax is a statement of how words are in fact connected. 'Philology is an empirical science',[2] and to formulate a syntactical law is to say that such and such a pattern has been observed in several sentences. Thus to explain a construction by referring to a grammatical rule is to say that the construction explained is another instance of a pattern which has been found in other cases, i.e. that parallels exist.

But it seems possible to take a further step and to maintain not only that the thesis is not proved but also that it is wrong. It seems to be the case that the main clause must contain an explicit noun or pronoun with which the verb of the relative clause agrees. This means that in a case like 1 Chron. 21: 17, where the relative clause is syntactically the predicate of the subject of the main clause, it is not an accidental and insig-

[1] *VT*, IV (1954), 299.
[2] M. Macdonald, 'The Philosopher's Use of Analogy', *Logic and Language* (First Series), ed. A. G. N. Flew (Oxford, 1951), p. 83.

nificant detail that the main clause is a nominal clause: on the
contrary this is necessarily so. In general, this rule seems not
to have been formulated in the grammars. I am aware of one
exception only: J. Pedersen's original and independent Hebrew
grammar (unfortunately available only in Danish), where the
section on the relative clauses contains the following rule: 'If
the principal clause is a *nominal clause*, the subordinate clause
may thus be its predicate.'[1] This is to say that 'I am the one
who...', 'This is that which...', etc., is in biblical Hebrew
expressed by a nominal clause. There are several instances in
Old Testament Hebrew with the predicate of such a nominal
clause consisting of a relative clause: Ezek. 38: 17 האתה־הוא
אשר־דברתי בימים קדמונים 'Are you the one of whom I spoke
in former days?'; Gen. 44: 5 הלוא זה אשר ישתה אדני בו 'Is not
this the one from which my lord drinks?'; Deut. 14: 12 וזה
אשר לא־תאכלו מהם 'And these are the ones which you shall not
eat:...'[2] This is of course the natural Semitic mode of expression: in the Koran, for instance, phrases like *huwa 'lladī yursilu
'r-riyāḥa* 'He is the one who sends the winds' (Sura 7: 55)
are frequent (cf. 6: 97 ff., 114, 165; 9: 33; 10: 23; 42: 24,
27; etc.).[3]

It may be added that our 'I am the one who...', etc., is in
Hebrew also often expressed by a participle where we have a
relative clause, as for instance in Josh. 24: 17, quoted above in
section III, or in 1 Sam. 4: 16 אנכי הבא מן־המערכה 'I am the one
who has come from the battle'. This construction seems to be
especially frequent in Deutero-Isaiah, for instance 43: 25 אנכי
אנכי הוא מחה פשעיך למעני 'I, I am the one who blots out your
transgressions for my own sake'; 51: 9 f. הלוא את־היא המחצבת
רהב מחוללת תנין : הלוא את־היא המחרבת ים 'Are you not the one
who cut Rahab in pieces, who pierced the dragon? Are you

---

[1] *Hebræisk Grammatik* (2nd ed. Copenhagen, 1933), §129 o, p. 275: 'Hvis
den overordnede Sætning er en *Nominalsætning*, kan den underordnede
Sætning saal. udgøre dennes Prædikat' (my italics).

[2] In these cases, of course, the subject of the relative clause is not identical
with that of the principal clause, so that the rule of concord does not apply
here.

[3] For further examples in Arabic see C. Brockelmann, *Grundriss der vergleichenden Grammatik der semitischen Sprachen*, II (Berlin, 1913), §385 b.

25

not the one who dried up the sea...?'; or 51 : 12 אנכי אנכי הוא
מנחמכם 'I, I am the one who comforts you'. But of the syntactical pattern presupposed by Schild I have not been able to
find any examples.

V

It is interesting to note that when Lindblom and Schild discuss
the syntax of אהיה אשר אהיה, it is exclusively a matter of arguing
for the suggested new analysis. The traditional understanding
of the structure of the sentence is said to be wrong but this is
simply stated, never demonstrated. Neither Schild nor Lindblom
has at all attempted to show precisely where the mistake is to
be found: there are in fact no arguments *against* the common
syntactical understanding. Apparently the correctness of the
new explanation is regarded as so evident that the older view of
the grammatical construction of the sentence is thought to dis-
appear as a possible alternative once the arguments for the new
view have been presented. But of course this is not necessarily
so. Even if the new explanation had been acceptable, the
traditional understanding would not of necessity have been
wrong: a sentence may be ambiguous and admit of more than
one grammatical analysis, and in such a case Schild's arguments for his understanding would not imply the denial of a
different explanation. It might have been a question of two
equally possible ways of understanding the disputed phrase, and
strictly speaking there is no basis for more far-reaching conclusions than this in Schild. The fact that there are no arguments against the usual translation in Schild's detailed paper
is of some importance when his own analysis is shown to be
inadequate: consequently no such arguments remain to be
refuted.

The reason why the advocates of the translation 'I am the
one who is' have not attempted to explain what is wrong with
the syntactical analysis which yields the translation 'I am who
I am' is probably simply that it is so difficult to refute; in fact
it seems entirely faultless. This becomes particularly clear if we
so to speak turn the problem over and ask what is the Hebrew

On the syntax of אֶהְיֶה אֲשֶׁר אֶהְיֶה

for the English sentence 'I am who I am' or 'I will be what I will be'. It would seem that this is naturally expressed by the sentence אֶהְיֶה אֲשֶׁר אֶהְיֶה. As is well known, this is a paronomastic construction which is normal in Semitic languages: *sami'a 'llāhu liman sami'a* 'Allah hears whom he hears'; *ḳāla ma ḳāla* 'he said what he said', and common also in Hebrew, as for instance in 2 Sam. 15: 20: אֲנִי הוֹלֵךְ עַל אֲשֶׁר־אֲנִי הוֹלֵךְ 'I go where I go'.[1] Accordingly 'I am who I am' may well be rendered אֶהְיֶה אֲשֶׁר אֶהְיֶה. It is sometimes thought that the imperfect form of the verb, אֶהְיֶה, is not quite appropriate in this connection. But it must not be forgotten that the whole phrase is a kind of word-play on the divine name יהוה—rather reminiscent of many folk-etymologies of names in the Old Testament—and this of course considerably restricted the author's choice of forms. It should perhaps be mentioned that neither Schild nor Lindblom discusses the paronomastic character of the disputed clause, which is all the more surprising as this is a feature which has been emphasized and dealt with in considerable detail by Th. C. Vriezen in his well-known and important article in the *Bertholet-Festschrift*.[2] To my mind Vriezen is entirely right in stressing the paronomastic character of the sentence, and it is certainly a mistake to disregard this feature altogether. It is however unnecessary to repeat here what has so convincingly been demonstrated by Vriezen.[3]

VI

The situation thus seems to be that the unusual translation revived by Lindblom and Schild presupposes that the sentence is construed in a way to which—despite affirmations to the

---

[1] See H. Reckendorf, *Über Paronomasie in den semitischen Sprachen. Ein Beitrag zur allgemeinen Sprachwissenschaft* (Giessen, 1909), pp. 156 ff., and cf. Th. C. Vriezen, ''Ehje 'ᵃšer 'ehje', *Festschrift Alfred Bertholet* (Tübingen, 1950), pp. 498 ff.   [2] See n. 1 above.

[3] It is however doubtful if Vriezen is right in making the paronomastic construction yield an 'intensive' meaning (*Festschrift Alfred Bertholet*, pp. 500 ff.). Paronomastic sentences of this type usually express indetermination, and there is no reason to try to avoid this shade of meaning in Exod. 3: 14. Cf. A.-M. Dubarle, 'La signification du nom de Iahweh', *Revue des sciences philosophiques et théologiques*, xxxv (1951), 7 ff.

contrary—there are no real parallels in the Hebrew of the Old Testament and which is not the natural way of expressing in Hebrew the idea which is supposed to be found in the passage. The traditional rendering on the other hand regards the sentence as one of many examples of a common and characteristic Semitic mode of expression which is often found also in Hebrew, and the translation is irreproachable from a grammatical point of view. Only one conclusion is possible: there is every reason to retain the syntactical analysis of אהיה אשר אהיה which has resulted in the classical rendering represented by almost all Bible translations. Unfortunately this means that we are back in the difficulties of interpretation which the new translation was designed to solve. But this is no argument against the grammatically correct rendering. And if we should have to admit that though the words are not difficult to translate, we do not quite understand their meaning and cannot give them an entirely satisfactory interpretation, this is not after all surprising: many sayings in the Old Testament are so ancient and have had so eventful and varied a history that we may well expect their original meaning to be sometimes irrecoverable. This does not, of course, exempt us from the duty to use every conceivable means to reach a solution. But perhaps we should admit more often than we do that we simply do not know. Old Testament scholars, too, would perhaps do well to ponder upon the famous and equivocal dictum of a great teacher at Cambridge: 'Whereof one cannot speak, thereof one must be silent.'

3

ומרחוק יריח מלחמה—JOB 39: 25

by P. A. H. de Boer

The war-horse possesses superhuman strength, velocity, and courage. His qualities are described in the poetry of Job 39: 19–25. The last part of the strophe reads like this in the usual translation

> and he smells the battle from afar,
> the thunder of the captains, and the shouting.

The Greek and the Syriac versions each have a reading which differs from the rabbinical text preserved in our Hebrew bible. Instead of the last line, 'the thunder of the captains, and the shouting' the Greek version reads '(and) with a bound (—at a leap—) and a cry (he goes out)'. It has been supposed that the translator misread the Hebrew word רעם, overlooking its first character. The Syriac rendering of these last words of the line runs as follows: 'and he is shaking (terrifying) the captains with his neighing.' These renderings may of course go back to Hebrew readings not preserved, but to me it seems more probable that the translators have tried to avoid, each in his own way, the difficult connection of the verbal form יריח with, as well as מלחמה, two other objects: the thunder of captains and shouting, battle-cry. The Greek as well as the Syriac translation render the verb by 'he smells (the battle)'.

The line 'and he—the war-horse—smells the battle from afar' contains also another difficulty. All hooved animals have a well-developed sense of smell and the horse is no exception. With his nose he sniffs and he snorts. 'His proud snorting is terrible', runs a possible translation of verse 20 *b*. But smelling something at a long distance is no peculiarity of the horse. It is because of this difficulty that commentators have supposed the Hiph'il of the verb ריח had a metaphorical sense. Arnoldus Boot interpreted it in this way, and, in his *Animadversiones sacrae ad textum hebraicum Veteris Testamenti* (London, 1644), refers for the metaphorical sense of the verb to Martinus Borrhaus's commentary of 1555, Valentinus Schindlerus's lexicon of 1612, and Johannes Mariana's scholia of 1620. In liber III, caput xi, paragraph 4 of Boot's work we read that הריח means 'sentire, persentiscere: quomodo etiam sumitur Jud. 16: 9 et Esa. 11: 3'. In Samuel Bochartus's *De scripturae animalibus* (Utrecht, 1692), one finds a more detailed discussion of the supposed metaphorical sense of the verb. In part I, liber ii, col. 151 the following observations are to be found: '"Et pugnam eminus praesagit". Sagire enim (inquit Tullius lib. 1 De Divinit.) sentire acutè est, Cicero in Epist. ad Atticum: odorari quid futurum sit. Itaque: pugnam odoratur, id est futurum praesagit.' Bochart refers further to Kimchi who brings forward the verbal form ירגיש, a form occurring in the Targum Jon. of Exod. 2: 3 with the meaning: to feel the scent of, trace, track. He continues with:

Nempe *odorem* pro sensu in genere *Hebraei* passim usurpant; ut cum de arbore dicitur Job 14: 9—ex odore aquae germinat, *odor* ibi pro *sensu*. Ita Jud. 16: 9 ut frangitur filum stupeum—cum odoratum est ignem, id est sensus ignis. Et Esa 11: 3, ubi de Christo,—et odoratus ejus erit in timore Domini. Odoratus, id est, sensus, judicium. Proinde sequitur, Non secundum aspectum oculorum judicabit, etc. Eo igitur sensu dici potuit equus *praelium odorari*, id est, sentire, vel praesentiscere.

In recent lexica, translations and commentaries a figurative sense has been ascribed to the noun ריח in some places. But the verbal form, which occurs in Job 39: 25, is rendered by to smell, to absorb the smell of.[1] As far as I know Tur-Sinai is the only recent commentator to question the exactness of the usual translation.[2] 'To smell from a great distance', he says, 'does not

---

[1] Suffice it to mention: 'to smell, perceive odour'—*BDB*; RV; RSV; W. B. Stevenson, *Schweich Lectures 1943* (London, 1947). 'riechen, wittern' —Gesenius–Buhl; G. Fohrer, *Kommentar* (*KAT*, xvi, Gütersloh, 1963). '(das Wehen eines luftförmigen Stoffs) spüren, riechen'—*KBL*. 'flairer'— E. Dhorme, *Le Livre de Job* (Paris, 1926), *Pléiade* (1956); C. Larcher, *La Bible de Jérusalem* (Paris, 1956); S. Terrien, *Commentaire* (Neuchâtel, 1963). In Syriac the rendering of the Aph'el of ריח by *praesentiscere* is given—Payne Smith, *Thesaurus Syriacus*, referring to Ephraim, ed. Romana 272c: the devil and his hosts scented out the coming of our Lord, *praesenserunt*. Brockelmann gives in his lexicon the following meanings of the Aph'el: 1. odoratus est (meton. de igni); 2. flavit; 3. praesagavit, Job 39: 25.

[2] N. H. Tur-Sinai, *The Book of Job, a new commentary* (Jerusalem, 1957), pp. 548 and 551.

fit the horse at all.' But he did not try to solve the problem by supposing a metaphorical sense for the verb הריח. He suggests that Job 39: 20–5 is a description of a bird of prey and not of a war-horse. Verse 19 does, of course, refer to a horse, but remains in Tur-Sinai's translation an isolated line of a strophe of which the remainder has perished. Other scholars have supposed that after verse 19 one line has been lost. A serious objection to Tur-Sinai's opinion would seem to be that he does not mention any texts from ancient sources which actually refer to the sense of smell as a peculiar quality of birds of prey. Do birds of prey smell from afar? The poet of Job 39 stresses the visual faculty of the bird of prey: 'From thence [from his place high in the mountains]', he says in verse 29 of chapter 39, 'he spies out a prey, his eyes pierce to the farthest distance.' It is not his sense of smell that has impressed the poet.

Dhorme, although translating 'And from afar he sniffs the smell of battle', suggests a more or less figurative sense for the verb by referring to the sense of the noun ריח in Job 14: 9 and Judg. 16: 9 in his explanation.[1] A tree cut down, a stump, flourishes anew מריח מים, 'at the scent of water', is Dhorme's translation of Job 14: 9. This rendering is close to the Vulgate which reads: 'ad odorem aquae', explained by Jacobus Tirinus (Antwerp, 1632), with 'ad tactum. Est catachresis, et enallage sensuum'. This analogical application of the noun ריח can be found in several translations and commentaries. Dhorme calls it 'an admirable image suggesting as it does the approach, the slightest contact'. He refers to Judg. 16: 9, rendering the expression בהריחו אש by 'as soon as it smells the fire'.

The rendering of מריח by 'at the scent of' seems to me open to discussion. The meaning of the preposition מן is 'out of', 'from', 'through'—very rarely is a meaning more or less similar to 'at' suitable. A more serious objection is in my opinion that the noun ריח everywhere has the meaning *smell given out*. 'Your anointed oils are fragrant', 'my nard gave forth its perfume', we read in the Song of Sol. 1: 3 and 12. The word also occurs with a similar concrete meaning in 2: 13; 4: 10, 11 (*bis*); 7: 9

[1] Dhorme, *Livre de Job*. English translation by Harold Knight, *A Commentary on the Book of Job* (London, 1967).

31

and 14 of the same Book. Hos. 14: 7 is very close to Song of Sol. 4: 11, 'and his fragrance like Lebanon', the scent given out by the cedars of Lebanon, an expression which is paralleled by 'the scent of your garments', i.e. the smell given out by your clothes. The smell of garments also occurs in Gen. 27: 27, next to the smell of the field and the smell of Isaac's son—three times in one verse the same expression, the smell given out. In Jer. 48: 11 Moab is compared to wine, wine that has not been emptied from vessel to vessel, 'so his flavour remains in him and his bouquet (ריח) is not changed'. Also instructive is Dan. 3: 27, a text referred to by Bochart, where we are told of Shadrach, Meshach, and Abednego coming out from the fire, that 'no smell of fire had come upon them', which stands for 'they did not even smell of fire'.

There remains Judg. 16: 9, quoted by Dhorme to support his rendering of Job 14: 9, 'at the scent of water'. Dhorme explains both Job 14: 9 and Judg. 16: 9 as an 'image'. I doubt whether it is right to render the Niph'al of נתק by 'se rompre'. Elsewhere the Niph'al means: be snapped, be torn apart, be drawn away. Cords of tents are torn loose, Isa. 33: 20 and Jer. 10: 20. 'A threefold cord is not quickly broken', Eccles. 4: 12. Dalman rightly remarks upon the inflammability of flax, quoting Isa. 1: 31. But his rendering of Judg. 16: 9 seems to me inaccurate: 'Werg—dessen Faden schon in der Nähe des Feuers auseinandergeht.'[1] The Revised Version translates the text with: 'as a string of tow is broken when it toucheth [note, Heb. *smelleth*] the fire.' Vincent, in *La Bible de Jérusalem*, which was published in 1956, the same year as Dhorme's translation appeared in *La Bibliothèque de la Pléiade*, also uses 'se rompre', cf. RSV: 'as a string of tow snaps when it touches the fire.' I suppose that the translations quoted have been influenced by the assumption that the expression is an image. I shall leave out of consideration whether expressions like 'to smell water' and 'to smell fire' are likely images for 'le plus léger contact'. Nor will I stress the inveracity of figurative language in which a root or stump, and a string of tow are endowed with a sense of smell. But it is, in my opinion, a serious objection to the assumption of meta-

---

[1] G. Dalman, *Arbeit und Sitte in Palästina*, v (Gütersloh, 1937), 28.

phorical language if the sentences are comprehensible without such an assumption. In Judg. 16: 9 it is said that Samson snapped the bowstrings, as a string of tow is snapped when it smells of fire. It is not the string of tow that smells but the flax-worker smells the string of tow. He may be using a flame to snap the string. When the string smells of fire he is able to snap it. Or, if a string of tow gets into touch with fire so that it smells of fire, one is obliged to tear it loose. Samson was able to snap the seven fresh bowstrings as if they were no more than a string of tow that smells of fire. The same simile occurs in Judg. 15: 14: '...and the ropes which were on his arms became as flax that has caught fire...' This supports my rendering of Judg. 16: 9.

The Hiph'il of the verb ריח has the meaning: 'to give out a smell', a meaning in full agreement with the clear sense of the noun ריח. And in Job 14: 9 the roots or stump of the supposed dead tree bud and flourish anew as a result of the smell of water. The opinion that water, unlike fire, has no scent has been advanced by Tur-Sinai[1] but seems to me untenable. Tur-Sinai did not realize that the text deals with water in contact with roots in the earth. The author of the passage in the Book of Job is alluding to the life-giving power of water. The scent of water can be compared with the scent of oil and perfume. Anointment and perfuming are evidence of power and life. The scent of water performs a similar task for the supposedly dead tree.[2]

The usual rendering of the Hiph'il of ריח by 'to smell, to perceive odour', and its explanation as feeling presentiments, do not receive support from the noun ריח whose unmistakable meaning is fragrance, perfume, stench—smell given out. Judg. 16: 9 can be translated and explained in accordance with this meaning of ריח. We may therefore be justified in doubting the

---

[1] *The Book of Job, a new commentary*, p. 235.

[2] P. Reymond, who has published an important monograph on water in the Old Testament—*L'eau, sa vie, et sa signification dans l'Ancien Testament* (*VTS*, VI, 1958)—did not give full attention to Job 14: 9. His observation, made on page 6 of his work, 'l'arbre dont parle Job 14: 9, sentant de loin l'eau du ruisseau, y envoie ses racines et retrouve vie', is an inexact paraphrase of the Hebrew text. As for the relation of anointment and life I may refer to my paper 'Vive le roi!', *VT*, v (1955), 225–31. Compare also Rivkah Harris's article in the *Journal of Cuneiform Studies*, IX (New Haven, 1955), 92 f.

correctness of the renderings and explanations usually given. And so in spite of the ancient versions and traditional and modern views it seems desirable to reconsider the meaning of a few passages.

The verbal form הריחו also occurs in Isa. 11: 3. A metaphorical interpretation, 'odoratus, id est, sensus, judicium', is given in Bochartus's work, as we have seen. The Greek and Latin translators may have altered or misread the Hebrew, probably reading והניחו, cf. Ezek. 24: 13 in the LXX, ἐμπλήσω. But their use of the term 'the spirit (of the fear of the Lord)' indicates their familiarity with the reading in Hebrew: הריח derived from the root רוח. The Peshiṭta version reads: 'and he shall be illustrious, or, shine forth (in the fear of the Lord)', using the verb *dnḥ*, a verb that is also known in Aramaic, and that corresponds to זרח in Hebrew. The author of this version may have read וזרחו, literally 'and his shining', instead of והריחו.

The non-figurative meaning 'to smell' has been kept by some commentators. Ibn Ezra stresses the reliability of perception by the sense of smell as contrasted with ear and eye. Calvin underlines the sharpness of perception by rendering 'et sagacem illum reddet in timore Domini'. Piscator (1546–1625) and others, like Bochartus, stress the power of judgement because of the next sentence in Isaiah, 'he shall not judge by what his eyes see', etc. Hugo Grotius derives his translation and explanation of the sentence from the meaning of the Qal of רוח, 'to relieve', 1 Sam. 16: 23 and Job 32: 20. His rendering runs as follows: 'Et consolari ipsius (id est, solatium).'[1]

Dillmann, whose commentaries excel in accuracy and brevity, ascribes to the verb 'to smell' in our passage the sense not of 'to perceive' but a satisfied stay, dwell upon (ב), 'das befriedigte Verweilen des Sinnes am'. His explanation of 'sein Riechen' is: 'sein Wohlgefallen', his delight.[2] This rendering, 'his delight', is found in most of the recent translations.

Many reject the authenticity of Isa. 11: 3a and consider the

[1] *Annotata ad Vetus Testamentum*, II (Paris, 1544), 21
[2] A. Dillmann, *Der Prophet Jesaja* (Leipzig, 1890), p. 118. Cf. J. Barth, *Etymologische Studien zum Semitischen insbesondere zum hebräischen Lexicon* (Leipzig, 1893), p. 65, who quotes Amos 5: 21 and Isa. 11: 3, translating 'Wohlgefallen haben', and bringing forward some parallels in Arabic.

line to be due to dittography. One of the supporters of this view is Duhm who has pointed out the problems with his characteristic clarity. In his well-known commentary on the Book of Isaiah we read on verse 3 a:[1] ' " "und sein Riechen ist an die Furcht Gottes" eine Variante mit sinnlosem Text. Wenn noch das verb. fin. stände,[2] dass wenigstens die Konstruktion erträglich wäre! Und wie riecht denn die Gottesfurcht? Diejenigen, die V. 3 a festhalten, müssten es wissen, aber sie sagen es nicht.' To assume a figurative sense for the verb 'to smell' is an attempt to get away from the real problem so clearly stated by Duhm. Skinner, who himself uses the rendering 'his delight', rightly observes that the expression is very awkward.[3]

Should we be tempted to deviate from the literal sense of הריח to get an understandable sentence? The explanation of הריחו in Judg. 16: 9 given above and the statement that scent/ smell does not mean 'odour perceived by', but 'odour given out', may give us freedom to leave the beaten track. The Hiph'il of ריח possibly has an intransitive sense (also?), similar to נתן ריח, used in Song of Sol. 1: 12. Such a meaning, 'to give forth scent, perfume', should make it possible to render Isa. 11: 3 a by: 'and his giving forth scent (is done) with the fear of the Lord.' ב הריח is used with the same meaning in Exod. 30: 38, as will be shown below.

Scent given forth is a manifestation of the power of life. I do not defend the authenticity of verse 3 a in its context. The line may be a gloss. If so it is a gloss in accordance with the trend of the passage. The qualities of the new prince—his inspiration, his wisdom, his piety—can also be called the manifestation of his observance of the Lord's will. To be gifted with the spirit of the Lord means to shine and to smell like a priest in the Lord's sanctuary who is anointed with oil and fragrance. In his observance of the will of the Lord the new prince gives evidence of his power.

[1] B. Duhm, *Das Buch Jesaia* (Göttingen, 1914), p. 82.
[2] G. Fohrer translates as if the Hebrew text reads a *verbum finitum*: [Er riecht nach Gottesfurcht], without an explanatory note, *Zürcher Bibelkommentar* (1960), p. 150.
[3] J. Skinner, *The Book of the Prophet Isaiah, chapters 1–39* (Cambridge, 1930), p. 105.

P. A. H. DE BOER

In Exod. 30 two instructions are given, one for the compounding of a special kind of anointing oil, for the anointing of the implements of the sanctuary and for the anointing of the priests, verses 22–30; and the other for a special kind of incense, perfume, for the sanctuary, 'where I shall meet with you', verses 34–6. Anointing oil as well as incense fabricated according to these instructions is called most holy. Both sets of instructions are followed by prohibitions on the use and compounding of the anointing oil and incense for profane purposes, verses 31–3 and verses 37–8.

In verse 38 we find: 'Whoever makes any like it לְהָרִיחַ בָּהּ shall be cut off from his people.' The words לְהָרִיחַ בָּהּ have been rendered in the LXX by ὥστε ὀσφραίνεσθαι ἐν αὐτῷ, cf. the Peshiṭta version lmrḥw bh. The rendering of the Vulgate is more explicative. It runs: 'ut odore illius perfruatur.' Recent translations follow either the Greek rendering or that of the Vulgate.[1]

In these renderings the fact that the purpose of compounding perfume is not 'to smell *thereto*' but to give forth scent *with* that perfume is overlooked. The purpose of both anointing and perfuming is to manifest oneself as healthy and full of power and life. The anointed implements of the sanctuary and the anointed priests are filled with divine life and glory through the holy anointing oil. The purpose of the holy perfume—the incense—is the same. It fills the place where the deity meets his believers with divine strength and grace. To shine with the anointing oil and be perfumed with the holy incense are the benefit and the privilege of the sphere of God, his sanctuary and his priests. Appropriation of these privileges is sacrilege. Such profanation should be punished by death. This penalty is also needed to

[1] 'to smell thereto', RV; 'pour en humer l'odeur', *La Bible de Jérusalem* (1956, 2nd ed. 1958): B. Couroyer; 'pour le respirer', Dhorme, *Pléiade* (1956); more neutral is the rendering given in the RSV: 'to use as perfume', to be found also in the English edition of M. Noth's commentary on *Exodus* (London, 1962). Evidently in the line of the rendering of the Vulgate is Noth's German text: 'um seinen Geruch zu geniessen' (*ATD*, v, Göttingen, 1959); 'um seinem Geruche zu ergötzen', H. Holzinger, *Kautzsch-Bertholet* (Tübingen, 1922); 'um sich an seinem Geruch zu erfreuen', G. Beer-K. Galling, *Kommentar* (Tübingen, 1939). Compare also D. Lys, 'Rûach', *Le souffle dans l'Ancien Testament* (Paris, 1962), p. 20: 'pour en sentir l'odeur, c'est-à-dire pour s'en régaler par l'odeur.'

secure the people against the after-effects of the sacrilegious acts performed by a member of the people. 'Whoever makes any like it to perfume with shall be cut off from his people.' The conception of divine smell and its correlation to sacrifice will be dealt with at a later date. I shall therefore be considering here neither texts like Lev. 26: 31 and Amos 5: 21—both of which use the term הריח ב—nor the other places where the deity himself is the subject of the verbal form הריח, nor the expression רֵיחַ נִחֹחַ. I shall confine myself here to passages of a more or less profane character, but I will not conceal my opinion that the meaning of the verbal form הריח proposed here has far-reaching consequences for the meaning of sacrifice.

In Gen. 27: 27 the subject of the verbs changes without any indication in the Hebrew text, a rather frequent phenomenon in the Hebrew literature. The usual rendering of the beginning of Gen. 27: 27 runs as follows: 'And he (Jacob) came near, and kissed him (Isaac); and he (Isaac) smelled the smell of his (Jacob's) garments, and blessed him, and said...' The ancient versions have the same interpretation. Any possible uncertainty is excluded in the reading of the Vulgate: 'Accessit, et osculatus est eum. Statimque ut sensit vestimentorum illius fragrantiam, benedicens illi, ait...' In recent translations one finds other small additions to exclude uncertainty about the subject of the verbs, as appears from the following quotations: 'Da trat er hinzu und küszte ihn; er aber roch den Geruch seiner Kleider; da segnete er ihm und sprach...'[1]; 'Il s'avança et le baisa. Isaac sentit l'odeur de ses habits et le bénit. Il dit...' (Dhorme, 1956); 'Il s'approcha et embrassa son père, qui respira l'odeur de ses vêtements. Il le bénit ainsi:...' (De Vaux, 1956); 'As he went up and kissed him, [Isaac] sniffed the smell of his clothes. Then, at last, he blessed him, saying...' (Speiser, 1964). Translating is interpretation.

The rendering of וירח by 'and he smelled', 'perceived the odour', ascribing a transitive sense to the verb, makes good

---

[1] H. Gunkel, *Genesis* (3rd ed. Göttingen, 1910), p. 312. His observation—which is beside the point—on 'Rassen- und Nationalgerüche' made B. Jacob so angry that the latter forgot to translate verse 27a in his commentary, *Das erste Buch der Tora, Genesis* (Berlin, 1934), p. 566.

sense. If we make Jacob instead of Isaac subject of וירח,
ascribing an intransitive sense[1] to the verb, we also get a
meaning that fits in with the course of events in the passage:
'And he (Jacob) came near, and kissed him; and he gave forth
the scent of his clothes. After that he (Isaac) blessed him, and
said...' The words 'and he gave forth the scent of his clothes'
can be rendered less literally by: 'and his clothes gave forth
their smell.'

In conclusion I come back to the text from the Book of Job.
There is no doubt that the horse described in the strophe Job
39: 19–25 is a war-horse. Horse means war-horse everywhere
in the Old Testament. For the authors of the Old Testament
texts the horse was a new weapon that changed the manner in
which war was waged. We may compare the appearance of
horses in the theatre of war with tanks or bombers in our days.
A tank, or a bomber, makes us think of war. Just so a horse in
ancient times. Even from a distance he recalls war and its
features, the thunder of captains and battle-cries.

If we assume that הריח has an intransitive meaning we are
rid of the difficulties in the rendering of Job 39: 25 that are
mentioned at the beginning of this study. We do not need to
take refuge in the supposition of meanings that sometimes lead
far away from the direct sense of the verb and the noun that is
at the root of it. The horse gives forth the scent of war. The
horse gives out a penetrating smell. His appearance, even seen
from afar, recalls a battle-field, and the air beaten with shouts.

I hope to have brought forward here sufficient arguments to
suggest the possibility of a new translation of the final lines of
the strophe on the war-horse:

> and even from afar he recalls war,
> thunder of captains, and battle-cry.

---

[1] P. Haupt has suggested that we should distinguish *verba voluntaria* and
verba involuntaria instead of the usual transitive and intransitive verbs,
American Oriental Society Proceedings (Boston and New Haven, 1894), p. ci.
F. R. Blake, who wrote a detailed article on the so-called intransitive
verbs in the *JAOS*, xxiv (1903), 145–204, does not mention the texts
dealt with here. He mentions in his list of intransitive verbs that indicate
states or conditions, under no. 352 רוח: Job 32: 20, become wide, pleasant.

4

WORDS AND MEANINGS IN EARLY HEBREW INSCRIPTIONS

by David Diringer and S. P. Brock

The nature of the few hundreds of extant Early Hebrew documents—though a great part of the inscriptions consist of only one or two words—is noteworthy. What is recorded is for the most part not the history of great events or of striking personalities, but the details of everyday life. Even the smallest documents furnish information which is of considerable value in supplementing our knowledge of the Bible, of the Hebrew writing and language, and of the life and customs of ancient Israel.

For instance, the ostraca of Samaria,[1] which contain various data regarding the nature and provenance of supplies of wine and refined oil, and are probably dockets relating to payment of taxes in kind to the king of Israel, throw much light on the language, religion and personal names of the inhabitants of the Northern kingdom in the ninth or eighth century b.c., as well as on its topography, and especially on its provincial and fiscal administration, of which very little, if anything at all, was previously known.

Philologically, the Samarian documents are extremely important as they represent the earliest preserved texts written in the Hebrew dialect of the Northern kingdom. In them we have the form ‎יֵן‎ (yēn) instead of the biblical ‎יַיִן‎ (yayin), 'wine', and ‎שֵׁת‎ instead of the biblical ‎שְׁנַת‎ or ‎שָׁנָה‎ (šenat or šānāh), 'year'.

While the Samarian ostraca provide us with examples of the dialect of the Kingdom of Israel, most of the other inscriptions illustrate that of Judah. These include the Gezer Calendar,[2]

---

[1] For text see D. Diringer, *Le Iscrizioni Antico-Ebraiche* (Florence, 1934), pp. 21 ff. Translations of selected ostraca in *DOTT*, ed. D. Winton Thomas, pp. 204 ff.

[2] The text, translation and commentary can now conveniently be found in H. Donner–W. Röllig, *Kanaanäische und aramäische Inschriften* (*KAI*; 1962–4), no. 182. English translation in *DOTT*, pp. 201–3.

now generally attributed to *c.* 1000 B.C., the Siloam inscription[1] of *c.* 700 B.C., the Lachish 'Letters',[2] written during Jeremiah's lifetime, about 590 B.C., numerous other ostraca, and so on. Some of the Judean documents contain new words or very interesting grammatical forms.

Even short inscriptions, like those of the weights, seals,[3] and jar-handle stamps, contain hitherto unknown words, names and city names, and grammatical forms. So, for instance, about fifteen Early Hebrew weights bear the inscription נצף, a hitherto unknown metrological term, and seven are inscribed with the term פים, a puzzling word which appears in 1 Sam. 13: 21. Until the discovery of the פים-weights, this passage had baffled all translators of the Bible (the RV translated: 'Yet they had a "file" for the...'), but now the obscurity is cleared up. We now know that in this passage פים indicates a weight and expresses the price which the Israelites had to pay to the Philistines for the sharpening of their ploughshares, axes, etc.

On the other hand, etymologically, the word פים is still puzzling. Various interpretations have been suggested, for example, that it may be an abbreviation of (לְ)פִּי מְ(שֶׁקֶל), 'according to the standard weight', or of פִּי יָ(שְׁנַ)ם, 'two fractions', i.e. fraction divided into two, or 'half'; or else that it may be related to the Sumerian term *šanabi* and the Accadian *šinipu*, meaning $\frac{4}{6} = \frac{2}{3}$ (as in Accadian *šinā* means 2, *pū* may mean $\frac{1}{3}$, and the Early Hebrew *pim* or *payim* would mean $\frac{2}{3}$). However, no satisfactory explanation of פים can be given, except that it was a metrological unit.

Another source for very brief inscriptions is provided by seal stones.[4] These, quite apart from their important contribution to our knowledge of the Israelite onomasticon, give a number

---

[1] G. A. Cooke, *A Text-Book of North Semitic Inscriptions* (Oxford, 1903), no. 2; *KAI*, no. 189; *DOTT*, pp. 209–11.

[2] H. Torczyner, *Lachish I: the Lachish Letters* (Oxford, 1938); revised text and translation (Diringer) in *Lachish III: the Iron Age*, vol. 1 (Oxford, 1953). Selections in *KAI*, nos. 192–9 (ostraca nos. 2–6, 9, 13, 19); *DOTT*, pp. 212–17 (ostraca nos. 1, 3 and 4).

[3] For the seals and weights discussed below, cf. Diringer, *Lachish III*, pp. 159 ff. and 263 ff.; S. Moscati, *L'Epigrafia Ebraica Antica 1935–50* (Rome, 1951), pp. 47 ff. and 99 ff.; *DOTT*, pp. 218 ff. and 227 ff.

[4] For references see preceding note.

of official titles, such as עבד המלך (cf. 2 Kings 22: 12), נער
(cf. 2 Sam. 9: 9), אשר על הבית (cf. 1 Kings 16: 9), בן המלך, etc.
This last should probably also be taken as a title of an office,
rather than implying actual royal stock, and the same evidently
applies to several occurrences of the phrase 'son of the king'
in the Old Testament (e.g. 1 Kings 22: 26; Jer. 36: 26, etc.).

A few seals, unfortunately usually of unknown provenance,
have Yahwistic names ending in -יו, rather than the more
familiar -יה or -יהו. This is in fact a Northern feature, as is
shown by the Samaria ostraca, where all the theophoric names
of this type have the ending -יו (probably *-yaw*), and it is no
surprise that a further name of this type, דליו, has now turned
up in an inscription at Hazor (no. 8).[1] In the course of transmission similar names of Northerners who figure in the Old
Testament have been normalized to the Judean orthography,
-יָה or -יָהוּ, but it is possible that the Septuagint reflects the
original orthography in a few cases: Elijah (MT אליה(ו)) thus
appears as 'Ηλειού, rather than 'Ηλία or 'Ηλίας (the normal
endings for such theophoric names in the Septuagint), which
perhaps presupposes אליו, rather than אליה(ו). In confirmation
of this one might point to passages where the resulting homo-
graphs in the consonantal script—אֵלִיָּו 'Elijah', אֵלָיו 'to him'—
have led to confusion in the textual tradition, e.g. 1 Kings 17: 2,
MT אֵלָיו, but LXX πρὸς 'Ηλειού.

From the seventh and early sixth centuries there is an ever-
increasing corpus of Hebrew ostraca in the form of letters, which
are invaluable for the study of the Hebrew language of this
period. In the Yavneh-Yam letter,[2] for instance, a petition from
a labourer to the local military commander (השׂר) dating from
the end of the seventh century B.C., the writer claims that he
had harvested, measured out, and stored the grain in accordance
with normal practice: ויקצר עבדך ויכל ואסם כימם... . In the
Old Testament the verb כול occurs in the *Qal* in a single
passage, Isa. 40: 12, where it is usually rendered 'contain, en-
close', or the like, but the 'Three' were correct in translating
ἐμέτρησεν, and the sense of the passage is evidently that of

---

[1] For the publication see below, p. 44, n. 1.
[2] *KAI*, no. 200 (with lit.).

'eating one's soup with a pin'. In the Gezer Calendar a noun, כל (kēl) 'measuring', from the same root, probably occurs.

The next two words in the Yavneh-Yam letter likewise throw light on the language of the Old Testament. The verb אסם (infinitive absolute, wᵉ-'āsōm, here) is not attested in biblical Hebrew, although the plural of the noun אסם occurs twice (Deut. 28: 8; Prov. 3: 10). The context of the verb in the letter suggests that it had the more specialized meaning of 'to store *grain*', and this would lend some support to the reading שֶׁבֶר which underlies the Septuagint's rendering of Prov. 3: 10: ἵνα πίμπληται τὰ ταμίειά σου πλησμονῆς σίτου, where the last two words represent a doublet to שבע of the MT. Finally, *kayyāmîm* must be an idiomatic expression meaning 'as usual', 'according to regular (periodic) practice' (Cross), and, though not exactly paralleled in the Old Testament, it probably has its counterpart in לַיָּמִים of Judg. 17: 10.

Although the Arad ostraca may eventually outstrip them in importance, it is of course the Lachish Letters that have hitherto most illuminated the Old Testament, and especially their approximate contemporary, the Book of Jeremiah. Here, from the wealth of interesting material—grammatical, syntactical, etc., as well as lexical—only a couple of examples can be selected. The dramatic ostracon no. 4, with its mention of משׂאת, a technical term for 'fire-', or 'smoke-signal', lends added vividness to Jer. 6: 1: על בית הכרם שׂאו משׂאת, 'raise a fire-signal on Beth-haccherem (modern Ramat Raḥel)', and reminds one of the equally dramatic use of fire-signals described by Clytemnestra in Aeschylus's *Agamemnon* (lines 281 ff.).

In the same Letter the writer, probably Hošaʿyahu, assures Yaʾoš that he has written down על הדלת all that Yaʾoš has written to him about. Here the exact meaning of דלת is much disputed: it may be, literally, a 'door', on which notices were put (cf. Deut. 6: 9 'and you shall write them on the door-posts (מזוזות) of your house'); but perhaps it might be best to take the word in the same sense as דלתות in Jer. 36: 23 (LXX σελίδας, correctly), where it has the technical meaning of 'column of writing on a papyrus scroll' (compare the Greek loan from Semitic *dlt*, δέλτος 'writing tablet'). In this case what is envisaged is an official log book, into which the day's orders were entered. A similar type of document actually survives in Egyptian, in Papyrus Anastasi III,[1] which contains a diary, dating from the thirteenth century B.C., kept by an official stationed at a frontier post in the Eastern Delta. And perhaps the very fragmentary Phoenician papyrus of the fourth/third century B.C., published by Aimé-Giron, belongs to the same category.

The two Hebrew ostraca from Tel Arad that have so far been published[2] promise well for the future, and from the many interesting linguistic features one might single out the striking substantival use of עוד in the phrase ומעוד הקמח הראשן, 'and from the remainder of the best quality flour'—a usage that finds no exact parallel in biblical Hebrew.

Despite their small extent, the surviving Early Hebrew inscriptions serve as a constant reminder of how limited a picture the vocabulary of the Old Testament gives us of the range that the spoken language must have had: thus the Siloam inscription has a vocabulary of some forty words, yet of these two— roughly 5 per cent!—do not occur in the Old Testament. It is especially the vocabulary of everyday life that is poorly represented in the Hebrew bible, and so, for example, it is only from the Samaria ostraca that we learn the term for the Israelite equivalent of soap, שמן רחץ.

Even documents differing widely in time can illustrate each other: the Moabite stone[3] thus reveals what is probably the correct form of a word that occurs both in Ecclus. 50: 3 and in the Copper scroll from Qumran, cave 3 (3Q15). On the Copper scroll there are four occurrences of a word that is transcribed by Allegro as אשוח, but by Milik as אשיח: as very frequently in texts from Qumran *waw* and *yodh* are very hard to distinguish, and palaeographically either reading could be the

---

[1] An English translation of the text in Papyrus Anastasi III can be found in *Ancient Near Eastern Texts*, second edition, ed. J. B. Pritchard (Princeton, 1955), pp. 258–9. The Phoenician papyrus mentioned below is *KAI*, no. 51.

[2] Y. Aharoni, 'Hebrew Ostraca from Tel Arad', *Israel Exploration Journal*, XVI (1966), 1 ff.

[3] Cooke, *North Semitic Inscriptions*, no. 1; *KAI*, no. 181; *DOTT*, pp. 195–8.

correct one. The passage in Ecclesiasticus is preserved in Hebrew only in the Cairo Genizah fragment B, and this manuscript reads אשיח (LXX λάκκος). Now in the Moabite stone, lines 9 and 23, the same, or a related, word occurs in the form אשוח (probably *'ešwaḥ*, 'reservoir, cistern'). The evidence of the passage in Ecclesiasticus at first sight suggests that there were two words, אשוח and אשיח, current successively. But in fact this need not necessarily be so, for, as it now turns out, the Genizah fragments of Ecclesiasticus almost certainly derive ultimately from Qumran manuscripts of that book, and so it is very possible that the scribe of the Genizah fragment B, faced with this—by his day—rare or obsolete word, written with a letter that could be read either as a *waw*, or as a *yodh*, in this case (by no means an isolated one) made the wrong choice. Thus it is very possible that אשוח is the correct form of the word in all its known occurrences.

Often, of course, one is in danger of arguing *per ignotum in ignotius*, and one such case is that of the mysterious אראל דודה in line 12 of the Moabite stone. Of the many suggested interpretations, perhaps the least unsatisfactory is that of Segert: 'the altar-hearth of its דוד, or beloved', which he takes to be the appellation of a god, drawing attention to the conjecture דודך, for דרך, 'way', of MT, in Amos 8: 14. The emendation indeed gives a much better parallelism with the preceding words: '"As thy god, O Dan, lives", and "as *thy beloved*, O Beersheba, lives".' The Septuagint here provides ὁ θεός σου, corresponding to דרך of MT, but Wutz neatly conjectured θεῖος ('uncle') for θεός, which in turn would presuppose the conjectured Hebrew reading דודך!

Likewise it would be pleasing if the editor's reading לפקח סמדר on a jar (inscription no. 7) from Hazor[1] were correct, for this would both give a nice parallel to ין ישן of the Samaria ostraca, and at the same time illustrate a passage in the Mishnah (Orlah, 1. 7), which speaks of סמדר (cf. Song of Sol. 2: 13, etc.) as a fruit—presumably because it was used for making a kind of wine (Dioscorides gives the actual recipe for making wine

---

[1] For the Hazor Inscriptions see Y. Yadin *et al.*, *Hazor II* (Jerusalem, 1960), pp. 70 ff.

from οἰνάνθη, the Greek equivalent of סמדר, in his *De Materia Medica*, v. 25). Unfortunately, however, it was quickly pointed out that the last letter of the inscription in question is definitely a *hē*, not a *rēš*, and so the second word must be a name (i.e. 'belonging to Peqaḥ (son of) sᴍᴅ/ʀʜ'), not a commodity.

Finally, it is interesting to reflect that less than half a century ago some scholars were able to hold that most of the books of the Old Testament had been written down first of all in cuneiform. Today, of course, the picture is completely changed, and, quite apart from the many impressions of papyrus left on clay seals, we are even fortunate enough to possess an actual papyrus palimpsest fragment containing part of a letter as the underwriting, and a list of names as the upper: both texts probably date from the seventh century B.C.[1]

[1] The papyrus palimpsest fragment is Murabbaʿât 17 ᴀ/ʙ, published in *Discoveries in the Judean Desert*, vol. ɪɪ (Oxford, 1961).

5

'ANOTHER LITTLE DRINK'—
ISAIAH 28: 1-22

by G. R. Driver

The prophet Isaiah often uses the figure of a vineyard or of wine,
now in describing the Lord's care for his people (27: 2-6) and
now in condemning his fellow-countrymen as a vineyard which
disappoints its owner (5: 1-3), and that of wine turned sour
for the disappearance of joy from the earth (24: 7-9); he also
depicts his defaulting fellow-countrymen as drunkards in several
poems (5: 22-3; 28: 1-13; 29: 9-10). The best known of this
last group is the famous denunciation of the drunken leaders
of Ephraim (cf. Amos 4: 1, 4-6), to whom he compares the
leaders of Judah (28: 1-22); and, as a number of expressions
in this last poem seem to have been misunderstood, it may be
thought to deserve a special study in the hope of clearing up
some of the obscurities.

I

The opening verses, denouncing the leaders of Ephraim, contain several dubious translations as commonly rendered (RV).

In verse 1 'the crown of pride of the drunkards of Ephraim'
poses the question how these words can be parallel to 'the
fading flower of his glorious beauty'; and what can be the
meaning of 'on the head of the fat valley of them that are
overcome with wine'?

Here the words of an unknown Greek poet may throw some
light on the meaning of this verse:

ἐμοὶ μέλει μύροισιν	I am careful to drench
καταβρέχειν ὑπήνην·	my beard with perfumes;
ἐμοὶ μέλει ῥόδοισιν	I am careful to wreath
καταστέφειν κάρηνα	my head with roses

(W. T. Bergk, *Poetae Lyrici Graeci* (Leipzig, 1853), p. 811, no. 7,
lines 5-8); and many similar ditties show that the flowers in

47

the garland are regularly in full bloom and bright with colour (cf. *ibid.* p. 826, no. 42, lines 3–4; p. 829, no. 49, lines 6–8). Fresh flowers and perfumes, then, may be expected also in a Hebrew drinking song.

In verse 1 ציץ נבל 'fading flowers' is a grammatically correct phrase, however inappropriate to the context; but in verse 4 ציצת נבל 'a (single) flower of a fading one' is a strange way of describing a 'fading flower' and grammatically hard to justify.[1] The Accadian *nib/plu* 'bud, young shoot, sprig' and the Judaeo-Aramaic נִבְלָא 'unripe figs' (Jer. 8: 13), as well as the Arabic *nabula* I 'was excellent' IV '(a palm) yielded a crop of ripe dates', suggest a Hebrew נבל 'young shoot, sprig' still carrying blossom, however it may have been vocalized.

The first difficulty in על ראש גיא שמנים הלומי יין 'on the head of the fat valley of (!) them that are overcome by wine' is, as this translation shows, grammatical; for 'the fat valley' is not in the construct state, so that 'them that are overcome by wine' cannot be in the genitive case dependent on it. This difficulty can be overcome by accepting the old correction of גִיא שׁ' into גֵּאֵי שׁ' 'men proud of fat things',[2] whatever that may mean; and 1QIs[a] now confirms this emendation.

The root G'Y is basically onomatopoeic, as the Arabic *ji' ji'* 'gee-gee', the cry urging camels to drink, shows; from this *ja'ja'a* 'called (camels) to water' is formed as a denominative verb, and another verb derived from the same base is the Arabic *ja'ā* 'contained, retained (e.g. water)'. Hence on the one side the Hebrew גאה 'surged' is used of any rising head of water in a stream (Ezek. 47: 5) and of the waves of the sea (Pss. 46: 4; 89: 10; Job 38: 11); and this use is extended to include growing vegetation (Job 8: 11), to a lion raising its head above the scrub (Job 10: 16), and lastly to men raising their heads in pride (*passim*). On the other side, inasmuch as a head of flood-water carries mud down with it, the root came to be used of anything coloured like mud as in the Arabic *ja'iya* '(a horse) was brown-coloured', from which *ju'atu* 'dusty colour mixed with red' and *jū'watu* 'rough black ground' are derived. The semantic de-

---

[1] Cf. *GK*, § 128*w*.

[2] J. Halévy, *Rev. Sém.* XXI (1913), 5 and L. Rost, *ZAW*, LIII (1935–6), 292.

velopment of the root, then, starts from the gurgling noise of
water which is imitated to urge camels to drink and then comes
to serve on the one side for the surging flood-tide rushing noisily
down stream and on the other side for the brownish muddy
colour of the water as it carries the like-coloured soil with it.
Thus גאון הירדן 'the muddy flood of the Jordan' exactly describes the colour of that stream, which is not a stream in which
anyone is likely to have taken much pride, except perhaps because it is perennial whereas most of the streams in Palestine
are intermittent; for it runs between wide banks of mud, its
bed is muddy and its water is mud-coloured.[1] A similar use of
the root may be seen in ויתאבכו גאות עשן 'and they [the
thickets] are thick with the murkiness of smoke', i.e. 'covered
with a murky pall of smoke' (Isa. 9: 17); for here the Hebrew
אבך 'was dense' may best be explained in the light of the
Arabic *'abika* 'was fleshy', while the Hebrew גאות 'murkiness,
surging' has as much the sense of colour as of surging upwards.
Which sense is uppermost must be determined in the light of
the immediate context in which the word occurs.

Here the sense of גאה 'surging, proud; muddy' must depend
on that of שמן 'fatness, oil'. What cannot be meant is 'men
proud of fats', which is sheer nonsense; the Hebrew שמן 'fatness'
is nowhere used for human fat, while a drunkard is not likely
to be proud of being a fat man, and in any case whether he is
fat or thin, tall or short, is immaterial to the context. Further
חלב 'fat' and פימה 'excessive fat' both describe fat on the human
body, and another word for it is otiose. Sa'adyah alone has
seen that שמנים 'fatnesses' can mean only 'unguents, perfumes'
in the context.[2] The drunkards then may be described as גאי
שמנים 'streaming with unguents' or 'perfumes', which agrees not
only with the custom of Greek tipplers as quoted above but also
with Hebrew practice; for the Hebrews freely used שמן 'un-
guent(s), perfume(s)' as a sign of happiness and hospitality
(Amos 6: 6; Mic. 6: 15; Pss. 23: 5; 133: 2; 141: 5; Eccles. 9: 8).
A possible objection to this interpretation of גאה 'streaming'

[1] Cf. G. A. Smith, *Historical Geography of the Holy Land* (London, 1931),
pp. 485–6.
[2] So Acc. *šamnu*, Heb. שמן 'oil', especially as odoriferous (Song of Sol.
1: 3; 4: 10).

is that גֵאוּת 'pride' implies giving a different sense or *nuance* to the same root within the same verse or paragraph; rather, this is a positive reason for accepting the new interpretation, inasmuch as such paronomasia is a common practice in West-Semitic literature, of which the Ugaritic *l'emm* 'rulers' and 'people' (Baal IV. i. 16–17) is the earliest instance. Hebrew examples are עשׂה 'worshipped' and 'made' (Exod. 32: 35; cf. Pesh., Targ. O. and Targ. Ps.-J.), למודים 'teaching' and 'pupils' (Isa. 50: 4), כסף 'food' and 'money' (Isa. 55: 1), נפשׁ 'plenty' and 'appetite' (Isa. 58: 10), אתנן 'effigy' and 'harlot's fee' (Mic. 1: 7), and מן 'by, through' and 'without' (Ps. 104: 24; cf. Isa. 53: 8).[1]

In verse 3 תֵּרָמַסְנָה 'it shall (not) be trodden down' is not a feminine plural form, requiring the alteration of עֲטֶרֶת 'crown' into עַטְרֹת 'crowns' (Meinhold) but a singular form with the emphatic *-nāh*, as in ידה...תִּשְׁלַחְנָה 'she put forth her hand' (Judg. 5: 26; cf. Obad. 13, where the same form occurs with the ellipse of the natural object, so that the text does not require emendation). The ending is perhaps incorrectly read *-nāh* in consequence of having been wrongly taken as a feminine plural form and ought rather to be read *-annāh* (cf. Arabic *-anna*) or *-ennāh* (Procksch) as an 'energic' feminine singular form.[2]

In verse 4 כבכורה 'like its first-ripe fig' must be corrected to כבכורה 'like a first-ripe fig' (Duhm with Aq., Theod., Vulg., Pesh., Targ.).

The next problem is raised by אשר יראה הראה אותה בעודה בכפו יבלענה 'which when he that looketh upon it seeth, while it is yet in his hand he eateth it up' (RV), a verbal translation which makes little if any sense. If however יִרְאֶה 'he sees' is emended to יֶאֱרֶה 'he plucks' (Houbigant), which LXX πρὶν εἰς τὴν χεῖρα αὐτοῦ λαβεῖν αὐτό supports, and if יִבְלָעֶנָּה 'he swallows it [the flower]' is read יִבֹּל עֵינָה 'its bloom will wither',[3] the whole phrase may be translated 'he who sees them plucks them, and their bloom withers while they are yet in his hand'.

---

[1] Whether הקיץ 'parleyed' and קיץ 'to be cowed' (Isa. 7: 6, 16) come from the same root or from different roots is not clear.

[2] Cf. *GK*, §47k.

[3] M. Scott, *Textual Discoveries in Proverbs, Psalms and Isaiah* (London, 1927), pp. 197–8.

The error may be ascribed to two causes: that the Hebrew עין 'eye' has not elsewhere the meaning here ascribed to it, which however the Syriac '*aina* 'eye' and 'bud' of a vine, like the Greek ὀφθαλμός and like the Latin *oculus* 'eye' and 'bud', shows to be possible extensions of the use of the word; and that a feminine noun is here taken with a masculine verb, which however is permissible when the predicate precedes the subject.[1]

In verse 6 משיבי מלחמה 'to those who turn back the battle' must be read with ל' 'to' introducing it, though accidentally omitted in the MT (Houbigant with Vulg. and Targ.); it can hardly be carried through from the preceding clause.

In verse 7 the current interpretations of the text are again open to question; for 'erring' through wine and 'going astray' through strong drink go ill with being 'swallowed up (!)' by wine; and 'erring in vision' and 'stumbling (!) in judgement' are not concepts *eiusdem generis* with those preceding them, while 'being swallowed up' by wine and 'stumbling in judgement' are both strange expressions in which verb and noun are ill suited to one another.

Here the Arabic *sajâ* I '(night) was quiet and dark', II 'wrapped (a corpse) in a shroud', V 'wrapped himself up' suggests a Hebrew שגה 'was wrapped up in, addicted to' as in באהבתה תשגה 'thou art wrapped up in love of her' and למה תשגה בני בזרה 'why, my son, art thou wrapped up in a strange woman?' (Prov. 5: 19, 20) and in ברב אולתו ישגה 'he is wrapped up (as though shrouded) in the abundance of his folly' (Prov. 5: 23); and the same verb appears in כל־שגה בו לא יחכם 'every one who is addicted to it (*sc.* wine) is unwise' (Prov. 20: 1; cf. Vulg. *quicunque his delectatur*).[2] Similarly the Arabic *taġiya* 'croaked, guffawed' and the reduplicated *taġtaġa* 'spoke confusedly' (cf. Hebrew תעתע 'mocked' and Arabic *ta'ta'a* 'stammered') point to a Hebrew תעה 'cackled, croaked, guffawed' (distinct from 'strayed'), here used of the bawdy shouts of drunken men. The same verb may also be seen in כי ילדיו אל־אל ישועו יתעו לבלי אכל 'when its young ones [those of the raven] cry to God, croaking for lack of food' (Job 38: 41, where ישועו

---

[1] *GK*, §145*o* (cf. Gen. 1: 14, etc.).
[2] Cf. G. R. Driver, *Die Welt des Orients*, I (Wuppertal, Stuttgart, 1950), 410.

G. R. DRIVER

is a gloss on יתעו, as the metre shows);[1] for wandering is inappropriate to nestlings, while תעה 'croaked' is singularly apposite to describe the 'hoarse croak of the old raven' and the 'discordant chatter' of a number of them together.[2] That תעה 'strayed' is used elsewhere in connection with drunkenness (Isa. 19: 13, 14) is immaterial; the context in every case must decide which verb is meant.

Next 'they are swallowed up of drink' (RV) means nothing; the mistranslation is due to confusing the Hebrew בלע = Arabic *bali'a* 'swallowed' with another Hebrew בלע = Arabic *balaġa* 'reached, reached out at, overcame', which is reported to be 'said frequently of wine' (Lane) and from which also *bulaġâni* 'two disasters', i.e. 'dire disaster' and *balâġâtu* 'slanders' are derived, and the Syriac *bla'* 'was beaten, struck; was struck down, overcome (by love, envy, desire, greed, stupor)' (Brockelmann); and this root is found in its various senses also in the Old Testament (2 Sam. 17: 16; Isa. 9: 15; Pss. 35: 25; 52: 6; 55: 10; 107: 27; Job 37: 20; Prov. 19: 28; Lam. 2: 16; Eccles. 10: 12).[3] Consequently the need to suppose yet another בלע = בלל 'confused' disappears.[4]

At the end of the verse 'they err in vision, they stumble in judgement' (RV) is an equally dubious rendering of the Hebrew text if only because 'vision' and 'judgement' are out of place in parallelism with 'strong drink' and 'wine'. Here $rō'ēh$ 'seer' (not 'seeing') must be read $rō'eh = rŏweh$ 'intoxication', as Theod. μέθη and Pesh. *rwāyûtâ* 'intoxication' show; so $rā'āh = rāwāh$ 'was drenched, saturated; swilled' occurs in a number of passages, as already recognized long ago by Geiger and others (e.g. Isa. 22: 9; 53: 10; Jer. 31: 14; 46: 10; Pss. 36: 9; 40: 13; 50: 23; 60: 5; 91: 16; Job 10: 15; 20: 17; 31: 7; 33: 21;

---

[1] Cf. G. R. Driver, *AJSL*, LII (1935–6), 167–8 and *OBL*, I (1957), 139.

[2] H. B. Tristram, *Natural History of the Bible* (London, 1868), pp. 200–1.

[3] B. Jacob, *ZAW*, XXXII (1912), 287; G. R. Driver, *ibid.* LII (1934), 52–3 and *JTS*, XXIII (1931), 40–1; A. Guillaume, *ibid.* N.S. XIII (1962), 321–2, and Driver, *ibid.* 369–70; also H. H. Graetz, *Koheleth* (Leipzig, 1871), p. 121; E. Dhorme, *Le Livre de Job* (Paris, 1926), p. 521; Driver *ap.* B. Gemser, *Sprüche Salomos* (*HAT*, 1963), pp. 77, 112 and B. Albrektson, *Lamentations* (Lund, 1963), pp. 114–15.

[4] J. Barth, *Beiträge Jesaia* (Carlsruhe, 1885), pp. 4–5.

52

Prov. 23: 31; cf. 1 Macc. 6: 34 and 3 Macc. 5: 2);[1] the Targ.'s 'after pleasant food' partly supports this interpretation of the word. A Hebrew פוק 'to reel, totter' (*BDB*) does not seem to exist, being a doubtful word in the very few passages cited for it (Amos 2: 13; Jer. 10: 4) and being unsupported by the cognate languages; contrariwise the Arabic *fâqa(w)* 'bent, broke, cracked, split; hiccoughed, panted, gasped; expired', Syriac *pāq* 'sighed' and *'etpaw(w)aq* 'gaped, yawned' and the Judaeo-Aramaic פִּיקָא 'subsidence, sinking; fainting, collapse' suggest something quite different, namely, 'to break apart, become cracked', e.g. in reference to idols (Jer. 10: 3; Vulg. and Pesh.); the derived nouns mean something similar in לפוקה ולמכשול לב 'for cracking up and giving way of courage' (1 Sam. 25: 31) and פק ברכים 'giving way of the knees' in panic fear (Nahum 2: 11).[2] Here either 'hiccoughed' as characteristic of some stages of inebriation or 'subsided' (*anglice* 'went under the table') is the sense required by the context. Accordingly, the Arabic *falla* trans. 'broke, cracked, dented, notched; routed (an army)', especially as seen in *falla 'anhu 'aqluhu* 'his wits (intermittently) forsook him' (cognate *fâla* 'was unsound in judgement'), supports a Hebrew פלילה 'loss of wits, collapse' or the like, distinct from פלילה 'intervention' (Isa. 16: 3) and פליל 'arbitration' (Exod. 21: 22); and the Hebrew פלילים 'routed' or perhaps rather 'crack-brained, maddened (with fear), panic-struck' (Deut. 32: 31, where the word is translated ἀνόητοι by the LXX) agrees with this interpretation of the word. Thus the phrase under discussion will mean 'they hiccough in (drunken) frenzy' or 'they collapse unconscious'. The alteration of פלִילִיה '(in) frenzy' into בפלילִיה 'in frenzy' (Houbigant) is needless; for the noun may stand in the accusative case qualifying the action described by the verb.[3]

In verse 10 (cf. verse 13) צו לצו צו לצו קו לקו קו לקו 'it is precept upon precept, precept upon precept; line upon line, line upon line' (RV) presents the principal difficulty in the

---

[1] A. Geiger, *Urschrift und Uebersetzungen...* (Breslau, 1857), p. 414; cf. *Jüdische Zeitschrift*, IV (1866), 283 (Zweifel *ap.* Geiger); V (1867), 191–2 (Derenburg); IX (1871), 120–3 (Geiger).
[2] Cf. A. Guillaume, *Abr-Nahrain*, I (1958–9), 13, 31 and D. R. Ap-Thomas, *VT*, VI (1956), 234.   [3] *GK*, §118*q*.

chapter; for no Hebrew צו 'precept', though formally possible, is known (while מצוה 'command, instruction' occurs some 170 times); and the translation of 'ל 'to' as 'upon', meaning apparently 'in addition to', is hardly justifiable. Further, what קו 'cord, chord (Ps. 19: 5), (musical) note, notation (Ecclus. 44: 5; 1QH 1: 28–9 and 1QS 10: 9)' can mean in the context is not clear; it can hardly mean a 'line' of written instructions to hearers of the eighth century B.C., of whom scarcely any can ever have seen or even heard of a written document. The Versions unfortunately throw no light on either of these words, and no useful purpose can be served by setting them out, beyond recalling that the Greek translator called ὁ Ἑβραῖος transliterates them as σαυλεσαυ and καυλακαυ (Field). Houbigant[1] in the eighteenth century thought that צו (ṣāw) and קו (qāw) might be the original names of two letters of the alphabet, namely, צ/ץ (ṣādê) and ק (qôf); so too Montgomery[2] and Kennett[3] explained them as part of a lesson in which a schoolmaster repeated 'ṣādê-wāw are for (the letter) ṣû, qôf-wāw are for (the letter) qû' to the pupils to whom he was teaching the alphabet. These letters may indeed once have had monosyllabic names based on their sounds, for which ṣādê and qôf will have afterwards been substituted as representing their forms;[4] but no direct evidence for these supposed original names has yet been found. Further, the question may well be raised why the prophet arbitrarily has chosen two letters from the middle of the alphabet and does not call it by the first two letters (cf. Syriac 'ālef-bait, 'alfâ-baitâ and Greek ἀλφάβητος 'alphabet'). Another point which has recently come to light is that 1QIs[a] has צי (ṣê or ṣî) for צו (ṣāw), thus weakening the suspicion that the two together are the names of letters of the alphabet. Lastly, does any schoolmaster or other person teach the alphabet to 'them that are weaned from the milk and drawn from the breasts' (RV), i.e. to infants not yet capable of speech?

---

[1] In *Bibl. Hebr.* IV (1753), 73–4.
[2] *JBL*, XXXI (1912), 141–2.
[3] *Schweich Lectures* (London, 1933), p. 12; cf. W. W. Hallo, *JBL*, LXXVII (1958), 338.
[4] Cf. G. R. Driver, *Schweich Lectures* (London, 1954), pp. 156–61.

Clearly the two words are chosen as echoing קִיא (*qî'*) 'vomit' and צֹאָה (*ṣō'āh*) 'excrement, filth'[1] in verse 8; but taking them to mean respectively 'vomit' and 'excrement' is senseless.[2] Equally clearly they are intended to suggest the nonsensical cries and shouts of the drunken revellers of verse 7. In this connection the variant צִי (*ṣî*), which is due to the sibilant preference for the *i*-sound,[3] while *u* as a back-vowel is preferred with *q* which is itself a back-sound, is important as showing that *ṣāw/ṣî* and with it *qāw* designate nothing but meaningless sounds. At the same time, although they reflect the shouts and cries of drunken revellers, they may well have recalled, if not actually been, real words. As such, two connections, more or less merging in one another, can be suggested for both of them. First, the Arabic *ṣawwu(n)* 'empty' and *ṣawwatu(n)* 'echoing sound' suggests the notion of some mere empty sound, void of meaning, for the Hebrew צַו; and this basic sense can be recognized not only in the biblical הוֹאִיל הָלַךְ אַחֲרֵי־צָו 'he [Ephraim] was content to pursue vain follies'(Hos. 5: 11, where the word is translated τὰ μάταια by the LXX), but also in the post-biblical הלכו אחרי צו 'they went after *ṣāw*' and הצו הוא מטיף '*ṣāw*: that is a driveller' (CD 7: 1). So too *dawwatu(n)* 'clamour' and *dawâtu(n)* 'uproar' may be taken as cognate, if strengthened, forms of these words. Second, the Arabic *qawiya* I 'was strong; was very hungry; was empty; was incapable', II 'corroborated',[4] IV 'twisted (a rope) with threads of various thickness', from which *qîyu(n)* 'waste land' and *qawâyatu(n)* 'strength, desert land' are derived, suggests what the Hebrew קַו may import. The underlying idea connecting these diverse meanings is that what is twisted is strong and hard, and that a twisted feeling in the intestines is a mark of emptiness in them, i.e. great hunger (cf. Syriac *ṭwâ* 'fasted' with Arabic *ṭawiya* 'was rolled

---

[1] Cf. צֵא 'dung' (Isa. 30: 22; LXX κόπρος).

[2] H. Schmidt *ap.* H. Gunkel, *Psalmen* (Göttingen, 1926), p. 77.

[3] C. Brockelmann, *Grundriss der vergleichenden Grammatik der semitischen Sprachen*, I (Berlin, 1908), 202–3.

[4] Hence the Arabic *taqwiyatu(n)* 'repetition' suggests that the Hebrew *qiwwāh* 'waited' means 'repeated' when followed by the name of the Lord as its direct object in the accusative case (Ps. 52: 11) or 'called repeatedly' on the Lord when standing in the same position (Ps. 40: 2).

up; suffered hunger' with Syriac *kfen* 'was hungry' and Arabic *kafana* 'spun; wrapped in a shroud'). Consequently such reduplicated forms as the Talmudic Aramaic קַוְקַו 'croaking (of frogs)', Syriac *qauqī* 'hooted' and the Arabic *qauqa'a, qauqā* 'cackled, clucked' are nothing but onomatopoeic reduplications of the same root (cf. Latin *caccare* 'to empty the bowels' and *cacabare* 'to cackle'). The Hebrew word, therefore, can without hesitation be taken as describing a confused medley of senseless shouts. Accordingly the sense of the verse will be that the drunkards mock at the prophet, asking him to whom does he think that he is imparting knowledge—to newly born infants; and he answers: 'No! only to tipplers and topers, one shouting "Hey!" to another's "Hey!" or "Ho!" to another's "Ho!" as they call for drinks all around!'

The repetition of the drunkards' cries is similar to the repetition of the vintagers' cries in

ויין מיקבים השבתי
לא ידרך הידד הידד לא הידד

> and I have stopped the flow of wine from the vats;
> no shout shall follow shout—no, not a shout

(Jer. 48: 33; cf. Arabic *dáraka ṣautahu* 'he made his voice follow on', i.e. 'he spoke continuously'). Further, such cries and shouts of tipplers as are here assumed are found in the poetry also of other nations, for example, in the English

> with a Hey and a Ho
> Tirra-ley, Tirra-low
> (Skelton)

and in the German

> *A! tara lara da!*

in Auerbach's cellar (Goethe).

What then does זעיר שם זעיר שם 'here a little, there a little' (RV) at the end of the verse mean? It cannot mean 'You boy there, you boy there' as Kennett's interpretation of the scene seems to imply; for schoolchildren, as argued above, are here out of place, and the Hebrew זעיר 'little' is used only of things, as it is here translated in the Versions, e.g. ἔτι μικρόν (LXX),

modicum ibi (Vulg.), *qalîl ltamán* 'a little for there' (Pesh.), and
קליל מן הדא כקליל מן הדא 'a little of this like a little of that'
(Saʿad.). Briefly, it is the tippler's call for another glass of beer
or wine, with which the famous 'another little drink won't do
us any harm' (George Robey) may not inaptly be compared.

What then is the force of שׁם...שׁם...'...there...there'? It
may mean 'there [i.e. here]..., there...' in the sense of 'to
him there...to him over there', although such a personal use
of this adverb is rare, if not unique. Or ought it to be read
שׁים...שׁים... 'put...put...' in the sense of 'lay on (the table)'
or 'bring' a little more wine? Anacreon's

φέρ᾽ ὕδωρ, φέρ᾽ οἶνον, ὦ παῖ	bring water, bring wine, boy

and

ἄγε δή, φέρ᾽ ἡμῖν, ὦ παῖ,	bring, do bring us, boy
κελέβην, ὅκως ἄμυσιν	a flagon that I may drink
προπίω	a long draught

(Bergk, *Poetae Lyrici Graeci*, p. 788, no. 62, line 1 and p. 789, no. 63,
lines 1–3) will illustrate the Hebrew phrase; but no ancient
version so reads this word, and the Massoretic vocalization is
favoured by the order of the words.

On this interpretation of the passage קו 'empty sound' in
verse 10 and verse 13, while echoing קיא 'vomit' in verse 8, is
followed by a totally different קו 'cord, plummet-line' in verse
17, where the paronomasia emphasizes the contrast. This kind
of assonance between words derived from totally different roots
but standing in close or immediate juxtaposition to one another
is a not uncommon phenomenon in Hebrew literature: e.g. שׁפל
'was low' and 'lazed' (Isa. 32: 19; *š* and *t*), נצח 'blood' and
'glory' (Isa. 63: 3, 6; *d* and *ṣ*), עיט 'lair' and 'birds of prey'
(Jer. 12: 9; *ǵ* and ʿ), שׁכח 'forgot' and שׁכח 'withered' (Ps. 137:
6; *š* and *t*), דל 'poor man' and 'open door' (Prov. 22: 22).

In verse 15 כרתנו ברית את מות 'we have made a covenant
with death' ought perhaps to be rendered 'with Death', i.e. the
god of death ruling in Sheol; for death may have been personified
or deified here as in other places in the Old Testament (e.g.
I Sam. 26: 16; 2 Sam. 22: 6; Isa. 5: 14; Jer. 9: 20; Hos.
13: 14; Hab. 2: 15; Pss. 18: 5, 6; 49: 15; 116: 3; Job 18: 13;

G. R. DRIVER

28: 22; Prov. 1: 12; 7: 27; 13: 14; 14: 12, 27; 16: 25; Song of Sol. 8: 6).[1] In such cases *māwet* 'death' ought probably to be read as *Môt* (cf. Phoenician Μωτ, Μουθ in Greek transliterations);[2] and the LXX transliteration of several proper names (e.g. אֲחִימוֹת Οχιμωθ and עַזְמָוֶת Αзμωθ; חַצַרְמָוֶת Σαρμωθ and יְרֵמוֹת Ιεριμου)[3] support such a vocalization of the name.

Further, in verse 15 חֹזֶה and in verse 18 חָזוּת 'covenant', as LXX συνθῆκαι, διαθήκη and Vulg. *foedus* rightly render them (Gesenius), have no connection with חזה 'saw' (cf. Arabic *ḥazâ* 'divined') but come from the same root as חָזֶה 'breast' (cf. Arabic *ḥadâ* I 'was opposite', III 'rivalled', VI 'ran parallel'), as the South-Arabic *ḥdyt* 'things that correspond, agreement' shows.[4] It must then be accented as *ḥōzeh* 'agreement', not as *ḥōzéh* 'seer' (König).

In verse 15 as in verse 18 the allusion in 'the covenant with death' is not to a secret agreement with the Assyrians to spare the tipplers when they overrun the land;[5] like the Latin *pax illis* (namely *Psyllis*) *cum morte data est*,[6] the expression is a figure of speech for taking every possible precaution to forestall disaster (cf. Hos. 2: 18; Job 5: 22–3).[7]

In both these verses the Hebrew *kî* (like the Ugaritic *k*) 'surely', when postponed, has not temporal but emphatic force.[8]

In the same verses the Hebrew שׁוֹט/שִׁיט 'torrent' must be distinguished from שׁוֹט 'scourge', which is not in place here, as LXX καταιγὶς and Theod. κατακλυσμὸς as well as Targ. נַחַל 'torrent' show. Several Jewish commentators (e.g. Ibn Janâḥ,

---

1 U. Cassuto, *Orientalia*, N.S. VII (Rome, 1938), 267; J. Baumgartner, *Theologische Rundschau*, N.F. XIII (Tübingen, 1941), 172; A. Pohl, *Biblica* (Rome, 1941), pp. 36–7; S. Rin, *VT*, IX (1959), 324; G. R. Driver, *JJS*, X (1965), 120 and G. Widengren, *Sakrales Königtum* (Stuttgart, 1955), p. 70.

2 Philo *ap.* K. Müller, *Fragmenta Historicorum Graecorum* (Paris, 1841–72), III, 565, ii. 1 and Eusebius, *Praeparatio Evangelica*, i. 10; cf. Virolleaud, *Syria*, XII (Paris, 1931), 206 and W. F. Albright, *JPOS*, XII (1932), 193.

3 G. R. Driver, *PEQ*, LXXVII (1945), 13–14.

4 G. R. Driver, *JTS*, XXXVIII (1937), 44; cf. C. Brockelmann, *Lexicon Syriacum* (Halle, 1928), p. 216.

5 W. R. Smith, *Prophets of Israel* (London, 1895), p. 284.

6 Lucan, *Pharsalia*, IX, 898.

7 R. Lowth *ap.* T. K. Cheyne, *Isaiah* (London, 1886), pp. 165–6.

8 Cf. G. R. Driver, *Canaanite Myths and Legends* (Edinburgh, 1956), p. 144.

'Another little drink'

Ibn Ezra and his contemporary Eliezer of Beaugency) accept this explanation of the word, which the Arabic *sauṭu* 'torrent', as in 'the Lord poured upon them a torrent of punishment' (Koran lxxxix. 12) and the Ethiopic *sōṭa* 'poured out', confirm.[1] In verse 16 יִסַּד 'it has been founded' must be read יֹסֵד 'founding' (Lowth with Aq., Symm., Theod., Pesh., Targ., Saʿad.) or מְיַסֵּד 'founding' (Weir *ap.* Cheyne) which 1QIsᵃ מיסד now confirms, and מוּסָּד may be taken as a *forma mixta* offering a choice of מוּסָד (Hophʿal) and מְיֻסָּד (Puʿal) 'founded', although it ought perhaps to be deleted as a dittograph (Cheyne with LXX, Syrohexapla, Hebrew MSS).

What אבן בחן 'tried stone' (RV), literally a 'stone of testing', means is not clear; for that this can be paraphrased as a 'tested stone' (*BDB*) is by no means certain, although it is so interpreted by several versions (Aq., Symm., Theod.: λίθος δόκιμος; Vulg.: *lapis probatus*); other renderings are 'costly stone' (LXX λίθος πολυτελής) and 'carved stone' (Saʿad. חגר צנאם). Possibly here the Hebrew *bōḥan* is identical with the Egyptian *bḫn-w* 'diorite, granite' or other hard, dark-coloured stone, quarried in the Wâdy Ḥamâmât and called *lapis niger* or *Thebaicus* by ancient writers; this was much used both in ancient monuments and as a touch-stone, which may be the reason for assimilating the Hebrew word to the Egyptian name (Sethe).[2] That it is the Egyptian *bnbn* 'pyramidion, top-stone' cut first but laid last with a view to testing and so ensuring constructional accuracy[3] is highly improbable; the Egyptian and Hebrew words do not correspond, the 'top-stone' cannot be identified with the 'corner-stone', and architectural accuracy is hardly in point. That this stone is a figure for the Lord as the 'Rock of Israel' (Isa. 30: 29)[4] is equally improbable, if only because it is the Lord who is laying the foundation. Rather, the allusion is based

---

[1] J. Barth, *Etymologische Studien...* (Leipzig, 1893), p. 14 and *ZAW*, xxxii (1912), 306 and xxxiv (1914), 60, and A. Požnanski, *ZAW*, xxxvi (1916), 119–20; cf. Maimonides, *Guide of the Perplexed*, iii. 23 on Job 9: 23 (Arabic *sailu* 'stream, torrent' in the Arabic version).

[2] L. Köhler, *Theologische Zeitschrift*, iii (Basle, 1947), 390 and T. O. Lambdin, *JAOS*, lxxiii (1953), 148.

[3] J. Jeremias, *ZNTW*, xxix (1930), 264–5 and E. E. Le Bas, *PEQ*, lxxviii (1946), 103–15.   [4] Cheyne, *Isaiah*, I, 166.

primarily on a recollection of the 'great stones, costly stones' of Solomon's temple (1 Kings 5: 17), then still standing in Jerusalem. Secondarily, in order to constitute an effectual substitute for the unreal 'refuge in lies' and 'shelter in falsehood' to which it is opposed, it must represent some existent reality, something of which the basis must be found in the prophet's own present, however far it must reach into the future; the chosen nation is imperishable, but God's justice requires that its unworthy members shall be swept away, when the rest purged and renovated will constitute the foundation of a new community, exhibiting the ideal character of the people as a 'holy nation' (cf. Exod. 19: 6).[1]

At the end of this verse לֹא יָחִישׁ 'he shall not make haste' (RV), as thus translated, barely makes sense; it means rather 'he shall not be shaken', as the Accadian *ḫâšu* 'to shake, to be agitated, troubled', the Arabic *ḥâsa(w)* I and VIII 'was perplexed, bewildered' and the Ethiopic *taḥaw(w)asa* 'was moved, shaken' clearly show[2] (cf. Ugaritic *ḥṯ* 'was aggrieved'), which Pesh. *nedḥal* 'he shall fear' and Targ. יְזַדְעֲזַע 'he shall be shaken' confirm.

In verse 17 as in verse 18 the metaphor in שׁוֹט שׁוֹטֵף 'an overflowing flood' and secondarily 'scourge', is readily intelligible; the Arabic *sauṭu* 'scourge' and also 'water overflowing from a fishpond like a scourge reaching out over the land' (Freytag) exactly illustrates it. Similarly in verse 18 מרמס 'land trampled down' refers properly to the land trampled down by the Assyrian army as it advances but is here adapted to the picture of that army as a flood sweeping over the land.

In verse 18 וְכֻפַּר 'and it [the covenant]...shall be disannulled' (RV) has been needlessly altered to וְתֻפַּר 'and it shall be ineffectual' (Houbigant with Targum).[3] Two reasons are given for the emendation: the one that the verb stands in the masculine gender with a feminine subject and the second

[1] S. R. Driver, *Isaiah: His Life and Times* (London, 1893), pp. 52 (1), 110; cf. E. König, *Jesaja* (Gütersloh, 1926), pp. 255–6, where a number of explanations are summarized.

[2] G. R. Driver, *JTS*, XXXII (1931), 253–4.

[3] Cf. F. Martin *ap.* A. Condam in *Livre d'Isaïe* (Paris, 1905), p. 184.

that the verb is not otherwise used in this sense.[1] The first objection rests on ignorance of Semitic usage, for Arabic grammar requires and Hebrew grammar permits the apparent incongruence when the predicate precedes the subject.[2] The second fails to combine the uses of the root with the renderings of the ancient versions; the Accadian *kapāru* 'to wipe away (e.g. tears)', the Syriac *kfar* 'wiped away, expunged; denied' and the Arabic *kafara* 'covered over; denied (a favour received)' permit a Hebrew כִּפֵּר 'wiped clean (e.g. the face),[3] blotted out (e.g. sin)', here applied to the annulment of an agreement. Symmachus reflects this interpretation of the verb with his ἐξαλειφ-θήσεται 'it shall be blotted out', while Pesh. *metkap(p)ar* 'deleted, denied' reproduces the actual Hebrew verb.[4]

At the end of the verse the Hebrew *kî* 'for; indeed', like the Ugaritic *k* 'for, indeed', has not causal but affirmative force when standing before a verb which is not at the head of the clause (e.g. Gen. 18: 20; 2 Sam. 23: 5; Isa. 7: 9; 10: 13; 54: 6; Pss. 44: 4; 49: 16; 60: 4; 73: 21; 89: 2–3; 102: 11; 118: 10–12; 128: 2; 138: 2; Lam. 3: 22; Lachish 6: line 3).[5]

In verse 19 ביום ובלילה 'by night and by day' is a gloss to show that בבקר בבקר 'morning by morning' ought not to be taken literally as meaning 'only in the mornings' but includes the intervening nights; that LXX has only ἐν νυκτί 'by night' confirms this suggestion. As it is also hypermetrical, it may well be deleted (Procksch).

II

The following translation of the poem may now be offered:

1   Oh! the proud garland of the drunkards of Ephraim
        and the flowering spray, so lovely in its beauty,
          on the heads of the revellers overcome with wine!
2   See! the LORD has one mighty and strong
        whom he sets to work on the land with violence,
          like a sweeping storm of hail,
          like a destroying blast of wind,

[1] Cf. Cheyne, *Isaiah*, II, 154.   [2] *GK*, §145*o*.
[3] W. R. Smith, *The Old Testament in the Jewish Church* (London, 1892), p. 381.
[4] Cf. G. R. Driver, *JTS*, xxxiv (1933), 34–8.
[5] Cf. G. R. Driver, *Canaanite Myths and Legends*, p. 144 (17).

like a sweeping torrent of waters, mighty and overflowing.
3   The proud garland of Ephraim's drunkards
           shall be trampled under foot,
4   and the flowering sprays, so lovely in their beauty
           on heads streaming with perfumes,
        shall be like early figs before summer,
        whose bloom, if he who sees them plucks them,
        is gone while they lie in his hand.
5 On that day the LORD of hosts will be a lovely garland,
        a beautiful diadem for the remnant of His people,
6 a spirit of justice for him who presides in a court of justice
and of heroism for those who repel the enemy at the gate.
7   These (others) too are given up to wine
           and bawl over strong drink:
Priest and prophet are given up to strong drink
           and fuddled with wine,
bawling over strong drink, given up to tippling,
           and hiccoughing in crack-brained frenzy,
8   when every table is covered with vomit,
           with excrement leaving no clean spot,
        (as they ask):
9   'To whom is the prophet giving instruction,
        'Whom will he make to understand what they hear—
'babes newly weaned, just taken from the breast?'
10 No, but it is 'Ho!' answering to 'Ho!', 'Hey!' to 'Hey!'
and 'another drop here, another drop there!'
11 So, when through barbarous speech and a strange language
        God speaks to this people,
12   when He says to them:
'This is true rest; let the exhausted have rest!
'This is repose', and they refuse to listen:
13   then the word of the LORD to them will be:
'Ho!' answering to 'Ho!' and 'Hey!' to 'Hey!'
and 'another drop here, another drop there!',
so that, as they walk, they will fall on their backs,
        be injured, trapped and caught.
14 Therefore listen to the word of the LORD, you arrogant men,
you who rule this people in Jerusalem.
15 You say: 'We have made a treaty with Death
        'and have entered into a pact with Sheol.
'that the raging flood sweeping by shall not touch us;
        'for we have taken refuge in lies
           'and sheltered behind falsehood'.

16 Therefore these are the words of the LORD God:
  'Look! I am laying a block of granite in Zion,
      'a precious corner-stone for a firm foundation;
        'so he who has faith shall not waver.
17   'I will use justice as a plumb-line
          'and righteousness as a plummet;
        'hail shall sweep away your refuge of lies
        'and flood-waters carry away your shelter.
18   'Then your treaty with Death will be annulled
        'and your pact with Sheol will be void.
        'A raging flood shall indeed sweep by,
        'and you will be (like) land flattened down.
19   'As often as it sweeps by, it will take you;
        'for morning by morning it shall sweep by.
    'So paying heed to rumours of it will bring only dismay;
20   'for "the bed is too short for a man to stretch himself
        'and the blanket too narrow to cover him"'.
21 But the LORD will rise up as he rose on Mount Perazim
        and storm with rage as he did in the Vale of Gibeon
    to do what he will do—how uncharacteristic its doing!—
    and to perform his work—how strange a work!
22   But now have done with your arrogance
          lest your bonds be tightened;
    for I have heard the end, an end that is decreed
      by the LORD God of hosts
      against the whole land.

The import of Isaiah's message now becomes tolerably clear.

The prophet, by way of rebuking and warning the leading persons in Jerusalem, points to the evil example of the leaders of the northern kingdom, Ephraim, who indulge in drunken orgies and so try to drown their anxieties when threatened by 'one mighty and strong', namely the Assyrian king by whose forces, advancing like a destructive storm, Samaria may expect soon to be invested and taken. Then their fine garlands will be trampled underfoot; and they will become like an early fig, a delicate fruit whose bloom disappears in the hand of him who has plucked it (1–4). Then the true glory of a nation, the prophet says, will be not its rulers garlanded with flowers, drenched in perfumes, swilling down strong drink, but the Lord of hosts who, when the crisis is past, will show himself a nation's 'lovely

63

garland' and 'beautiful diadem', the source of justice and
of martial virtues for those who survive (5–6).

Let his hearers, is the prophet's thought, take warning from
their neighbours and put their trust in the Lord.

Far from it, the prophet says: these too, namely the leading
men among his compatriots in Judah, are carousing in the face
of coming disaster; priest and prophet, who ought to be giving
them sound advice and guidance, are themselves overcome by
wine, seated at tables covered with filth (7–8).[1] So, when he
tries to warn them of their danger, all that they can do is
mockingly to ask him if he supposes that he is teaching or
giving instruction to babes, to infants newly weaned. No, he
answers, he knows only too well that he is addressing drunkards
capable only of uttering maudlin shouts and sottish cries as they
call for 'another little drink', for drinks all round (9–10).

So, he goes on, when God answers them through barbarians
whose speech is equally outlandish, i.e. Assyrian invaders, warning them not to involve themselves in political intrigue in the
hope of warding off what is coming but to stay quiet, they will
not listen to him (11–12). This then will be the Lord's word to
them: 'Go on with your drunken orgies and lull yourselves with
wine into fancied security; but in the end you will stumble and
fall on your backs, drunkards as you are, and collapse into the
hands of the enemy' (13). Therefore, says the prophet, you
arrogant rulers of this people in Jerusalem, listen: You say that
you have made a treaty with Death and have entered into a
pact with Sheol to spare you when the flood comes, that you
have safeguarded yourselves by falsehood and treachery, regardless of the fate of the people committed to your charge (14–
15)—but, says the Lord, I am building a 'sure foundation',
built on principles of justice and righteousness, on which the
religious community will be rebuilt; the 'raging flood' will
sweep you away and your agreement with the powers below will
be annulled and will fail you. A 'raging flood' will indeed come,
and you will be like flood-swept land (16–18). As often as it
sweeps by, it will carry you away; for it will be a process pro-

---

[1] Cf. B. Meissner, *Babylonien und Assyrien* (Heidelberg, 1920), p. 419, where
a sculpture depicting an Assyrian drinking scene is reproduced.

longed from day to day, so terrible that merely to hear of it will
bring dismay (19); for the situation brought about by your
schemes will be intolerable, like sleeping in a bed that is too
short or with a blanket that is too narrow (20). For the Lord
will rise up as he did in times long ago, in the days when he
gave David victory over the Philistines (cf. 2 Sam. 5: 20–1 and
1 Chron. 14: 11–12, Baal-Perazim; 2 Sam. 5: 25 and 1 Chron.
14: 16, Gibeon) to fulfil his purposes, alien and strange to his
nature as they may seem; so cease from your mockery, or you
will be handed over to the enemy bound as for execution; for
I have heard of the fate that the Lord has decided for the
country (21–2).

III

The main purpose of this article is the attempt to find a solution
to the various problems presented by the Hebrew text of the
poem discussed in it.

A subsidiary object is to draw attention to the methods which
ought to be employed in such a task. The exegete must always
remember that all that has survived of the Hebrew language
as used over 1,000 years is found in a volume that can be
carried in the pocket; consequently ἅπαξ εἰρημένα abound, and
no amount of juggling with concordances and dictionaries,
either by forcing the sense or by substituting a word that one
knows for one that no one understands, will reveal the sense of
the passages in which they occur.

The hard and only proper way is to examine the translations
given in the ancient versions and to explain these in the light
of the cognate (Babylonian and Assyrian, Aramaic and Syriac,
Arabic and Ethiopic) languages, whereby many lost Hebrew
words may be recovered. Even their mistranslations may be
helpful; for example, LXX ὡς σευτλίον ἡμίεφθον 'like a half-
ripe beet' for the MT מכמר (א)כתו 'like an antelope (caught) in
a net' (Isa. 51: 20), though nonsensical, restores an otherwise
unknown word to the biblical vocabulary; for they read it as
כמר כתום (omitting the א with 1QIsᵃ) 'like garlic artificially
ripened', taking the first word as the Aramaic תום = Hebrew
שום 'garlic' and postulating as the second word a Hebrew

כמיר/כמור 'artificially ripened', which the Accadian *kumurrû* 'heaping up of dates for artificial ripening', the post-biblical Hebrew כִּמֵּר = Judaeo-Aramaic כַּמֵּר 'heaped fruit on the ground' support. Quite otherwise, a mistranslation in one passage may reveal a lost word which will fit into another passage. For example, the Hebrew חֹשֵׁשׁ 'chaff', which the Arabic *ḥuṭṭu* 'floating particles of straw, sand' confirms, is rightly so translated in 'ye shall conceive chaff; ye shall bring forth stubble' (Isa. 33: 11), as the parallel 'stubble' shows; but it is also mistranslated φλόξ 'flame' (Symm.) and *ardor* 'heat' (Vulg.), which the Arabic *ḥissu* 'burning cold' (cf. Latin *urere* 'to burn' as used of cold) proves to be a genuine word. Hence 'as the dry grass sinketh down in the flame' (Isa. 5: 24, RV), which is impossible if only because 'chaff' and 'dry grass' cannot be combined and chaff is not used as fuel, is an error for 'as the heat of the flame dies down' (Vulg. *calor flammae*; cf. LXX).

When all the possibilites of translation and mistranslation have been exhausted, the time comes to resort, independently of the ancient versions, to the vocabularies of the cognate languages, especially those of the Assyro-Babylonian and Arabic languages, which are vast.

Another danger is that of introducing something alien to the natural history, life and customs and thought, of ancient Palestine. For example, the translation of חפרפרות (*sic*) 'beetles' as 'moles' (RV after Jerome) is absurd (Isa. 2: 20); for these creatures do not exist in Palestine. The suggestion to translate them as 'mole-rats' (Procksch) is superficially attractive; but the Hebrew חֹלֶד (Lev. 11: 29) = Arabic *ḥuldu* 'mole-rat' rules this out; this is described as a blind creature resembling a mole, living underground and feeding on onions and leeks and can therefore be only the mole-rat (*Spalax typhlus*).[1] However, the root *ḥpr* 'dig' allows also a Hebrew חפרפרה 'beetle' with which the Egyptian *ḥprr* 'beetle' (*Scarabaeus*) agrees. This makes burrows in the earth and pursues slugs and earth-worms underground; the female makes balls of dung and hides them in suitable places underground, and both she and the male rest

[1] Cf. G. W. Freytag, *Lexicon Arabicum–Latina*, I, 513 with H. B. Tristram, *Fauna and Flora of Palestine*, in *Survey of Western Palestine* (London, 1888), p. 14.

during summer in their subterranean retreat.[1] What the prophet means, then, is that all idols of silver and gold must be cast away to 'dung-beetles and bats', i.e. to the dung-heaps which the beetles haunt and the caves and ruins which bats render foul with their droppings.[2]

Equally important is the duty of keeping Babylonian and Assyrian as well as Egyptian sculptures in view, which, in the complete absence of Hebrew works of art, are the sole means of studying the life and customs of the people of the ancient Middle East, so to say, at first hand.

The last danger is that of regarding even the most trifling *obiter dicta* in the Old Testament as setting forth theological doctrine; for example, in taking words for 'intoxication' and 'crack-brained frenzy' as theological terms for prophetic 'vision' and priestly 'judgement' or interpreting drunken shouts of 'Ho!' and 'Hey!' as words for 'precept' and 'rule', i.e. 'moral and political recommendations'[3] or a 'succession of judgements'.[4] The ancient Hebrews were 'men of like passions with ourselves', not living only and unceasingly in realms of high theology!

I have very great pleasure in offering this article, such as it is, to my first Hebrew pupil and for many years my colleague in preparing a new edition of 'Brown–Driver–Briggs', to which he has undertaken ἐν εὐκαιρίᾳ σχολῆς to devote the years of his coming retirement.

⁵العالم بلا عمل مثل الغيم بلا مطر

[1] J. E. Carpenter, *EB*, VI (1910), 666, 668, 673.
[2] H. B. Tristram, *Natural History of the Bible* (1868), pp. 45–6.
[3] Cf. Cheyne, *Isaiah*, I, 164–5.
[4] J. Skinner, *Isaiah*, I (Cambridge, 1915), 224.
[5] 'A scholar without work is like clouds without rain.'

6

RENAMING IN
THE OLD TESTAMENT

by Otto Eissfeldt

The Old Testament accords great significance to the giving of
names as such; so it does too to the renaming of places and
persons. A survey of the examples of this to be found in the
Old Testament or at least of the most important of them would
seem therefore to offer new insights into the nature of Israelite
and Jewish culture and religion. In view of the wealth of relevant
material, this present survey must be restricted to those cases
which present a genuine renaming, in other words where both
the old and the new name are given. The replacing of a name
formerly used for a particular class—such as that related in
1 Sam. 9: 9 in which ראה 'seer' is replaced by נביא 'prophet'—is
also not considered; nor are general utterances concerning the
granting of a new name of a kind represented by Isa. 62: 2,
according to which Jerusalem is to be renamed with a 'new
name' (שם חדש) determined by Yahweh himself. Nor are those
relatively few cases included in which there are cited for a particular entity two or three names belonging to two or three
different languages, as for example in Gen. 31: 47–8 and Deut.
3: 9. In the former the stone heap erected by Laban and Jacob
is termed by Laban יגר שהדותא, but by Jacob גלעד (both denoting 'heap of witness'); in the latter there is added to the
Hebrew name of Mount Hermon the note that 'The Phoenicians
call Hermon (חרמון) Sirion (שרין), and the Amorites call it
Senir (שניר)', and we thus have three names for the same
mountain belonging to three different languages.

The following discussion is also limited in another direction,
namely, that it simply cites the information provided by the
Old Testament without in general examining this information
to see whether it is historically reliable or belongs in the realm
of poetry and saga.

I

The Hebrew language, in addition to קרא 'name' which can also mean 'rename' as is shown by Judg. 1:17, has for the idea of renaming the term סבב in Hiphʻil and Hophʻal. It is to be found in Num. 32:37–8 which runs: 'But the Reubenites build Heshbon, Elealeh, Kiriathaim, (38) Nebo, and Baʻal-meʻon with changed names (מוסבת שם), and Sibmah; and they gave names to the cities which they had built.' However, the interpretation of the words מוסבת שם as presupposed by the above translation is not completely certain; they are often understood rather as a warning which has been subsequently inserted in the text against pronouncing the names of the alien deities Nebo and Baʻal which are contained in the town names Nebo and Baʻal-meʻon. In that case, מוסבת in Num. 32:38 cannot be utilized as evidence for the meaning 'rename' for סבב. However, סבב 'rename' is quite clearly attested in 2 Kings 23:34; 2 Chron. 36:4. Here it is related that Pharaoh Necho made 'Eliakim' the son of Josiah king over Judah in his father's place, and changed his name to 'Jehoiakim' (ויסב את־שמו יהויקים). The same is true of 2 Kings 24:17 which tells how the king of Babylon made 'Mattaniah', the uncle of the deposed and deported Jehoiachin, king over Judah in his place, and renamed him 'Zedekiah' (ויסב את־שמו צדקיהו).

The naming of places and persons, and so too their renaming, is a privilege of high importance, not only in the Old Testament, but at all times and in all areas. Here we are concerned with a right which expresses the authority which the one who gives the name or who renames exerts over the one who is named or renamed. The way in which this right is revealed may differ; it may in one instance indicate conquest, and even exploitation of the one named or renamed, or it may carry with it protection and patronage. The former rather than the latter is likely to be intended in Gen. 2:19–20 where it is related that 'the man gives names' (ויקרא האדם שמות) to all animals and—as we may read between the lines—exercises authority over them. But the latter is undoubtedly the case in the word of Yahweh to Israel in Isa. 43:1: 'Fear not! I have redeemed you, named you with your name [קראתי בשמך], you are mine.'

II

If we examine first the renaming of places, we may observe that this is usually occasioned by the fact that the places in question have changed ownership. This is true of the renaming of the town of 'Kiriath-'arba'' (קרית ארבע) as 'Hebron' (חברון, Gen. 23: 2); of the renaming of 'Kenath' as 'Nobah' (Num. 32: 42) with the name of its conqueror Nobah; of the renaming of the region of 'Argob' conquered by Ja'ir as 'villages of Ja'ir' (חות יאיר, Deut. 3: 14); of the renaming of the Canaanite town of 'Leshem' or 'Laish' (Josh. 19: 47; Judg. 18: 29) as 'Dan', after the name of its conquerors, the tribe of Dan; of the renaming of 'Kiriath Sepher', which became 'Debir' after it had been conquered by Othniel, the son-in-law of Caleb (Josh. 15: 15–17); of the renaming of the town of 'Zephath' (Judg. 1: 17) as 'Hormah', when it was conquered and put to the ban by Judah and Simeon; of the renaming of the 'fortress of Zion' (מצדת ציון) taken by David by a sudden attack, as 'city of David' (עיר דויד) (2 Sam. 5: 7–9; 1 Chron. 11: 7); of the renaming of the Edomite fortress of הסלע 'the rock' as 'Joktheel' (יקתאל) when it fell into the hands of the Judaean king Amaziah (2 Kings 14: 7).[1]

The replacing of the older place-name 'Luz' (לוז) by the later 'Bethel' (בית-אל), mentioned in Gen. 28: 19, looks similar to the cases which have just been dealt with, involving change in the ownership of the settlement, but actually it is a special case. In fact it is not a matter of consciously replacing an older name by a later one, but of giving a name to a place, which had not previously been settled, on account of a theophany. This name, the 'House of El', has then been applied later to a town called 'Luz' very near it to the west, and the older name has fallen into disuse. There is clear indication of this in Josh. 16: 2, where part of the southern border of the tribe of Joseph is described as running 'from Bethel to Luz'. In Judg. 1: 22–6, on the other hand, 'Bethel' and 'Luz' appear as two names for the same

---

[1] On the identification of 'this rock' (הסלע), captured by the Judaean king Amaziah and renamed Joktheel, see 'Notes and News', *PEQ*, xcviii (1966), 123–6.

place; it is only the information that the Canaanite, who had made it possible for the Israelites to capture the city, moved to the land of the Hittites (i.e. well into north-west Syria), and there founded a new city and called it 'Luz', which shows that Luz had been the older name of the Canaanite city. Moreover, Gen. 28: 19 ('Jacob called the name of that place (המקום) Bethel; but the name of the city (העיר) was Luz at the first') makes a clear distinction between the 'cult-place' (המקום) Bethel and the 'city' (עיר) Luz. In the same way as Bethel originated through a theophany, so also 'Penuel' (פנואל, Gen. 32: 32), or 'Peniel' (פניאל, Gen. 32: 31), is the name given to the 'place' (המקום) as a result of the meeting of El with Jacob described in Gen. 32: 23–33. But, unlike Bethel, there is no indication whether there had already been a settlement at or near this place beforehand, or what it had been called, or what was its relationship to the city and fortress of 'Penuel' (פנואל), which according to the evidence of Judg. 8: 8 f., 17 and 1 Kings 12: 25 existed in the twelfth to tenth centuries B.C.

Besides change in the ownership of settlements, renaming might be brought about by other events which happened to them or threatened them. According to Gen. 50: 11 a great mourning ceremony in Egyptian style was held for Jacob at a place in Transjordan called the 'Threshing-floor of the Thorn-bush' (גרן האטד), and this led to the renaming of the place as the 'Mourning of the Egyptians' (אבל מצרים). Exod. 17: 1–7 relates how the place in the Sinai peninsula formerly known as 'Rephidim' (רפידים) was renamed by Moses 'Proof and Con-tention' (מסה ומריבה), because the Israelites 'contended' (ריב) with Moses and put Yahweh to the 'proof' (נסתם, verse 7) there. In Jer. 19: 6, Jeremiah warns his people that the place near Jerusalem called 'Topheth and the Valley of the Son of Hinnom' (התפת וגיא בן־הנם) would be called the 'Valley of Slaughter' (גיא ההרגה), because there, as also throughout the land, the bodies of the slain would be heaped up. Similarly Ezek. 39: 11 proclaims that Gog and his entire following will be buried in the 'Valley of the Travellers' (גי העברים), which will then re-ceive the name the 'Valley of Gog's Multitude' (גיא המון גוג).

III

Renaming of persons and groups of persons, like that of places, is frequently due to the fact that they have come under new masters. This is obvious in the case of the two Judaean kings 'Eliakim' and 'Mattaniah', who were renamed 'Jehoiakim' by Pharaoh Neco and 'Zedekiah' by Nebuchadnezzar king of Babylon respectively (2 Kings 23: 34; 24: 17). To this class belong also the renaming of 'Joseph' as 'Zaphenath-Paneah' (צפנת פענח) by Pharoah (Gen. 41: 45), and of 'Daniel' and his three companions, 'Hananiah, Mishael and Azariah', as 'Belteshazzar, Shadrach, Meshach, and Abednego' by Nebuchadnezzar or his officer, the chief of the eunuchs (Dan. 1: 7). Of course these renamings, especially in the case of Joseph, are not in any way intended to express merely the dependence of the men so named on their royal masters; they indicate rather a kind of adoption into the household which is equivalent to conferring on them a high honour. Such high distinctions are also the renamings of Abram and Sarai, which are made with a view to the glorious future of their descendants: 'Abram' (אברם, 'the Father is exalted') becomes 'Abraham' (אברהם, 'Father of a Multitude of Nations', Gen. 17: 5),[1] and 'Sarai' (שרי, 'Princess') becomes 'Sarah' (שרה, 'Queen', 'who will be a mother of nations, and will bring forth kings', Gen. 17: 15). Other renamings of persons and groups are due to various fortunes of those concerned. Gen. 35: 18 relates how Rachel gave birth to her second son at the cost of her life, and called him 'Son of my Misfortune' (בן־אוני); but the fortunate father Jacob altered this sorrowful name into a correspondingly joyful name 'Son of Good Luck' (בנימין)—in spite of the fact that he had lost his favourite wife when she gave birth to his second son by her. Jer. 20: 1–6 tells how Pashhur ben-Immer (פשחור בן־אמר), the priestly leader of the temple guard at Jerusalem, had the prophet Jeremiah whipped and put in the stocks because of what he thought to be the defeatist tone of his preaching, and then Jeremiah uttered this threat: 'Yahweh does not call you

---

[1] On Abram/Abraham cf. G. Sauer, 'Bemerkungen zu 1965 entdeckten ugaritischen Texten', *ZDMG*, cxvi (1967), 235–41, see p. 241.

Pashhur, but Terror on every side' (לא פשחור קרא יהוה שמך כי אם־
מגור מסביב). This threat is based on his forecast of a terrible
misfortune in store for Pashhur. In Ruth 1: 20 there is the
moving request of Naomi, on her return home to Bethlehem from
Moab, that her friends and acquaintances there should no more
call her 'Pleasant' (נעמי) but 'Bitter' (מרא), explaining that the
Almighty has 'dealt very bitterly with her' (המר שדי לי מאד).

IV

In the changes of personal names which have just been dealt
with the relationship between the old and the new names often
depends on a play on the sound or on the meaning of the
words. This is obvious in the cases of 'Abram/Abraham' (Gen.
17: 5), 'Sarai/Sarah' (Gen. 17: 15), and 'Naomi/Mara' (Ruth
1: 20). In the prophecy of Jer. 20: 1–6, where Pashhur's name
is changed to 'Terror on every side' (מגור מסביב) and the
fearful threat against him and his family and friends is added,
it is disputed whether any such relationship of paronomasia or
play on the meaning applies to the names 'Pashhur' and 'Terror
on every side', and this can scarcely be decided with certainty.[1]
The same is true of the change of 'Joseph' to 'Zaphenath-
Paneah' (Gen. 41:45), and of 'Daniel' and his three companions
'Hananiah, Mishael and Azariah' to 'Belteshazzar' and to
'Shadrach, Meshach and Abednego' (Dan. 1: 7). These five
new names, which moreover have possibly suffered some textual
distortion, can be understood in a variety of ways. So also it
has to remain undecided whether the changes of 'Eliakim' to
'Jehoiakim' by Pharaoh Neco (2 Kings 23: 34) and of 'Mattaniah' to 'Zedekiah' by Nebuchadnezzar (2 Kings 24: 17) have
any other reason than the desire for an impressive sign that
both these kings of Judah are creatures of their foreign overlords.

The changes of place-names are mostly due to events which
have happened to them, or—in the case of new names involving

---

[1] Cf. W. Rudolph, *Jeremia* (*HAT*, 3rd ed. 1968), p. 128f., who cuts out
מסביב as a secondary addition dependent on Jer. 20: 10 (6: 25), and finds
in מגור no 'etymological play on the name Pashhur', but prefers to understand the new name מגור as 'purely objective' in the sense that Pashhur
'becomes terror personified'.

a threat—to events which will happen to them. This applies
to 'Kenath/Nobah' (Num. 32: 42), 'Argob/Villages of Ja'ir'
(Deut. 3: 14), 'Leshem' (Josh. 19: 47) or 'Laish' (Judg. 18:
29)/'Dan', 'Stronghold of Zion'/'City of David' (2 Sam. 5: 7–
9), and 'Threshing floor of the Thornbush'/'Mourning of the
Egyptians' (Gen. 50: 11). Something like paronomasia or play
on the meaning occurs when places are named as a result of
events in their history in so far as the new names happen to
contain reminiscences of these events. Thus the change of
'Rephidim' to 'Massah and Meribah' is brought into relation
with the fact that the Israelites had 'contended' (ריב) with
Moses and put Yahweh to the 'proof' (נסתם) there, while the
change of the name of the city of 'Zephath' to 'Hormah' (חרמה)
goes back to the fact that Judah and Simeon had put the place
to the 'ban' (ויחרימו). A play on the sound or the sense of the
words may also be the connecting link between the old name
in Jer. 19: 6, 'Topheth and the Valley of the Son of Hinnom'
(התפת וגיא בן־הנם), and the new one which will apply in the
future, the 'Valley of Slaughter' (גיא ההרגה), and also between
the 'Valley of the Travellers' (גי העברים) in Ezek. 39: 11 and
the 'Valley of Gog's Multitude' (גיא המון גוג). But if such
connections ever existed, they are no longer apparent to us. The
reasons for the change of 'Sela' (הסלע, 'the Rock') to 'Joktheel'
(יקתאל) in 2 Kings 14: 7 also remain impossible to determine.

v

Three or four cases of renaming persons or groups deserve
special attention, because the new names conferred on them are
theophoric names, and therefore have significance for the history of religion. It is related in Gen. 32: 29; 35: 10; 2 Kings
17: 34 that 'Jacob' was to be renamed 'Israel' by a supernatural being, called 'El' or 'Elohim' or a 'man' or a 'messenger', who wrestled with him beside the Jabbok. Hos. 12: 4–5
also alludes to this. In Gen. 32: 29 the being says to Jacob:
'Your name shall no more be called Jacob, but Israel (ישראל),
for you have striven with God and with men, and have prevailed' (שרית עם־אלהים ועם־אנשים ותוכל). In Gen. 35: 10 God

tells Jacob, 'Your name is Jacob; no longer shall your name be called Jacob, but Israel shall be your name', and this is immediately followed by 'So he called his name Israel' (ויקרא את־שמו ישראל). 2 Kings 17: 34 concerns the laws which Yahweh had commanded the children of Jacob 'whom he named Israel' (אשר שם שמו ישראל). Hos. 12: 4–5 also refers to Jacob: 'In the womb he took his brother by the heel, and in his manhood he strove with God. He strove with the angel and prevailed, he wept and sought his favour' (ובאונו שרה את־אלהים וישר אל־מלאך ויכל בכה ויתחנן־לו). Though this passage evidently presupposes a tradition which differs slightly from the other Jacob-traditions, it contains the word-play on ישר and שרה in the change of Jacob's name to 'Israel', and to that extent agrees with the other passages under consideration.

It can only be pointed out briefly here, that at the back of these narrative sequences, before they were put into story form, there lies an event in the history of the tribe of Jacob. Belonging originally to the Syrian–Arabian desert or to Mesopotamia, they transferred their allegiance to the El[1] who resided at one of their semi-nomadic stopping-places. Besides making explicit acknowledgement of this El, as attested in Gen. 33: 20 'El is the God of Israel' (אל אלהי ישראל), they also reshaped their own neutral name Jacob into one which would witness to the majesty of El, ישראל. Our tradition is probably correct when it assumes that Israel means something like 'El is Lord', and when it regards this position of lordship as manifested primarily in his victory over his own and his worshippers' enemies.[2] But the presupposi-

---

[1] Cf. my essay 'Der kanaanäische El als Geber der den israelitischen Erzvätern geltenden Nachkommenschaft- und Landbesitzverheissungen', which is to appear in the Brockelmann Memorial Volume in 1968.

[2] On Israel, cf. Sauer, *ZDMG*, cxvi (1967), 239–40. 'Israel' and 'Jerubba'al' (discussed below, p. 78) are names of historical entities, the former the name of a group of tribes, the latter of an individual. But the explanations given of these names in Gen. 32: 29; 35: 10; 2 Kings 17: 34 (Hos. 12: 4–5); and in Judg. 6: 32—'You have striven with God and with men and have prevailed' for the former, and 'May Ba'al contend against him, because he has torn down his altar' for the latter—are of a fictional, narrative kind and have no historical content. It is noteworthy that the verbal elements in 'Israel' and in 'Jerubba'al', viz. שרה and רבב, which appear to mean something like 'to be great', are in both cases explained as meaning 'to

tion of an antagonism towards El, which underlies the explanation of the name Israel as it has come down to us in the Old Testament, belongs to the shaping of the tradition (itself containing a historical fact) into the form of a story, as has been already suggested. Similar shaping of traditions occurs frequently elsewhere in the Old Testament, especially in Genesis. It can even be asserted that this is what gives to the patriarchal narratives their distinctive character.

The second example of the change of a neutral personal name into a theophoric one comes at the end of the list of the twelve representatives whom Moses sent to spy out Canaan, which is given in Num. 13: 1–16 (P). Here we are informed that 'Moses called Hoshea the son of Nun Joshua' (ויקרא משה להושע בן־נון יהושע, verse 16). This information deserves far more attention than is usually given to it. There seems in fact to be here a reminiscence of a particular practice, namely the replacement of neutral names by theophoric Yahweh names. This may indeed be a historical reminiscence in so far as it informs us that after the adoption of the cult of Yahweh by the Israelites or by certain forerunners of later Israel, such changes of name actually took place. The remarkable thing is that a statement of this kind is contained only in the latest strand of the Hexateuch, i.e. P, with its 'Hoshea/Joshua' (הושע/יהושע), whereas the older strands always use the one form Joshua, and have nothing to say about Hoshea as an earlier name for the man. But also with regard to the use of the name Yahweh, it is the youngest Hexateuchal source P—along with the next youngest E—which alone contains the memory of a historical fact.

strive', 'to fight', 'to contend' or the like. Cf. further O. Eissfeldt, 'Jakob-Lea und Jakob-Rahel', *Festschrift H. W. Hertzberg* (Göttingen, 1965), pp. 50–5, see p. 53, where there is a discussion of the narrative concerning the birth of the twelve sons of Jacob in Gen. 29: 31–30: 24; 35: 16–20, and the following is said: 'The explanations provided by the narrative for the names of the twelve sons of Jacob in fact without exception give expression to the feelings of their mothers; they are purely fictional and contain no reference to the history of the tribes which are traced back to these twelve sons.' The same is true for the explanations given for the two names under discussion here, 'Israel' and 'Jerubba'al'; they have no historical content and all we can do is examine the names themselves to see how far any historical information can be extracted from them.

The third example comes in the account of the replacement of the neutral name 'Gideon' (גדעון) by 'Jerubbaʿal' (ירבעל)[1] in Judg. 6: 25–32. When the citizens of Ophrah demand that Joash should deliver up his son Gideon to execution after he had destroyed the Baʿal altar of Ophrah and the cultic pole that stood by it, Joash replies: '"Will you contend for (ל) Baʿal? Or will you defend his cause? Whoever contends for (ל) him shall be put to death by morning. If he is a god, let him contend for (ל) himself, because his altar has been pulled down." Therefore on that day he was called Jerubbaʿal, that is to say, "Let Baʿal contend against (ב) him", because he pulled down his altar' (verses 31–2). This passage presents the critic with numerous problems, both linguistic and historical. We must confine ourselves to a clear exposition of what the text which has come down to us means, and that depends first and foremost on the explanation of the new name 'Jerubbaʿal' which Joash gave his son Gideon, and so on the meaning of ירבעל. Whereas the preposition ל used in dependence on 'contend' must mean *for*, in Joash's explanation for giving his son Gideon the new name Jerubbaʿal the preposition ב (which also occurs in dependence on 'contend') can only mean *against*. Jerubbaʿal is here therefore undoubtedly explained to mean 'Let Baʿal contend against him'. Whether this explanation is correct, and whether a father is to be credited with giving his son a name which opens up such dangerous perspectives, must be left on one side. Suffice it to say that, according to the evidence of his words against Baʿal 'If he is a god, let him contend for himself' (verse 31), Joash did not put much faith in Baʿal, and so need not have regarded his son's new name 'Let Baʿal contend against him' as dangerous. In any case, Judg. 6: 25–32 provides us with an illuminating glimpse of the time when Yahweh, newly arrived in Canaan, must have taken up the struggle with the Baʿal who was native to the place.

A final example of the replacement of a neutral personal name by a theophoric name is the information recorded in 2 Sam. 12: 25 that David changed the name of his second son by Bathsheba, 'Solomon', to 'Jedidiah' (ידידיה, 'Beloved of

---

[1] Cf. p. 76, n. 2.

Yahweh'), on the instructions of the prophet Nathan—or rather gave him this as an additional name.[1] Unlike the three examples which have just been dealt with, this one does not give evidence of a significant moment in the history of Israelite religion, but it does at any rate belong to a time when the struggle between Yahweh and Ba'al, which we have seen in Judg. 6: 25–32, had been decided in favour of the Yahweh religion.

---

[1] When it says in 2 Sam. 12: 25 וישלח ביד נתן הנביא ויקרא את־שמו ידידיה בעבור יהוה, it is to be understood that Yahweh, speaking through the prophet Nathan, gave to the child called Solomon by his parents a surname signifying salvation, Jedidiah, 'Beloved of Yahweh for Yahweh's sake', and that he thereby guaranteed that his life would be preserved. It is not, then, to be taken, as usually happens, to mean that David entrusted the training of his son Solomon to the prophet Nathan, who then gave the child the surname Jedidiah. For 2 Sam. 12: 24b, where it says that Yahweh 'loved' (יהוה אהבו) the newborn child, and 12: 25 conclude the narrative of David's sin against Bathsheba and Uriah. This had led to the death of the first child of the union of David and Bathsheba. These final verses then assert that Yahweh takes their second child into his special protection.

7

SOME DIFFICULT WORDS
IN GENESIS 49

by J. A. Emerton

The importance of early Old Testament poems for the study both of Israelite history and of the Hebrew language has long been recognized. Among such passages is the Blessing of Jacob in Genesis 49, which is often dated in the time of the united monarchy, although it may be composed of a number of originally independent poems, some of which are perhaps considerably older. The purpose of the present article is to examine a few obscure words in the chapter in the light of recent scholarly work,[1] in the hope of either establishing or disproving some theories and also, in one or two places, of leading the discussion a little farther forward. It is a pleasure to dedicate the article to Professor D. Winton Thomas, who has elucidated the meaning of so many obscure words and difficult passages in the Old Testament.

SIMEON AND LEVI

Verse 5 is translated as follows in the RV (from which the other renderings at the beginning of each section are taken):

> Simeon and Levi are brothers;
> Weapons of violence are their swords.

The word מְכֵרֹתֵיהֶם, rendered 'their swords', is found only here, and no theory about its etymology has won general acceptance. Most recent writers have adopted one or other of the older

---

[1] See J. Coppens, 'La bénédiction de Jacob', *Volume du Congrès, Strasbourg 1956* (*VTS*, IV, 1957), pp. 97–115, and J. De Fraine, *Genesis* (Roermond en Maaseik, 1963), for further references. I am indebted to Professor G. R. Driver for drawing my attention to some of the works cited in the present paper and for helpful criticisms of the first draft.

theories, although some[1] have brought forward new arguments for them. The only completely new suggestion of which I am aware has been advanced by B. Vawter.[2] He notes that the Jerusalem Targum renders the word מן טליותהון 'from their youth', and that the Peshiṭta has mn kynhwn, 'by their nature', and he suggests that the original Hebrew was משרתיהם, which he translates 'from their very birth', and that the letters kaph and shin in the old script were confused. He explains the emended text with the help of Ugaritic ṯrr, 'small', Accadian šerru, 'child', and Aramaic שָׁרָא, 'to begin', and שֵׁרוּ, 'beginning'; he also compares the Hebrew kᵉṯib שרותך in Jer. 15: 11.

The Jerusalem Targum is a free rendering, but Vawter may be right in thinking that מן טליותהון corresponds to מכרתיהם. However, his emendation is unconvincing for several reasons. First, Ugaritic ṯrr may be ignored, since an Aramaic cognate should begin with taw, not shin, and the meaning of the word is disputed.[3] Nevertheless, Vawter can still compare the other alleged cognates. Second, the meaning 'beginning' does not fit Jer. 15: 11 and, in the absence of the support of a Hebrew word there, it is rash to emend Gen. 49: 5 in order to obtain a hapax legomenon. Third, Vawter does not consider whether the renderings of the Jerusalem Targum and the Peshiṭta can have been derived from the same Hebrew consonants as those of the Massoretic Text. The mem was probably regarded as the preposition meaning 'from', and the rest of the word may have been derived from a root containing the letters kaph and resh. One possibility is that the translators connected the word with כּוּר, which seems to be used of the womb in a Hebrew text from Qumran (1QH3: 10) and probably denotes the female pudenda once in the Babylonian Talmud (Shabb. 140 B).[4] The

---

[1] M. J. Dahood, CBQ, xxiii (1961), 54–6; C. H. Gordon, HUCA, xxvi (1955), 60. Cf. also E. Ullendorff, VT, vi (1956), 194.

[2] CBQ, xvii (1955), 3 f.

[3] G. R. Driver, Canaanite Myths and Legends (Edinburgh, 1956) and J. Aistleitner, Wörterbuch der ugaritischen Sprache (Berlin, 1963), both explain it differently.

[4] M. Jastrow, Dictionary of the Targumim, the Talmud Babli and Yerushalmi, and the Midrashic Literature (New York and London, 1903), pp. 154, 625, rejects the reading in favour of one found in the Aruch, but it may be

fact that it is a masculine noun, whereas the obscure word in Gen. 49: 5 appears to be feminine, would not necessarily have deterred the translators from explaining the latter by means of the former. If they understood the Hebrew to mean 'from their [mother's] womb' (cf. Job 3: 10), their renderings are easily explicable. A second possibility is that the translators had in mind the Hebrew מְכֹרָה or מְכוּרָה,[1] which appears to mean something like 'origin' in Ezek. 16: 3; 21: 35; 29: 14; in the last of these passages, Theodotion's rendering is recorded in the Syro-Hexaplar[2] as *dylydwt' dylhwn*, 'of their birth'. If the *mem* was translated as a preposition, the translators (in so far as they were worried about such questions) may have regarded the word as a noun without preformative *mem* identical in meaning with one that had it; thus מָעוֹז and עֹז are sometimes[3] treated as synonyms in the Targum, and forms such as מַאֲכָל and אֹכֶל have very similar meanings. Since the translations of the Jerusalem Targum and Peshiṭta can be explained without postulating different Hebrew consonants in Gen. 49: 5, Vawter's emendation is without support.

JUDAH

Verse 10:

> The sceptre shall not depart from Judah,
> Nor the ruler's staff from between his feet,
> Until Shiloh come;
> And unto him shall the obedience of the peoples be.

The principal difficulty lies in the third line (עַד כִּי־יָבֹא שִׁילֹה), which does not make sense as rendered above: no satisfactory explanation of 'Shiloh' has been offered, and there is no adequate reason to accept the ancient opinion (B. Sanh. 98 B)

suspected that the less delicate reading is original. A connection between the word and 1QH3: 10 was suggested by J. Baumgarten and M. Mansoor, *JBL*, LXXIV (1955), 190.

[1] The Peshiṭta's rendering was similarly explained by C. J. Ball, *The Book of Genesis* (Leipzig, 1896), p. 107. Various scholars have explained the Hebrew word in Genesis from the one in Ezekiel; cf. E. F. C. Rosenmüller, *Scholia in Vetus Testamentum*, I (Leipzig, 1821), 692.

[2] A. M. Ceriani, *Monumenta Sacra et Profana, VII. Codex Syro-Hexaplaris Ambrosianus* (Milan, 1874).

[3] Cf. *VT*, XVII (1967), 140.

that the word is a name of the messiah. Various ways of reading the text have been suggested, but only three will be considered here.[1]

First, W. L. Moran has argued[2] in favour of the old opinion[3] that שִׁילֹה should be divided into two words and pointed שַׁי לֹה, that יָבֹא should be vocalized יוּבָא (although he does not regard the change as absolutely necessary), and that the line should be translated, 'Until tribute is brought to him'. Moran's reading of the line is possible, but it lacks support in any ancient version and departs from the pointing of the Massoretic Text. It is still necessary to ask whether the traditional vocalization can yield a satisfactory sense, and it will be argued below that it can.

Second, it has been suggested that the difficult word should be pointed שֵׁ(י)לָה, the name of Judah's youngest son by Shua (Gen. 38: 5). Gen. 38 tells how Judah failed to obey the levirate law and to give Shelah to Tamar, the widow of his eldest son. Before A. B. Ehrlich[4] accepted the reading שֵׁי לֹה, he favoured the view that the word meant 'Shelah'; he suggested that Judah told Tamar to wait until Shelah had grown up, and that 'until Shelah comes' became a proverbial saying meaning 'never'. The possibility that the word should be read 'Shelah' was noted by several commentators[5] who did not accept the pointing, but it was adopted by W. Schröder[6] in 1909, apparently in ignorance of his predecessors, and by E. Burrows[7] some time before 1938. Burrows worked out a complicated theory that the city of Shiloh, or Sheloh, had been inhabited by a clan of Judah claiming

---

[1] For an account of older views, see S. R. Driver, *J. Phil.* xiv (1885), 1–28, and A. Posnanski, *Schiloh. Ein Beitrag zur Geschichte der Messiaslehre. Erster Teil* (Leipzig, 1904).

[2] *Biblica*, xxxix (1958), 405–25.

[3] Cf. S. R. Driver, *J. Phil.* xiv (1885), 12 f., 16; Posnanski, *Schiloh*, pp. 117 f., 126, 270.

[4] *Randglossen zur hebräischen Bibel*, i (Leipzig, 1908), 245 f. His earlier view was published in 1899.

[5] See the commentaries of W. H. Bennett (Edinburgh, n.d.), H. E. Ryle (Cambridge, 1914), and J. Skinner (2nd ed., Edinburgh, 1930).

[6] *ZAW*, xxix (1909), 186–97.

[7] *The Oracles of Jacob and Balaam (The Bellarmine Series,* iii) (London, n.d. but preface and *imprimatur* 1938).

descent from Shelah, and that the verse refers to the migration of the clan to Bethlehem after Shiloh's destruction; Jesse was, he thinks, one of the refugees, and so David's rise to the king-ship was the sequel of Shiloh's, or Shelah's, coming to Beth-lehem. He suggests that David was believed to be, in a sense, a descendant of Shelah through Elimelech, as well as of Perez through Boaz. The theory contains so much speculation that it cannot be regarded as very probable.

Yet another attempt to interpret the reading 'Shelah' has been made by E. M. Good,[1] who was unaware that anyone but Ryle had thought of it. He translates verse 10: 'The staff shall not [ever again!] depart from Judah, nor the "lawgiver's em-blem" from between his legs, until Shelah comes to whom [properly] belongs the obeisance of the peoples.' Good sees in the passage an ironical polemic against the tribe of Judah written by someone who favoured the Joseph tribes. Shelah, he thinks, is contrasted with Perez, the son who was born in discreditable circumstances to Judah and Tamar, and who was the ancestor of David (1 Chron. 2: 5–15; Ruth 4: 18–22). He claims to find allusions to the uncomplimentary story about Judah in Gen. 38. The word 'feet' is said to be used because it can be a euphemism for the male sexual organ, and the words 'staff' (שֵׁבֶט) and 'lawgiver's emblem' (מְחֹקֵק) are intended to remind the reader of Judah's מַטֶּה in Gen. 38: 18. The binding of a donkey to a vine in 49: 11 is foolish, since the animal would eat the plant; Good rejects the opinion that the verse speaks of conditions of such plenty that the loss of a vine does not matter—a time when, to use twentieth-century terms, men light cigars with five pound notes. He thinks that שֹׁרֵקָה ('choice vine') is used in verse 11 to suggest to the reader the vale of Sorek (שֹׂרֵק), close to Timnah which is mentioned in Gen. 38. Finally, verse 12 refers to Judah's eyes (עֵינַיִם) in order to make the reader think of the place Enaim in Gen. 38: 14, 21. The alleged allusions are not very convincing. If the poet wanted to refer to Judah's מַטֶּה, why did he not use the same word? Why, too, did he use the feminine שֹׁרֵקָה, which is found only here in the Old Testament, when the masculine שֹׂרֵק was better suited to his purpose? In any case, the

---

[1] *JBL*, LXXXII (1963), 427–32.

name Sorek does not actually occur in Gen. 38. Good's supposed allusions to the story of Tamar are rather far-fetched, and cannot be taken seriously. Moreover, he does not make plain what he believes to be the meaning of Gen. 49: 10. He comments, 'Judah, by impregnating the woman who should have been Shelah's wife by the levirate law, had foregone his ancestry of the Davidic monarchy, which by rights belonged to Shelah'; but his words fail to explain precisely what is meant by 'until Shelah comes'. Nor is it easy to understand what he is trying to say about Judah's ancestry of the Davidic monarchy; even if Shelah had been given to Tamar, Judah, his father, would still have been the ancestor of Shelah's descendants.

Good also claims to detect allusions to the kidnapping of Joseph recorded in Gen. 37, but his arguments are no more convincing. Moreover, it is difficult to see why the story of Joseph should have been regarded as especially discreditable to Judah. In the E form of the story, Judah is not singled out for blame and is no worse than his brothers; in J, however, Judah appears in a favourable light as the one who did not want to kill Joseph (37: 26), who later promised Jacob to be surety for Benjamin (43: 9), and who even offered to be a slave in Benjamin's place (44: 20 ff., 33 f.). Good's theory must be rejected.

Third, the vocalization of the Massoretic Text has had its defenders. The Hebrew of the problematic line can be translated, as in the RV[mg], 'Till he come to Shiloh'. It then refers to the extension of Judah's power until[1] the tribe comes to Shiloh. J. Lindblom has suggested[2] that the oracle dates from the period when David was king in Hebron, and that it looks forward to the extension of his authority until it reaches Shiloh, the site of the former sanctuary that had contained the ark; Shiloh was, he thinks, a 'representative name' standing for the northern tribes. O. Eissfeldt,[3] followed by H. J. Zobel,[4] has

---

[1] 'Until' does not necessarily imply that Judah's authority will cease when it reaches Shiloh. Cf., for example, 1 Sam. 15: 35; 2 Sam. 6: 23.

[2] *Congress Volume, Copenhagen 1953* (*VTS*, I, 1953), pp. 78–87.

[3] *Volume du Congrès, Strasbourg 1956* (*VTS*, IV, 1957), pp. 138–42, reprinted in O. Eissfeldt, *Kleine Schriften*, III (Tübingen, 1966), 417–20.

[4] *Stammesspruch und Geschichte* (*BZAW*, xcv, 1965).

maintained the somewhat different view that the verse expresses hopes for the future of Judah in the period before the destruction of Shiloh (*c.* 1050 B.C.). They believe that, in the period before 1050 B.C., various tribes laid claim to primacy over the others, that Judg. 8: 1–3 and 12: 1–6 reflect such a claim by Ephraim, and that the later passage in Mic. 5: 1–3, which makes a similar claim for Judah, is based on an old tradition. In the time of Gen. 49: 10, Judah, which had previously had little to do with the northern tribes, hoped to dominate them in place of Ephraim and to be acknowledged at Shiloh as the leading tribe.

Moran has contested the theories of Lindblom and Eissfeldt for several reasons. In the first place, he objects that Shiloh is nowhere else spelt שִׁילֹה. Since, however, it is found in other places as שִׁלוֹ, שִׁילוֹ, and שִׁלֹה, he is scarcely justified in finding fault with yet another way of spelling the word. Secondly, he maintains that the word עַמִּים, used of those who are to be subject to Judah, should denote foreign peoples, not Israelite tribes. While the argument is perhaps not conclusive, it is true that the word is most naturally understood of foreign peoples, and the objection has force against Eissfeldt's theory. It carries no weight, however, against Lindblom, who understands the verse to refer to a 'political dominion over foreign nations' (p. 83; cf. p. 84). Lindblom could have added that a reference to foreigners would have been very appropriate to the time when David was king in Hebron, since he had already come into conflict with the Amalekites and established some kind of relationship with non-Israelites in the south (1 Sam. 30), since an extension of his kingdom would be possible only if the Philistines were subdued, and since he may already have had hopes of taking the Jebusite city of Jerusalem. Thirdly, Moran objects that Shiloh is not a very suitable symbol of authority over other Israelite tribes. There is no evidence that the supremacy of any one tribe ever made itself felt at Shiloh, and it was unlikely at a time when the tribes prized their independence. Moran's argument against Eissfeldt seems justified, and it may be added that Judg. 8: 1–3 and 12: 1–6 do not necessarily speak of the kind of authority over other tribes that is, *ex hypothesi*, meant in Gen. 49: 10. Once again, however, the objection is irrelevant to Lindblom's theory. Fourthly, Moran claims that his theory alone 'really offers parallelism with the following colon'; however, if the coming to Shiloh denotes the extension of Judah's sovereignty, the meaning of the line is very close to that of the parallel.

Two of Moran's arguments are thus unconvincing, and two tell against Eissfeldt, but not against Lindblom. Yet another consideration favours Lindblom against Eissfeldt. Gen. 49: 10 appears to imply that there is already a leadership in Judah which will be extended until it reaches Shiloh, and the implication is more appropriate to Lindblom's view that David is already king in Hebron. Lindblom's theory, therefore, offers a more satisfactory interpretation of the Massoretic Text than Eissfeldt's. Moran dismisses Lindblom's explanation on the ground that Shiloh is unlikely to have been used to symbolize control over the northern tribes after its destruction, but it is difficult to agree with him that the site of the shrine must necessarily have lost all significance so rapidly. Lindblom's interpretation of the Massoretic Text has thus not been disproved, and there is no reason to prefer Moran's theory. Indeed, although Moran's view is not impossible, Lindblom's has the advantage that he does not alter the vocalization of the Hebrew.

DAN

Verse 16: דָּן יָדִין עַמּוֹ כְּאַחַד שִׁבְטֵי יִשְׂרָאֵל

> Dan shall judge his people,
> As one of the tribes of Israel.

It has long been recognized that the verb may denote, not judging in the narrow sense, but vindicating, perhaps even defending in battle. Commentators have been divided over the interpretation of 'his people'. Some think that the people are the members of the tribe of Dan. Dan will defend his own members and maintain his existence among the tribes of Israel. But who is Dan? It is hardly the eponymous ancestor who will defend his descendants, and so it must be supposed that the tribe is somehow distinguished from its people whom it will defend.

Though such an explanation may not be impossible, it is rather strained and not entirely satisfactory. Others suppose that 'his people' means Israel as a whole. But when did the tribe of Dan vindicate Israel as a whole? Some have thought of the stories of Samson, but it may be suspected that the view of Samson as a vindicator of all Israel is later in date than the Blessing of Jacob. Alternatively, it might be suggested that, if M. Noth is right in supposing that there was an office of judge of Israel[1] in the amphictyony postulated by him, the verse may mean that a member of the tribe of Dan will fill the office; the use of the root דין, rather than שפט, would occasion no difficulty. However, even if the uncertain theory that there was such an office is accepted, it does not give a satisfactory meaning to the verse. It may be doubted whether the existence of a Danite holder of the office would have justified the statement that the tribe of Dan was itself judging the other tribes. It is therefore difficult, even if not impossible, to find a meaning for the verse on the supposition that the verb means 'to judge' or 'to vindicate'. Moreover, the play on words is perhaps too obvious, and contrasts with the other examples in the chapter, whether direct as in verses 8 and 19, or indirect as in verse 13 (where there is no need to emend יִשְׁכֹּן to יִזְבֹּל in order to make the pun on 'Zebulun' explicit), 14 f., 20, and 22 (see below). The presence of so obvious a play on words in verse 16 cannot be dismissed as impossible, but it would be better if a more subtle one could be found.

In view of the difficulty of the verse, it is interesting to note the suggestion of C. Rabin[2] that the verb does not come from דין, 'to judge', but from a root (which he also finds in Gen. 6: 3; 30: 6) cognate to Arabic *danâ*, 'to be close', and the related *dûna*. He says, 'if the passage refers to the Laish period, an assurance that "Dan is close to his people" (and will assist

---

[1] *Festschrift Alfred Bertholet zum 80. Geburtstag gewidmet* (Tübingen, 1950), pp. 405–17.

[2] C. Rabin (ed.), *Studies in the Bible (Scripta Hierosolymitana*, VIII, Jerusalem, 1961), p. 389. An Arabic idiom was earlier used to overcome the difficulty by J. D. Michaelis, *Supplementa ad Lexica Hebraica* (Göttingen, 1792), p. 422: '*Dan remetietur populo suo, ut ulla tribus Israelis*, i.e. paria cum illis faciet fortitudine ac victoriis.'

them if necessary) is anything but trivial'. Rabin's theory avoids
the problems of the usual explanations, but it is not without its
own difficulties. If, as he thinks, the verse comes from the time
after Dan had settled at Laish, then the northernmost part of
the country is not very appropriately described as near. If, on
the other hand, it were to be dated in the period of the Danite
settlement in the south, there would be no point in stating the
obvious. Nor does a reference to Dan's possible assistance to the
rest of Israel seem the most natural point to make about so
small a tribe. Another difficulty is that a preposition might have
been expected after the verb, as in Arabic. Nevertheless, unlike
the majority of scholars, Rabin has seen that the usual interpretations of the verse are unsatisfactory, and has shown a possible
way out of the difficulty. Perhaps the verb comes from a root
different from that of the common verb 'to judge'. Although
radices hebraicae non multiplicandae sunt praeter necessitatem, there is
a case for postulating a new meaning here. A passage where a
poet is seeking a play on words is the kind of place where a rare
verb might be expected, and the presence of a different root
from the one denoting judgement would make the play on words
more subtle. Perhaps a more suitable root than the one suggested
by Rabin can be found.

What is the verse trying to say about Dan? Dan was a small
tribe and had to migrate from the south because it was hard
pressed by the other inhabitants of the region (Judg. 1: 34;
17–18; cf. 13–16); and in Gen. 49: 17 it is compared to a
snake of small size. Yet the words 'as one of the tribes of Israel'
suggest that Dan will have a status similar to theirs (cf. כְּאַחַד
or כְּאַחַת in Gen. 3: 22; Josh. 10: 2; Judg. 16: 7, 11; 17: 11;
1 Sam. 17: 36; 2 Sam. 2: 18; 9: 11; 13: 13; Ezek. 48: 8; Obad.
11; Ps. 82: 7; Ruth 2: 13; 2 Chron. 18: 12). The verb probably
refers, therefore, to some quality or activity that will make Dan
comparable to the other tribes, despite its small size. Some
support for this view may be found in verse 17, which may contain a similar idea even if it was originally an independent
saying; the point of verse 17 is that Dan, though small, is very
deadly and far from insignificant.

A suitable meaning can be obtained if the verb is derived

from a root דנן and pointed יָדֹן (unless a by-form דין is postulated). The root may be regarded as cognate to Accadian *danānu*, 'to be strong', from which Ugaritic *dnn* should probably be explained.[1] According to G. R. Driver,[2] the root is also found in a Hebrew text from Qumran (1QH5: 13), where he thinks that ודנת יגוני means 'and the vehemence of my pain', but the phrase has been explained in different ways by other scholars and cannot bear much weight as evidence for the existence of the root in Hebrew. Whether or not the root is found in the Qumran literature, I suggest that it should be postulated for Gen. 49: 16. Professor Driver, who first drew my attention to the fact that the verse is difficult and to the possibility that a new root should be sought, has suggested to me that the *casus pendens* construction is used (cf. verses 19 and 20, assuming that the letter *mem* at the beginning of the latter should be attached to the end of the former); if so, the verse may be translated:

> Dan—his people will be strong,
> As one of the tribes of Israel.

Despite its small size, Dan is a tribe to be reckoned with, and will maintain its position as a full tribe of Israel.

JOSEPH

Verse 22: בֵּן פֹּרָת יוֹסֵף בֵּן פֹּרָת עֲלֵי־עָיִן

> Joseph is a fruitful bough,
> A fruitful bough by a fountain.

The phrase בֵּן פֹּרָת is difficult, and many commentators have resorted to emendation. It has often been suggested that the verse contains a play on words alluding to Ephraim, which was part of the House of Joseph. If a play on words is present, it is perhaps probable that the allusion is, not to אֶפְרַיִם, 'Ephraim', but to אֶפְרָתִי, 'Ephraimite', which is more like פֹּרָת. The allusion, if it is regarded as likely, offers some support for the Massoretic Text against such emendations as פָּרָה, in which the play is more remote.

---

[1] H. L. Ginsberg, *The Legend of King Keret* (*BASOR* Supplementary Studies, II–III) (New Haven, Conn., 1946), p. 45. Driver and Aistleitner agree.
[2] *The Judaean Scrolls* (Oxford, 1965), p. 435.

Fresh light is perhaps shed on פְּרָת by the form פורת, which is used of the Euphrates in two texts from Qumran (1QapGn21: 12, 17, 28; 1QM2: 11). It has been observed[1] that the name is also spelt *pwrt* in Christian Palestinian Aramaic, that Josephus spells it φοράς (*Ant.* i. i. 3 [§ 39]), and that it is *Furât* in Arabic; despite the caution of Y. Kutscher,[2] the spelling at Qumran probably reflects a pronunciation nearer than the Massoretic Text's usual פְּרָת to the original Accadian *Purattu*. It therefore seems possible, or even likely, that פֹרָת in Gen. 49: 22 is a way of spelling the word meaning the 'Euphrates'.

If the word as traditionally vocalized may denote the Euphrates, it is worth recalling that J. M. Allegro suggested[3] some years ago that פֹרָת should be pointed פְּרָת and understood to mean the Euphrates. The meaning sought by him can now be obtained without changing the vowel points. Allegro also suggested that the word בֵּן here denotes, not 'son', but the 'ben-tree', which he had previously detected[4] in Isa. 44: 4. The Arabic *bânun* is used of a kind of moringa, but that meaning does not fit the two Old Testament passages, because the moringa grows in dry places, not near water. Allegro noted, however, that the Arabic word is also applied (incorrectly, according to Lane) to a species of willow. Similarly, בִּינָא, which normally means 'tamarisk' in Aramaic and Syriac, has been thought by many to denote a willow or poplar in B. Gittin 68 B. Finally, he thought that the Accadian *bīnu* is used of a poplar, although the Chicago dictionary has more recently expressed[5] support for the meaning 'tamarisk'. Since Allegro believed that there is evidence that the ben-tree could be identified with the poplar, he suggested that Gen. 49: 22 refers to the *Populus euphratica*, and translated the first part of the verse, 'A Euphratean poplar is Joseph'.

[1] J. van der Ploeg, *Le Rouleau de la Guerre* (*Studies on the Texts of the Desert of Judah*, II, Leiden, 1959), p. 74; Y. Yadin, *The Scroll of the War of the Sons of Light against the Sons of Darkness* (E.T., Oxford, 1962), p. 266; J. A. Fitzmyer, *The Genesis Apocryphon of Qumran Cave I* (*Biblica et Orientalia*, XVIII, Rome, 1966), p. 133.

[2] C. Rabin and Y. Yadin (eds.), *Aspects of the Dead Sea Scrolls* (*Scripta Hierosolymitana*, IV, Jerusalem, 1958), p. 24.

[3] *ZAW*, LXIV (1952), 249–51.   [4] *ZAW*, LXIII (1951), 154–6.

[5] A. L. Oppenheim (ed.), *The Assyrian Dictionary*, II (Chicago, 1965), 239–42.

Allegro's theory is not satisfactory as it stands. It is unlikely that an ancient Hebrew anticipated the scientific description of a kind of tree as a *Populus euphratica* or thought that a tree found commonly in Palestine was a Mesopotamian species. Yet Allegro may have pointed the way to the correct solution of the problem. It is possible that the poet does, indeed, speak of a 'ben-tree of the Euphrates', but does not intend 'Euphrates' to define the species; he may mean simply a species found in both Palestine and Mesopotamia, but have in mind a particular example of the species growing near the Euphrates. Why, then, does he speak of the Euphrates? Two reasons may be suggested. First, the verse may be compared with places in the Song of Songs where there is a tendency to speak of particular examples of things found in particular places: thus 4: 1 and 6: 5 speak, not of goats in general or even of goats on any mountain, but of goats on Mount Gilead, and 7: 4 refers to pools in Heshbon (cf. also 1: 14; 3: 9; 4: 11). Second, the poet wishes to describe a flourishing tree growing near a river where it is well watered (cf. Num. 24: 6; Jer. 17: 8; Ps. 1: 3), and here makes the water supply doubly assured by mentioning a spring. The Euphrates was known to be a great river, far greater than any in Palestine, and had the added advantage of giving a play on words. If this view is accepted, Allegro's suggestion that a tree is named may be justified, but the difficulty of supposing 'Euphrates' to be part of the definition of the species is avoided. Nor is it necessary to follow him in holding that the species was a poplar. The meaning 'tamarisk' is better attested in cognate languages, and there are kinds of tamarisk that grow near water.[1] The first part of verse 22 may therefore be translated:

> Joseph is a tamarisk of the Euphrates,
> A tamarisk of the Euphrates near a spring.

After I had noticed the possible connection between Gen. 49: 22 and פורת in the Qumran texts, I heard a paper read by Professor W. F. Albright to the Society for Old Testament Study in July 1967, in which he made a similar point. He, however, gives to בֶּן the meaning 'son'.

[1] G. E. Post (revised by J. E. Dinsmore), *Flora of Syria, Palestine and Sinai*, 1 (Beirut, 1932), 223.

8

TWOFOLD ASPECTS OF HEBREW WORDS

by Georg Fohrer

I

A. It has been demonstrated from several examples that Israelite thought presents an idea or an event under two aspects, or, so to speak, allows it to pivot on two foci, in order that the idea or event might be understood in its entirety. Thus the same event may be depicted as intervention by Yahweh on the one hand, and as human activity on the other, but much more frequently the divine and the human factors are seen side by side or even interwoven. Various representations stand side by side and are interconnected: of the human hero, who brings help and victory, of the help of Yahweh who himself uses human heroes, and of Yahweh as sole helper who allows no human activity beside his own.[1] Further, two interconnected ideas form the central core of the religion of Yahweh: God's sovereignty which is expressed *inter alia* in the concept of the 'Jealous God', in the assertions of Yahweh's Lordship, in the titles 'King' and 'Shepherd'; and the relationship between God and man which appears *inter alia* in the concept of man as *imago dei*, in the personal character of faith, and in the burnt offering or communion offering (זבח).[2] Finally, in the religion of Yahweh divine and human activity are correlated. Yahweh does not act without considering human activity, or indeed in opposition to this activity, although he is independent of it. Instead, there is harmony between the actions of the two parties. This too is the case in the fatal crisis of the non-believer, as the Egyptian plagues

[1] I. L. Seeligmann, 'Menschliches Heldentum und göttliche Hilfe. Die doppelte Kausalität im alttestamentlichen Geschichtsdenken', *TZ*, xix (1963), 385–411.
[2] G. Fohrer, 'The Centre of a Theology of the Old Testament', *Nederduitse Geref. Teologiese Tydskrif*, vii (1966), 198–206.

before the Exodus from Egypt testify: man's unwillingness and the blindness and hardening brought about by Yahweh leave the unrepentant sinner to become more and more deeply entangled in his own destruction. In the same way man's goodwill and Yahweh's readiness to forgive belong together and form two aspects or parts of a whole: the salvation of an existence which is sinful and subject to death.[1]

B. The position is no different with regard to the meaning of Hebrew words. It is well known that in the first instance the basic meaning of given roots is decisive and applies equally to the words derived from the root. Such words can denote several processes or objects which correspond to the basic idea. Thus, מְכַסֶּה, derived from כסה 'to cover', denotes several things which have in common that they cover something: the covering of a bed (Isa. 14: 11), or clothing (Isa. 23: 18), the deck of a ship (Ezek. 27: 7) and, anatomically, the fat covering the entrails (Lev. 4: 8). The word מַפֶּלֶת, derived from נפל 'to fall', denotes several things which have in common that they have fallen or can be made to fall: the carcass, i.e. a fallen animal (Judg. 14: 8) and a felled tree-trunk (Ezek. 31: 13); or the word denotes the actual fall or collapse (Ezek. 26: 15, 18).

The twofold aspects of Hebrew words begin to be apparent in cases where words are used both in a literal sense and in a transferred sense. This occurs very frequently in Hebrew, so a single example will serve for clarification. קָנֶה denotes literally a reed (1 Kings 14: 15), and with a transferred meaning other things which are tubular: a stalk of grain (Gen. 41: 5), the shaft of a lamp-stand (Exod. 25: 31 ff.), a measuring rod (Ezek. 40: 5) or the humerus (Job 31: 22 for the shoulder joint).

Further, a word can be used both in a spatial and in a temporal sense. The word קֶדֶם has basically the meaning 'in front' (Ps. 139: 5). In its spatial aspect, for the Israelite, with his eastward orientation, it denotes the actual point of the compass which lies 'in front' of him. In its temporal aspect it denotes time 'before',

[1] G. Fohrer, *Überlieferung und Geschichte des Exodus* (*BZAW*, xci, 1964), pp. 60 ff.; 'Jesaja 1 als Zusammenfassung der Verkündigung Jesajas', in *Studien zur alttestamentlichen Prophetie (1949–1965)* (*BZAW*, xcix, 1967), pp. 159–63.

that is, 'antiquity' or 'primaeval time'. Similarly, the word קֵץ
'end' is to be found in its spatial aspect with the meaning
'border' (Ps. 119: 96) or 'goal' (Job 6: 11) and in a temporal
aspect 'the time of the end' (Dan. 8: 19).

Finally, arising from its basic meaning, a word can be applied
with a positive and a negative aspect. נקב I means primarily
'bore a hole, pierce' and then from 'perforate, prick' extends
to 'determine, designate', as well as 'distinguish'. This last
can have a positive meaning on the one hand, like 'the notable
men (נְקֻבֵי) of the first of the nations' (Amos 6: 1), or on the
other hand a negative meaning as in the expression 'to curse
(distinguish unfavourably) the name (of Yahweh)' (Lev. 24:
11, 16).

II

Further stages in the direction of the twofold aspect of word
usage can be seen in the following four groups of words:

A. Hebrew shares with other languages the semasiological
development of a word denoting a thing into a word denoting
a person: a word which originally denoted a thing is used to
denote a person.[1] This development may even proceed in two
stages, in that a word denoting a thing first becomes a personal
adjective and this then becomes a noun. For example, Accadian
qurbum 'nearness, relationship' to 'near, related' and to 'relative, neighbour'. In Hebrew this development was sometimes
complete at an early date and is no longer to be found in extant
texts. Thus מַלְאָךְ 'sending, motion' to 'messenger', תּוֹשָׁב 'sitting,
residing (permitting to reside)' to 'inhabitant' and תַּלְמִיד
'teaching' to 'pupil'. In other cases both aspects are still
represented: בַּיִת denotes 'house' and the family living in it,
הֲלִיכָה the 'way' and the 'caravan' which travels along it, מַצָּב
'standing place' and the 'outpost' or the 'garrison' stationed
there.

B. A word can denote an activity as well as the person who
performs it. The best-known example is קֹהֶלֶת, feminine participle

[1] W. Eilers, 'Zur Funktion von Nominalformen. Ein Grenzgang zwischen
Morphologie und Semasiologie', *Die Welt des Orients*, III, 1/2 (1964), 80–
145.

of קהל, which is originally the action of leading the general assembly and the discourse there, and is then applied to the person who performs this activity, the leader and preacher of the assembly. The same holds good for the words סֹפֶרֶת and פֹּכֶרֶת הַצְּבָיִים (Ezra 2: 55, 57). Originally they denoted the court office of scribe and the activity of the catcher of gazelles, and then those who filled the office or performed the activity; finally they became personal names. Admittedly in these cases, too, only the last step of the development is on record. On the other hand both aspects are clearly recognizable in the word זָקֵן, although the development is in the opposite direction: זָקֵן is equally 'old man' and, in the plural, the rank of 'Elders' with their special functions in the context of Israelite society.

C. Other words denote equally a part as well as a larger whole: thus הַר 'mountain' and 'mountain range', תַּפּוּחַ 'apple' and 'apple-tree'. The case is similar with גְּבוּל, which can mean 'boundary' and the 'district' enclosed by the boundary.

D. More frequently words are used concurrently with both concrete and abstract meanings, where the former need not always be the primary meaning.[1] Thus, from אדר (with the double sense of noble and strong) is derived אַדֶּרֶת first 'splendour' or 'glory' (Ezek. 17: 8), then the king's 'royal robe' (Jonah 3: 6) and also the 'cloak' of a prophet who proves his power or even works miracles (1 Kings 19: 19; 2 Kings 2: 8, 13 f.). The concrete meaning of אָוֶן 'uncanny power, condition of tabu' is implied several times (Num. 23: 21; Deut. 26: 14; 1 Sam. 15: 12; Isa. 1: 13; 29: 10) but most clearly in the name which the dying Rachel gives to her son (Gen. 35: 18); yet the more abstract meaning 'evil, wickedness' predominates. The question of the primary meaning of אַף II remains open; it denotes on the one hand 'nose', on the other 'anger', and, in the dual, 'face' yet the verb אנף is found only with the meaning 'to be angry'; of course, it is possible that a basic though irrecoverable meaning 'to snort' preceded it, from which all the rest may be derived.

---

[1] M. A. van der Weiden, '"Abstractum pro concreto", phaenomenon stilisticum', *Verbum Domini*, XLIV (1966), 43–52, gives examples from Ugaritic and Old Testament texts.

The juxtaposition of concrete and abstract aspects is further to be found in הֶבֶל, which denotes ephemeral 'breath' and 'transitoriness, nothingness'; in זְרוֹעַ 'arm', the plural of which serves to denote 'military forces'; in חֲלַקְלַקּוֹת, which, besides the 'smooth places' of a path, stands for 'smoothness, deceit' in behaviour; in טַעַם which besides 'taste' in food or drink passes through the intermediate 'perception of such a taste' to denote 'discrimination, understanding'; in יוֹבֵל, primarily 'ram' and later the 'year of release', through the blowing of the ram's horn which accompanied it; in כֵּן III which denotes the 'stand' as well as the place where someone stands, and the place which someone occupies, his 'office'; in כְּתָב which has the meanings 'document' and 'mode of writing'; in קֶרֶן, which is used for 'horn' (with various concrete meanings) and for 'strength, power', of which the horn is a symbol. All these examples, which could be multiplied, show that one and the same word can be in current use with concrete and abstract meanings at the same time.

III

Hebrew displays not a few verbs and nouns which view a single event from two aspects, and in this way indicate a greater whole. Combining the double notions of before and after, cause and effect, they denote the consequence of an event as well as the event itself, the result which is effected by an action as well as the action itself.

A. אוֹן I denotes primarily a man's 'procreative power', so that Jacob singles out the 'firstfruits of my strength' before the others in his oracle on Reuben (Gen. 49: 3) just as does the ordinance on the inheritance of the first-born (Deut. 21: 17). Besides, the word has the general meaning 'strength', so that it can be said of Jacob 'in his manhood he strove with God' (Hos. 12: 4). Then follows the second aspect which proceeds from the idea that the man with such strength is able to acquire 'property', as the result or consequence of forceful action (Hos. 12: 9; Job 20: 10).

אשם (Qal) means 'to incur guilt', as the whole body of Israel incurs guilt or falls into sin when it unwittingly commits a sin

99

(Lev. 4: 13). Over against this stands the second aspect that the guilt which a man brings upon himself by slandering another must be 'expiated' (Prov. 30: 10). The same meaning is most likely in Ps. 34: 22 f.

בּוּשָׁה is on the one hand 'the shame' which, like the feeling of terror that can fill a man, is visible in the expression of his face (Ezek. 7: 18). The consequence of being thus put to shame (which indeed follows certain wrong doing) is on the other hand the 'disgrace' which covers a man or a people, or clings to them (Obad. 10; Mic. 7: 10; Ps. 89: 46).

בַּז and בִּזָּה certainly denote predominantly 'plunder', i.e. booty snatched by plundering. But apart from this result of the act of plundering, the word denotes also the act itself, as in Dan. 11: 33 where the parallel expressions 'sword, flame, captivity' only permit the rendering 'plunder(ing)'.

חֶבֶל 1 denotes the 'cord' or 'line' which is used for many different purposes. The cord serves also for measuring portions of land which are divided or allocated accordingly. Thus Amos threatens the High Priest of Bethel with the division of his land by line (Amos 7: 17), and the Psalmist declares that Yahweh apportioned with a line the peoples of Palestine to Israel (Ps. 78: 55). The result of this activity provides a measured 'portion of land' like Manasseh's portions (Josh. 17: 5) or the 'district' of the Judeans (Josh. 19: 9).

חַטָּאת presents a twofold aspect like אָשָׁם: 'sin' on the one hand and 'atonement, sin offering' on the other. The second aspect is particularly clear in Mic. 6: 7b, where פֶּשַׁע also shows its second aspect, normally overlooked in comparison with its first aspect, 'opposition, revolt'. 'Shall I give my first-born as a transgression offering (פשע) for myself, the fruit of my body as a sin offering (חטאת) for my life?'

חַיִל shows a similar double aspect to אוֹן: 'strength' as the faculty of achieving, producing or obtaining something, and 'property, fortune' which are the results of the application of such strength. Whoever has possessions and adds to them is in consequence a worthy and well-to-do man with property, who is fit for military service (אִישׁ חַיִל) or even belongs to the élite (Neh. 3: 34 of Samaria).

חַרְצֻב denotes on the one hand the 'bond' laid upon another (Isa. 58: 6) and on the other hand the 'affliction' which results from being bound with bonds (Ps. 73: 4).

יְגִיעַ often means the 'toil' and 'labour', as where Job regards man as having been made by the work of God's hands (Job 10: 3); and also the produce or result of labour: the 'gain' or 'profit' which may be put in jeopardy once more (Gen. 31: 42; Jer. 3: 24).

יחם (Pi'el) clearly shows a double aspect. The verb means both 'to be on heat' (Gen. 30: 41) and—in the case of a woman or a female animal—'to conceive' as the result or consequence of being on heat (Ps. 51: 7).

יְשׁוּעָה and יֵשַׁע, 'help, deliverance' (derived from the verb ישע 'to help, deliver'), have acquired in eschatological prophecy the further meaning of the 'salvation' which is brought about by deliverance, so that once again the double aspect of cause and effect appears.[1]

מוּסָר is primarily the 'chastisement' with a rod required above all by wisdom teaching (Prov. 13: 24; 23: 13). The result of the 'chastisement' which serves to inculcate wisdom's rules for living then becomes the 'chastening' achieved by keeping the rules—self-discipline, which brings wisdom and guarantees life (Prov. 1: 2 f.; 4: 13).

מִכְתָּב expresses 'writing', a written symbol or a kind of writing, whether written by God or engraved with a signet (Exod. 32: 16; 39: 30). The same word also means the 'document' which results from the use of writing (2 Chron. 21: 12) or a written edict (2 Chron. 35: 4).

מלא and its derivatives show the two aspects very clearly: 'to fill' and (as its consequence) 'to be full'.

מַעֲשֶׂה presents the same picture. In accordance with the derivation from עשה it is concerned at the same time with 'deed' and 'work', and therefore with the 'product' which results from them, e.g. baker's work (Gen. 40: 17), a grating (Exod. 27: 4), wrought metal (Num. 31: 51) or cast metal work (2 Chron. 3: 10).

[1] G. Fohrer, 'σῴζω κτλ, B. σῴζω und σωτηρία im Alten Testament', *TWNT*, vii, 970–81.

מְצוּדָה 1 in Ezekiel means both the 'net' used by the hunter (Ezek. 12: 13; 17: 20 transferred to Yahweh) and the consequence of its successful use: the prey caught (Ezek. 13: 21).

נסע (Qal) denotes, from the basic meaning 'to pull out', the pulling up of tent pegs (Isa. 33: 20). Usually tent pegs are pulled out of the ground to break camp, in order to set out. Therefore the verb often has the meaning of the consequence or result of pulling up the tent pegs: 'to break up, set out'.

פֹּעַל means primarily 'deed, work, activity', but at the same time also—like יְגִיעַ—'gain' (2 Sam. 23: 20) and 'wages' for work (Jer. 22: 13; Job 7: 2).

צַיִד 1 resembles מְצוּדָה in that, as well as 'hunt' (Gen. 10: 9), it denotes also the result of the hunt: 'the game bag'.

רָעָה finally is the 'evil' which someone does and the 'disaster' which he encounters in consequence. So even this part of the doctrine of retribution is regarded also as a totality with two aspects.

B. In some cases the kind of effect envisaged in the second aspect is further distinguished as a positive or a negative consequence.

עָמָל denotes primarily 'labour' and 'toil'. The end to which labour leads is expressed in twofold fashion by the same word: on the one hand it is the 'acquisition', achieved by labour (Ps. 105:44), and on the other 'trouble, sorrow' (Isa. 10: 1; Ps. 7: 15).

פְּעֻלָּה 'work, deed' can likewise have two consequences: on the one hand 'recompense' acquired through work (Isa. 40: 10) and 'wages' for work (Prov. 11: 18), and on the other 'punishment' as the wages of sin (Isa. 65: 7; Ps. 109: 20).

C. In the case of a few words Hebrew exceeds its use of two aspects and expresses the totality of an event by means of three aspects. Thus אָשָׁם denotes 'guilt' (Gen. 26: 10) and the 'sin-offering' which is presented for its expiation (Lev. 5: 6ff.) and 'guilt offering' or 'compensation' (1 Sam. 6: 3f.). בֹּשֶׂם is 'balsam bush' (Song of Sol. 5: 1), the 'balsam oil' extracted from it (Exod. 35: 28) and the 'sweet savour' obtained from the latter (Exod. 30: 23). דִּין is a 'legal claim' (Isa. 10: 2), the 'law suit' brought on account of it (Prov. 22: 10), and the 'judgement' which concludes the suit (Ps. 76: 9). מָוֶת mostly means 'death', but sometimes also the 'dying' which precedes it or the 'sickness' which causes it (Jer. 15: 2), and the 'kingdom of the dead' which the dead enter (Isa. 38: 18). סוֹד is the 'circle of intimates' (Gen. 49: 6) which holds a 'confidential discussion' (Prov. 15: 22) and then makes a 'plan' or 'decision' (Amos 3: 7). עָוֺן means 'sin' (Ps. 18: 24), the 'guilt' which it incurs (Jer. 50: 20) and its consequent punishment (Gen. 4: 13). It is clear from these words that the twofold aspect of before and after, cause and effect, repeats itself in the threefold aspect, since the first result becomes at once the starting-point for a second result.

D. The word מַכָּה perhaps presents even a fourth aspect. It means primarily 'blow' (Deut. 25: 3) and its resultant 'injury' (Isa. 1: 6), then the 'plague' which follows ceaseless beating (Isa. 14: 6) and the 'defeat' brought about by beating and wounding (1 Sam. 14: 30). But in this case also it is a matter of the repeated application of the twofold aspect of before and after, act and consequence, cause and effect.

9

חסד AND תודה IN THE
LINGUISTIC TRADITION
OF THE PSALTER

by A. E. Goodman

The dispersion of the Jews which commenced with the fall of
the kingdom of Judah in 586 B.C. was but the beginning of a
long process of disintegration, which, in spite of efforts towards
national restoration, continued to grow in extent throughout
the succeeding centuries. A resultant problem was that of com-
munications, both geographical and linguistic. An ever-
increasing number of Jews lived in foreign countries and spoke
a foreign tongue, while even in the home land Hebrew did not
survive, save amongst the higher classes of society, as the spoken
language, but gave place gradually but steadily to Aramaic, the
cognate Semitic tongue of the Aramaeans.

It is against this background that we may trace the beginnings of translations of the Old Testament, or parts of the
Old Testament, into these 'foreign' tongues, the Aramaic translations or 'Targums' for the Jews of Palestine and Babylonia,
the Alexandrian or 'Septuagint' version, in the first instance
for the Jews in Egypt, and subsequently the authoritative bible
of Hellenistic Jewry, and the Syriac 'Peshiṭta' for the Jewish
communities settled in northern Mesopotamia. It is easy to
over-simplify the history of the formation of these versions. The
process in each case was lengthy and complex. We know of three
separate recensions of the Pentateuch Targum; the Peshiṭta
underwent repeated revision at the hands of the Syriac-speaking
Christians so as to bring it into conformity with the Septuagint,
while the Septuagint, in turn, became widely used by the
Christian Church, but was rejected as the authorized version
of Hellenistic Jewry in favour of what were felt to be more
accurate and trustworthy versions of Scripture—notably those
of Aquila, Theodotion and Symmachus.

Throughout the history of these and other versions which derive directly or indirectly from the Hebrew Old Testament, two basic aims are apparent: (1) The communication of Holy Scripture in as precise and accurate a manner as possible, and (2) the maintenance of correct exegesis in conformity with authoritative doctrine. That both these aims were justifiable, and that in general the manner of their attainment is praiseworthy, is beyond question, but equally unquestionable is the incidence of problems both of translation and of exegesis which had inevitably to be encountered.

The history of the transmission to posterity of the Old Testament Psalms may be said to extend from the early verbal Aramaic paraphrases delivered by the Meturgeman or 'Interpreter' in the post-exilic synagogue, to the most recent of the post-reformation translations of today. Since the Psalms have occupied a position of such prominence in both Jewish and Christian worship during a period which now exceeds two millennia, it is not surprising that we should find highlighted in them some of the problems of translation and interpretation which have beset those whose vocation has been, in the tradition of the Meturgeman, to transmit the Scriptures to the People of God. An examination of the Old Testament terms חסד and תודה and their treatment in the linguistic tradition of the Psalter illustrates certain aspects of these problems.

The Hebrew word חסד in Old Testament usage ranges in meaning and import from the proper relationship that needs must exist between human beings who are bound by a mutual covenant, or who may be said to belong together in any other way, and that which, on the Godward side, does in fact exist between God and his people. The psalmist's avowal, 'To thee, O Lord, belongs חסד' (Ps. 62: 13), indicates חסד in its fullest sense as being an integral part of the divine character, and the demand by the mouth of the prophet for 'חסד and not sacrifice' (Hos. 6: 6) carries with it the clear implication that man is called upon to exhibit in himself, in loyalty and response to God, nothing less than this same divine attribute.

תודה, on the other hand, with which is closely associated the verbal form הודה, is in the Old Testament used almost exclusively of man's attitude in worship to God.[1] Both these words express grateful acknowledgement for what he is and does. If they are to be derived from the root ידה *to throw* or *cast*, they may possibly possess overtones of physical gesture, as for example the throwing up of the hands in worship or in sacrificial ritual. The one solitary instance where God ironically undertakes himself to acknowledge man (Job 40: 14) merely underlines the essentially human action towards God which תודה and הודה imply. תודה is man's response in worship to God's חסד. The remarkable thing is that, though the Old Testament literature straddles so lengthy a period of changing and varying circumstances, the two words חסד and תודה have to such a marked degree not only maintained their vital and central position in the vocabulary of Hebrew theology, but have remained unchanged in themselves in the basic religious truths which they enshrine.

חסד AND ידה IN THE PSALTER

A. *The Hebrew Psalms*

Of the very large number of occurrences of חסד in the Psalms, three only are used of man: Ps. 109: 12 'let there be no one to extend חסד to him'; Ps. 109: 16 'because he remembered not to shew חסד'; and Ps. 141: 5 'let the righteous smite me, it would be חסד'. In all other cases חסד is used exclusively of God. It is thus in the Psalms, *par excellence* a divine attribute. 'To thee, O Lord, belongs חסד' (Ps. 62: 13) suggests something very much more than an anthropomorphic projection of human ethos upon God. The term חסד in the Psalms has become in effect almost completely de-secularized, and the חסידים, who are so called by virtue of the fact that they practise חסד, do so by following nothing less than the divine example. There is thus a development apparent in the Psalms of the meaning and implication of חסד. It is in effect a shifting of emphasis rather than a change of meaning. חסד in the Psalms is above all the divine prerogative, exhibited by God in his dealings with man.

---

[1] In Neh. 12: 31, 38, 40 of thanksgiving choirs, so also perhaps Jer. 30: 19. See *BDB s.v.*

תודה in the Psalms, as elsewhere in the Old Testament, is predominantly a liturgical term used, like the verbal form הודה with which it is connected, of ritual worship. Whether תודה and הודה are to be associated with the root ידה, 'to throw, cast', or whether there were two separate roots, one meaning 'to throw' and the other (in the Hiph'il) 'to give thanks', 'confess',[1] both words are indicative of action rather than of reflection. Thus the frequent references to זֶבַח הַתּוֹדָה in the Psalms and elsewhere in the Old Testament indicate a sacrificial action on the part of the worshipper by virtue of which thanksgiving is rendered to God. But whereas זבח התודה is basically a ritual offering made in the Temple in conformity with the Levitical law, there are signs in the Psalms of a change in emphasis. Just as God is said to require 'חסד and not זבח' (Hos. 6: 6), so the point is made in Psalm 51: 19 that 'the sacrifices of God are a troubled spirit, a broken and contrite heart, O God, shalt thou not despise'. In Psalm 50: 13, 14 the worshipper is directed to offer the sacrifice, not of bulls and goats, but of תודה. Here תודה stands as it were in its rights, the 'sacrifice' enjoined being not only one which *results in*, but one which *consists of*, the offering of תודה to God. תודה in the Psalms is an active expression of thanksgiving in liturgical worship, and in this sense is frequently used to mean a thanksgiving song. Accompanied by the avowal of sin, תודה develops further into 'confession'.[2] But it is clearly distinguishable both from 'thankfulness' and from 'contrition' either of which can be expressed in biblical Hebrew by circumlocution, but neither by terminology.

B. *The Versions*

Allusion has already been made to the problem of communication which arose as a direct result of the Dispersion. A further problem which had serious repercussions on the translation and transmission of the Old Testament Scriptures was brought about by the rise of Christianity. Nowhere was this more acutely felt than in the case of the Psalter. The history of the Greek and Syriac versions of the Psalter shows a continuous tension, not

---

[1] For the former view, see *BDB*; for the latter, see *KBL s.v.*
[2] See Ps. 51: 18, 19.

only in the realm of linguistic interpretation, but also and more impressively in that of theological exegesis.

There is indeed some indication that this kind of problem was liable to arise within Judaism itself independently of Christianity. The treatment which Psalm 68: 19 received at the hands of the Versions is a case in point. Here the reading לָקַחְתָּ 'thou didst receive' is supported by the Septuagint ἔλαβες. The Peshiṭta on the other hand renders *wyhbt* 'and thou didst give'; similarly the quotation of this verse in Ephes. 4: 8 has ἔδωκε 'he gave', while the Targum, in a Haggadic paraphrase, refers the words to Moses—'O prophet Moses...thou didst teach the words of the law, thou gavest them—יהבתא להון—as gifts to the children of men'. There is evidence here of a tradition, even possibly a controversy, distinctly Jewish in character, regarding a correct interpretation of Scripture: can God be said to 'receive'? does he not rather 'give'?[1]

The earliest Version of the Psalter was that of the Greek Septuagint, translated from the Hebrew in the second century B.C. at Alexandria. The dating of the Syriac Peshiṭta Version is not so easy to determine. The numerous instances of conformity with the Septuagint have tended to mask or obliterate its character as a version translated basically from the Hebrew. Its use at an early date by the Syrian Christians would suggest the second or third century A.D.

The Aramaic Targum of the Psalter in its present form dates from the ninth century A.D., but numerous instances of similarity between it and the Peshiṭta Psalter suggest that behind this Targum is a chain of tradition, extending from at least the beginning of the Christian era. In spite of the fact therefore that the Aramaic Targum on the Psalms is in its present form a late version, and that for textual criticism its value is limited, it would be a mistake to dismiss it as useless. Late recensions of a text frequently have embedded within them strands of ancient tradition which have escaped the treatment of revisers, and we may expect to find in this Targum traces of its early history

[1] See W. E. Barnes, *The Peshitta Psalter according to the West Syrian Text* (Cambridge, 1904), pp. xlii f.; J. Armitage Robinson, *St Paul's Epistle to the Ephesians* (London, 1904), pp. 179 f.

which in turn throw light upon early biblical transmission and exegesis.

The Psalms Targum follows the Massoretic Text to which has been added a quantity of Haggadic material. An illustration of this has already been noted. In rendering passages in which the Hebrew has תּוֹדָה, however, the Targum version sometimes exhibits a consciousness that the Temple sacrifices are no longer possible. Efforts to meet this difficulty are of two kinds: (a) the introduction of a Haggadic explanation, e.g. 'Since the day when the sanctuary was laid waste I did not receive the flesh of fat sacrifices, nor did the priests sprinkle before me the blood of bucks; subdue the evil inclination, and it will be before the Lord like the sacrifice of thanksgiving כניכסת תודתא and pay thy vows unto the Most High';[1] or (b) by the use of a word other than תודתא, the normal Aramaic equivalent of the Hebrew תודה, e.g. שבחא (Ps. 26: 7), תושבחתא (Ps. 42: 5), אודותא (Ps. 100: 4), each of which emphasizes a non-sacrificial conception of praise. On the other hand, in Ps. 116, in which the Jerusalem sanctuary is specifically mentioned, the sacrificial nature of the thank-offering referred to in verse 17 is emphasized by the rendering of the Hebrew זבח תודה by the explicit דבח ניכסתא, 'the sacrificing of the sacrifice'.

The direct acknowledgement of God by the worshipper as the possessor of חסד, which the verb הודה would readily suggest to an Aramaic-speaking Jew, was an approach which the Targum appears to deprecate, and in so doing reflects a known tendency in post-exilic Judaism to avoid over-familiarity with the deity. Thus, in the oft-repeated refrain, 'Praise the Lord, for he is good, for his חסד is everlasting', the imperative הודו is rendered in the Targum by the more impersonal שבחו.[2]

The various Targum renderings of חסד in the Psalter fall into two categories: (a) חִסְדָּא, which is merely an Aramaized form of חסד, and (b) derivatives of the root טוב or טאב amongst which are טובא, טיבותא and the plural form טַבְוָן (or טַבְיָן), perhaps from a sing. טַבְוָא (טַבְיָא). One sees here, as in the Syriac

---

[1] Ps. 50: 13, 14, and cf. verse 23.
[2] Pss. 136: 1, 2, 3, 26; 105: 1; 107: 1; 118: 1; cf. also Pss. 42: 6, 12; 43: 5; 111: 1; but Pss. 106: 1; 118: 29 have אודו.

Peshiṭta Psalter, evidence of the apparent impossibility of finding any one Aramaic term which can adequately represent the different shades of meaning expressed by the Hebrew חסד. Broadly speaking, טוּבָא suggests 'inherent goodness' and 'a merciful disposition' while טֵיבוּתָא and טַבְוָון 'beneficence', 'active kindness', but these terms, as well as חִסְדָּא, are used in the Targum Psalter either indiscriminately, or at best at the whim of the translator, and together produce what can only be described as an impoverished rendering of the Hebrew.

The LXX Psalter was prepared, as was the rest of the LXX, by Jews for Jews. The fact that the Psalter was so prepared only by about the second half of the second century B.C., that it passed into the hands of the Church at an early stage, and was readily seized upon by Christians as a useful source-document for anti-Jewish polemic, and that in any case the current trend in Palestinian Judaism was towards a more scrupulous adherence to the Hebrew text than it was felt the LXX as a whole provided, makes it likely that the LXX Psalter was seldom if ever used in the Palestinian synagogues. But it was used widely by the Church and is regularly quoted in the writings of the New Testament. The style of the LXX could not be described as elegant, in some ways it is clumsy, even at times to the point of being uncouth. But to give it its due, the LXX translation was by and large a faithful representation of the Hebrew text, and was not affected by the kind of religious propaganda with which it later became involved. In the Psalms some effort has clearly been made to preserve the poetic structure, and the vocabulary has not been adopted in any haphazard fashion, but deliberately and in harmony with other parts of the LXX version. We therefore do not find in the LXX renderings of חסד and תודה in the Psalms evidence of any considerations other than those arising from the normal linguistic problems of translators from one language to another. In the Psalms, חסד is invariably rendered by ἔλεος, and elsewhere in the Old Testament this is the normal rendering; a number of other words, such as δικαιοσύνη, ἐλεημοσύνη, δίκαιος, ὅσιος, οἰκτείρημα, are also to be found as renderings, but among these only δικαιοσύνη and ἐλεημοσύνη (common in Proverbs) occur more than a very small number of times or even more than once.

It is perhaps not without significance that in the LXX Psalter תודה is rendered in two ways: (a) by αἴνεσις 'praise' (7 times) and (b) by ἐξομολόγησις 'acknowledgement' (5 times), while the verb הודה is (with one exception only)[1] rendered by ἐξομολογέομαι. A preponderance of instances of this latter verb for הודה and of αἴνεσις for תודה is to be seen elsewhere in the Old Testament. It is difficult to avoid the conclusion that the translators were conscious of a distinction in the basic conception of 'praise' and 'acknowledgement' respectively, and that though תודה might on occasion be equated with הודה in the sense of acknowledgement, and similarly that הודה could on occasion be rendered by the verb αἰνεῖν *to praise*, there nevertheless existed two distinct entities in the sphere of worship which it was important not to confuse.

The situation in the case of the Peshiṭta Psalter is different. Here, though the translation was basically from the Hebrew, and there is some evidence of early Targumic influence, it is unlikely that it was made for Jews, but for the Syriac-speaking Church. Its many affinities with the LXX suggest that recourse was had to the latter in its preparation, and that in any case it was subject to constant revision to bring it into conformity with the Greek text. Nevertheless the Peshiṭta Psalter was not a Hellenistic but a Semitic version, and as such retained much that was Semitic and non-Hellenistic.

The Peshiṭta Psalter renders חסד either by *rḥm'* (*pl.*) or by *ṭybwt'*. *rḥm'* (*pl.*) like the Hebrew רַחֲמִים denotes 'compassion' felt for, and either explicitly or implicitly shown to another or others. *ṭybwt'* on the other hand possesses a more objective connotation. Derived from the root *ṭwb*, Pāʿel, *ṭayeb* 'provide, prepare', it may be said to denote 'loving-kindness' in its action and content. This may take the form of the imparting of a favour, such as a 'blessing', 'grace', or, in a general sense, a 'gift'. The preparedness of the recipient to accept such a favour constitutes, according to the Syriac idiom, an expression of gratitude or indebtedness to the giver. Hence we find fre-

---

[1] Ps. 31 (32): 5 (ἐγνώρισα).

חסד *and* תודה *in the Psalter*

quently the compound expressions *qbl ṭybwt* 'he was thankful', and *qwblṭybwt* (written as one or two words) 'thankfulness'.

Though *ṭybwt* for חסד is common in the Peshiṭta Psalter and in the Old Testament generally, the compound expressions *qbl ṭybwt* and *qwblṭybwt* occur in neither. This is at least in part due to the unique linguistic climate of the Hebrew Old Testament and of the Hebrew idiom. Thanksgiving in the Hebrew sense was a concrete act of praise effected either by means of an offering, by word of mouth, or by a song. When a Hebrew wished to thank, he praised. As we have noticed above, it is apparent in the LXX that the Hellenistic Jewish world was already encountering a problem here. Whether or not there was ever any really clear-cut distinction in Hebrew between 'praise' on the one hand, and 'confession' and 'acknowledgement' on the other, there is reason to suppose that the Hellenist translators felt that in the Greek version there should be.

The desire to bring the Syriac text of the Psalter into close conformity with that of the LXX is clearly demonstrated by the renderings, in each version, of תודה. Where the LXX has ἐξομολόγησις, the Peshiṭta renders always *twdyt'*. Where the LXX has αἴνεσις, the Peshiṭta has, with four exceptions,[1] *šwbḥ'*. In the later Syro-hexapla, however, we find in three of these passages, that the Peshiṭta *twdyt'* has been replaced by *šwbḥ'*, while in Ps. 69: 30 the retention by the Syro-hexapla of *twdyt'* is readily understandable since *šwbḥ'* already occurs in the first half of the verse.

The Syriac compound expression *qwblṭybwt'*, 'thanks', 'thankfulness', is not found in the text of the Peshiṭta Psalter or elsewhere in the Old Testament. It occurs twice in the New Testament (Rev. 4: 9; 7: 2), 'glory and honour and *thanks*', where it stands for εὐχαριστία. The verbal form of the expression is found in the Peshiṭta of Luke 17: 9, where μὴ ἔχει χάριν τῷ δούλῳ 'does he thank the servant?' is rendered *lm' ṭybwth mqbl dhw 'bd'*, the Old Syriac having *lm' ṭybwth dnpš 'hyd 'bd' hw*, 'does that servant hold a favour for himself?'. Here, as elsewhere in the New Testament, *ṭybwt'* represents χάρις. Since the latter is the normal LXX equivalent of חֵן, it might appear that to

---

[1] Pss. 50: 14, 23; 56: 12; 69: 30 (all *twdyt'*).

8   II3   AWA

'hold' or 'receive' *ṭybwt'* is to be understood by comparison with the oft-recurring Old Testament phrase מצא חן and the less frequent נשא חן, to *find* or *obtain favour*. However it is noteworthy that nowhere in the Old Testament does the Peshiṭta translate חן by *ṭybwt'*, but in nearly every case by *rḥm'* (*pl.*) 'mercy'. *ṭybwt'* on the other hand is the normal Old Testament Peshiṭta rendering for חסד. The explanation no doubt lies in the fact that though *rḥm'* (*pl.*) was a suitable enough rendering of the Old Testament חן, it proved inadequate to represent χάρις in its Hellenistic, and even more so in its specifically Christian, connotation. There is a sense therefore in which it may be said that in the Syriac *ṭybwt'*, חן and חסד are both represented, and that the acceptance of *ṭybwt'* implies the acceptance of them both.

Amongst the variety of Psalm titles that were introduced into the Peshiṭta Psalter at different times by the Syriac-speaking Church, are a number which include the expression *qwblṭybwt'*, a 'thanksgiving' (psalm).[1] These titles bear no relationship to those of either the Hebrew or the LXX, and appear to be merely explanatory notes. There is evidence also of the use of *qwblṭybwt'* to represent εὐχαριστία in its special connotation of Eucharistic thanksgiving.[2]

CONCLUSION

An examination of the terms חסד and תודה in the linguistic tradition of the Psalter throws into relief the richness of these terms, in particular of חסד, and the consequent problems of translation and interpretation amidst a changing theological scene. The development of the concept of thanksgiving can be seen to range from a basically ritual thanksgiving offering to a

---

[1] See in the edition of Samuel Lee, Pss. 18, 30, 56, 57, 61, 103, 111, 123, 137, 143. Cf. also the title to the first of the Syriac Apocryphal Psalms (= LXX Ps. 151). M. Noth, 'Die fünf syrisch überlieferten apocryphen Psalmen', *ZAW*, XLVIII (1930), 1–23. Cf. also J. A. Sanders, *The Psalms Scroll of Qumrân Cave 11 (11QPsᵃ)* (*Discoveries in the Judaean Desert*, IV, Oxford, 1965), p. 58. The Qumran text reads: הללויה לדויד בן ישי 'A Hallelujah of David the son of Jesse.'

[2] See R. Payne-Smith, *Thesaurus Syriacus* (Oxford, 1879–1901), col. 3474.

more personal and spiritual act of praise, accompanied by the acknowledgement of God's חסד and man's sinfulness. This receives further emphasis in Hellenistic Judaism, while, with the advent of the Christian religion, the concepts of חסד and חן come together in the Syriac *ṭybwt'*, while εὐχαριστία, *qwblṭybwt'*, in the context of the Eucharistic Liturgy, is indicative of a simple expression of gratitude for grace received.

10

TORAH IN DEUTERONOMY

by Barnabas Lindars, S.S.F.

The supreme place of the law in Judaism is evident not only
in the rabbinic writings, but also in the New Testament and
in the non-canonical books of late Judaism. The word תורה can
mean the Pentateuch and even the whole of the Old Testament.
It sums up in one word the central ideas of the Jewish religion.
To those familiar with this pre-eminence of תורה in the later
development it sometimes comes as a surprise to discover that
the word is comparatively rare in the earlier literature of the
Old Testament, and that, when it does occur, it has a very
different meaning. It is customary to trace the course of development along a line from a primitive priestly usage, in which
תורה denotes 'instruction', through the work of the codification
of the law in the exilic age, to the 'religion of the book' of
post-exilic Judaism. It is widely recognized, however, that the
cardinal point in this development is not the Priestly Code as
such, but the Book of Deuteronomy.[1] It is in this work that such
phrases as 'this book of the law' and 'the words of this law'
first make their appearance. But even a cursory reading of
Deuteronomy reveals that these phrases are rare, and are mostly
confined to the editorial matter, whereas the concept of law
is expressed much more frequently by a variety of synonyms,
generally used in combination and in the plural form, משפטים,
חקים, מצות, and עדות. Why תורה was chosen by the Deuteronomic editors to express 'law' is not immediately self-evident.[2]

---

[1] This point is obscured, however, by G. Östborn, *Tōrā in the Old Testament:
a Semantic Study* (Lund, 1945), the fullest treatment of the subject. Although
it contains a wealth of valuable information, it suffers from an excessive
preoccupation with the problem of etymology and from a confusing
arrangement of the material, which frequently disregards the literary
stratification of the sources.

[2] The question is raised by Östborn, *Tōrā in the Old Testament*, p. 62, but
only to deny that it is really new in Deuteronomy. If the present study
appears to be a return to the older critical orthodoxy, it may be pointed

Nor is it readily apparent why it achieved its dominating position so quickly. Obviously there was a well-developed concept of law in old Israel. Indeed there is no shortage of ancient legal texts in the Old Testament. The position, then, is not at all the same as it is with ברית, for which it can be argued, even if unconvincingly, that the concept as well as the word is almost unknown before Deuteronomy.[1] In this case we have sufficient evidence for the concept of law, and the question arises why תורה was not already the usual word for it. In fact it is more likely that תורה comes into currency in the time of the Deuteronomists as a result of growth in the range of meaning of the term itself, which now becomes the appropriate word for an idea which has previously been expressed in other ways. But it must also be asked whether the choice of this word, rather than any other, corresponds with a modification in the concept of law itself. We need to ask not only how תורה assumes the semantic range required for it to apply to the existing aspects of the concept of law, but also whether any of those aspects lie close to the central meaning of תורה, and so could explain the Deuteronomists' predilection for it.

I

In seeking to establish a change in the use of תורה at a well-developed stage of the language, it can hardly be expected that much help will be gained from etymology, the more so as this in fact remains an unsolved problem. Engnell briefly summarizes the prevailing tendencies by grouping them under the names of

out that the reaction away from it is due for reassessment in the light of current trends.
[1] Cf. the posthumous work of R. H. Pfeiffer, *Religion in the O.T.* (London, 1961), p. 55: 'Every mention of the covenant of Jehovah with Israel in the Bible is later than 621', echoing the extreme position of R. Kraetzschmar, *Die Bundesvorstellung im A.T.* (Marburg, 1896), pp. 6, 122. The chief difficulty has always been the silence of the canonical prophets, but cf. W. Eichrodt, *Theology of the O.T.* (English translation, London, 1961), I, 51. It is now universally agreed that both covenant and law go back to the time of Moses, and therefore we must assume the existence of a law-code, whether oral or written, from that time.

three scholars, Gesenius, Wellhausen and Delitzsch.[1] The first group derives הורה/תורה from ירה 'to throw', the Hiph'il meaning 'to point with the finger' (cf. Prov. 6: 13) in much the same way as שלח יד. This leads to 'instruction' as the normal meaning of תורה. The second follows the same derivation, but it explains the meaning of the Hiph'il as 'to cast lots' in order to obtain an oracle, so that תורה is an oracular response. The third group takes תורה to be a loan-word from Accadian *tērtu*, which also probably has the ultimate meaning 'oracle'. In this case the Hiph'il verb has to be regarded as a back-formation from the noun. But as *tērtu* is itself derived from *wa'aru/āru*, (i. 1) 'to go', (ii. 1) 'to send (a message)',[2] the connection with the Accadian word can be accepted without resorting to the theory of a loan-word. The advantage of this proposal is that it allows the meaning of 'oracular response' for תורה, which has left some traces in Old Testament usage, without necessarily introducing the idea of casting lots, for which there is no evidence at all.

Whatever be the true solution to the problem, it can scarcely be denied that there is likely to be some connection with the Accadian usage, and this, in its turn, forces us to look for the original setting of תורה in cultic practice. Although 'instruction' frequently seems to be an adequate rendering, it would be a mistake to take this in a general sense. If an oracle is involved, תורה (which can denote both the action of giving a message, and the content of it, i.e. the message itself) is primarily a specific direction in response to a query, and the broader notion of instruction is to be regarded as a result of the generalizing tendency common in semantic development. There are three main streams of the usage of תורה in the Old Testament, which correspond with the three classes of men most influential in the history of ideas in Israel, the priests, the prophets and the wise men.[3] The first two, at least, of the three are closely associated

---

[1] I. Engnell, *Israel and the Law* (Uppsala, 1954), p. 2.

[2] Hence this root (ירה iii) is not used in the Qal in Hebrew, cf. *KBL*.

[3] This classification is followed by Östborn, *Tōrā in the Old Testament*, but first he has two chapters on 'The Deity as Imparter of *Tōrā*' and 'The King as Imparter of *Tōrā*'. But God does not give תורה except through such functionaries as prophets and priests; and it is precisely the absence of

with the cult. These three parallel streams continue into the post-exilic period quite apart from the new development found in the Deuteronomic literature.

The classic passage for the priestly usage[1] is the Blessing of Levi (Deut. 33: 8–11). The cultic functions of the Levites are enumerated in verse 10. They 'teach (יורו) Jacob thy ordinances (משפטיך), and Israel thy law (תורתך)'. This duty is given pride of place, before that of sacrifice, to 'put incense before thee, and whole burnt-offering upon thy altar'. In the priestly laws of Leviticus and Numbers תורה is best translated 'rule' or 'regulation', e.g. זאת תורת 'this is the rule of....' (Lev. 6: 2, etc.), תורה אחת להם 'the same regulation applies to them both' (Lev. 7: 7, etc.). The possibility that this function includes some oracular method of determining the divine will is suggested by the E passage Exod. 18: 13–23, which may refer to the separation of secular justice from the sanctuaries at some time during the period of the monarchy.[2] Here routine cases are to be judged by local courts of representatives of clans and families, but difficult cases are to be reserved for Moses himself, who will 'make them know the statutes of God and his decisions (תורתיו)' (verse 16, cf. 20). The duty of the priests to give תורה is attested in the prophetical books, and continues in exactly the same way in the prophets of the restoration.[3] In Leviticus and Numbers תורה always means 'rule' or 'regulation', as just mentioned, but it never refers to the law as a whole, in spite of the fact that these works were compiled after Deuteronomy. Thus the use of it in this sense throughout 1 and 2 Chronicles, Ezra, Nehemiah and Daniel 9 depends not on the Priestly Code, even though these books have obvious affinities with the priestly literature, and

this word in connection with the king's position as law-giver or law-speaker of the covenant-law which makes the Deuteronomic usage so remarkable.

[1] Cf. H. H. Rowley, *Worship in Ancient Israel* (London, 1967), pp. 101 f.; J. Begrich, 'Die Priesterliche Tōrā', *Gesammelte Studien* (München, 1964), pp. 232–60.

[2] Or perhaps earlier, as the organization into rulers of thousands, etc., makes use of the existing institution of the military levy, cf. M. Noth, *Exodus* (English translation, London, 1962), *ad loc.*

[3] Thus Ezek. 7: 26 (cf. Jer. 18: 18); 22: 26; 43: 11, 12; 44: 5, 24; Zeph. 3: 4; Hag. 2: 11; Mal. 2: 6, 7, 8, 9.

even though it is the Priestly Code, or rather the Pentateuch, to which it refers in them. On the contrary it is to be traced to the influence of the Deuteronomic literature, and the link is provided by such passages as Zech. 7: 12 and Mal. 3: 22.

The prophetic usage[1] of תורה may also have a cultic origin. This accords with recent work on the prophets, which has largely removed the idea of a fundamental opposition between priest and prophet, which was formerly prevalent in critical scholarship. According to 1 Sam. 9: 9 it was customary to go to the 'seer' to gain an answer from God, and there is nothing intrinsically impossible in the use of תורה to describe a prophetic oracle. But in fact the word only rarely occurs in this sense. The verb is used in Judg. 13: 8, a passage which does not seem to be affected by the Deuteronomic editing, to denote the directions which Samson's mother is to observe. It is the priestly manner of speaking, but the subject is the 'man of God' (cf. 1 Sam. 9: 6). The noun תורה occurs in Amos only in a late addition (2: 4). It is found three times in Hosea (4: 6; 8: 1, 12), and its use here will require consideration later on, but it is not relevant to our immediate purpose. In Isaiah, however, it actually denotes the prophetic word (1: 10; 2: 3;[2] 5: 24; 30: 9; possibly also 8: 16, 20). The context makes it clear in each case that the oracle consists of some direction which the people have rejected (or will gladly receive, 2: 3). Isa. 30: 9 is particularly instructive, because it is concerned with the prophet's struggle with the king's advisers, 'who carry out a plan, but not mine'. The תורה which they refuse may, then, be compared not only with priestly instruction, but also with the advice of the wise men. In Hab. 2: 18 מורה שקר [3] is applied to an idol, which should be able to give oracles. References to תורה in Jeremiah mostly belong to the Deuteronomic style of the prose passages, but in

---

[1] Cf. J. Lindblom, *Prophecy in Ancient Israel* (Oxford, 1962), p. 157.

[2] = Mic. 4: 2. This passage is generally ascribed to the time of the exile (e.g. Lindblom, *Prophecy in Ancient Israel*, pp. 383 f.), but once it is conceded that תורה here means an oracle there is no compelling reason to put it so late as this. It is ascribed to Isaiah himself by G. von Rad, 'The City on the Hill', *The Problem of the Hexateuch and Other Essays* (English translation, Edinburgh, 1966), pp. 232–42, and by R. E. Clements, *Prophecy and Covenant* (London, 1965), p. 49, n. 3.

[3] Also 2: 19 הוא יורה, but this is probably a gloss.

6: 19 'my law' is parallel with 'my words', and can be interpreted to mean the prophetic teaching. It could, however,
equally refer to the covenant law, which the people have rejected.[1] The references in Deutero-Isaiah must be held over
for discussion later. Zech. 7: 12 has already been referred to in
the preceding paragraph. This leaves only Job 22: 22, where
תורה is parallel to Yahweh's 'words'. Here again the idea is
instruction derived from Yahweh, and whether it is gained from
prophecy or from priestly direction, or even from the Wisdom
teaching, is not specified.

In the Wisdom literature תורה is used in a quite general way
of the instruction of the wise men. We have already seen a hint
of this in Isa. 30: 9 and perhaps in Job 22: 22. It is possible that
Jer. 8: 8 also belongs here, though the scribal activity which
is there mentioned might be the codification of law in the
Deuteronomic sense. In Prov. 1: 8; 3: 1; 4: 2; 6: 20, 23; 7: 2;
13: 14 it is used of the teaching which is imparted in the education of the young. Here the idea of 'regulations', which we have
seen suits the priestly usage, is likely to be the underlying notion,
rather than a body of instruction. This meaning continues even
in so late a passage as the acrostic poem on the virtuous house-
wife (Prov. 31: 26).

These three streams of the employment of תורה agree in that
there is never any stress laid on the method by which the ruling
is obtained, whether it be by priestly regulation, prophetic
oracle, or educational instruction. It must be assumed that the
method used is that which is appropriate to the person giving
תורה. The priest in his teaching office may use mechanical
means of obtaining answers to questions, such as the Urim and
Thummim, but the actual examples of priestly teaching appear
rather to be the application of a tradition of expertise in
ceremonial matters on which he bases his authoritative ruling
in particular cases. The prophet's teaching is derived from his
special capacity to speak the word of God, and is thus bound
up with the whole problem of the nature of the prophetic ex-

---

[1] If so, it belongs to the Deuteronomic development outlined below, p. 131,
but unlike the other references there given it is parallel to the work of the
Deuteronomists, rather than dependent on them.

perience. Similarly the wise man gives guidance from his fund of practical wisdom and traditional knowledge. When תורה is applied to the law, we should expect it in the first instance to refer to the explication of law, an authoritative ruling on the manner in which a law is to be kept, or on the scope of its operation. If the ceremony of covenant renewal included recitation of the law, as most scholars think today, it is to be expected that the priests, or other covenant officials, would give תורה in explanation of it (rather like the 'targumizing' in Neh. 8: 7 f.). Some passages which can be taken to support this supposition will be discussed later.[1] When the Deuteronomists apply this word to the covenant law as a whole, it implies that the distinction between primary and secondary aspects of law has been done away. Our next step, then, is to consider the concept of law in old Israel, before we turn to Deuteronomy itself.

II

It is widely held today that the oldest collection of laws in the Old Testament is the Ten Commandments, although in both places where they are recorded (Exod. 20: 1–17; Deut. 5: 6–18) they are given in slightly amended and expanded forms.[2] They are considered to be the stipulations of the original covenant between Yahweh and Israel, comparable to the stipulations of the Hittite vassal treaties. This setting adequately accounts for the fact that they are called, not actually 'commandments' (מצות), nor even תורות, but simply 'words' (דברים). They are neither ethical norms nor expedients for the good ordering of society, but the divine requirements for maintaining the covenant relationship. They thus refer to the practical aspects of Yahweh's exclusive claim on the people's allegiance, and they protect his sovereign rights over them. It is no accident that they are in apodeictic form. This is similar to the Hittite treaty between Hattusilis and Ramses II, in which the apodeictic form

[1] See p. 132.
[2] Cf. J. J. Stamm, *The Ten Commandments in Recent Research* (English translation with additions by M. E. Andrew, London, 1967), p. 69. Although he criticizes attempts to derive the covenant from the Hittite vassal treaties, he recognizes the value of these treaties for comparative study.

is used for the stipulations (i.e. the sections on mutual renuncia-
tion of aggression and on the succession to the throne), though
these are each followed by a series of regulations for possible
contingencies arising from them, which are naturally in casuistic
form.[1] The Decalogue does not include contingent matters. It
is the divine *fiat*, which can countenance no deflection on pain
of death. It thus exerts the strongest moral compulsion, because
disobedience can only spell disaster. Indeed, disaster is usually
to be traced to breach of one of the Commandments.[2]

The present position of the Book of the Covenant (Exod. 21–
3), almost immediately following the Decalogue, might be
taken to correspond with the casuistic explanations in the example of a Hittite treaty just mentioned. It is true that the
casuistic form predominates in this collection, but obviously the
connection with the Decalogue is not nearly so simple as this.
It is more likely to be a collection from a later time, with its
own internal history of amendments and expansions, originating
at a comparatively developed stage in the formation of the
tribal confederacy, if not at the time of the institution of the
monarchy.[3] It may well be, as Alt has maintained, that much
of the contents has been taken over from Canaanite law, though
it is doubtful whether the casuistic form can be taken as the
criterion for separating Canaanite from Israelite elements.[4] The
point which concerns us here is that the collection is not called
דברים, nor is the word תורה applied to it. It does not hold the
fundamental position of the Decalogue. It is introduced as the

---

[1] Cf. G. Mendenhall, *Law and Covenant in Israel and the Ancient Near East*
(Pittsburgh, 1955), p. 7. Translation in *Ancient Near Eastern Texts*, ed.
J. B. Pritchard (Princeton, 1955), pp. 201–3.

[2] Thus Achan's sin (Josh. 7: 21) consists in coveting (חמד) and taking
possession of the metal objects devoted to Yahweh. Though similar to
the tenth Commandment, it is really an infringement of the first, Yahweh's
sovereign rights. The necessity for a 'ransom' when the census is taken
(Exod. 30: 12) suggests that David's sin in numbering the people (2 Sam.
24) in some way cut across these rights. Cf. J. R. Porter, 'The Legal
Aspects of the Concept of "Corporate Personality" in the O.T.', *VT*, xv
(1965), 361–80.

[3] Cf. O. Eissfeldt, *The Old Testament: an Introduction* (English translation,
Oxford, 1965), pp. 212–19.

[4] A. Alt, 'The Origins of Israelite Law', *Essays on O.T. History and Religion*
(English translation, Oxford, 1966), pp. 79–132.

'ordinances' (מִשְׁפָּטִים 21: 1). This implies that it is the promulgation of the שׁפט, the officer of the sacral union of tribes who
is responsible for the maintenance of the covenant. There is no
separation of judicial functions, such as is implied by the later
passage, Exod. 18: 13–23, referred to above. The provisions of
this collection have the force of law, not because they belong to
the original basis of the covenant, but because they have been
promulgated within the institutional framework of the sacral
confederacy based upon it. This would presumably have taken
place at the covenant renewal ceremony, so that the application
to it of the phrase 'the book of the covenant' (Exod. 24: 7) is
not a misnomer, even though it has come about artificially in
the process of literary redaction. In fact, of course, the phrase
refers to the Decalogue (24: 3, where וְאֵת כָּל־הַמִּשְׁפָּטִים is clearly
an editorial addition to the original אֵת כָּל־דִּבְרֵי יהוה).

The writing of 'the words' on stone tablets is recorded a
second time in the composite chapter, Exod. 34. Here again it
means the Decalogue (actually mentioned in verse 28). The
view has been canvassed that this is not the same as the Ten
Commandments of Exod. 20, but the so-called Ritual Decalogue,
contained in 34: 11–26. But recent scholarship has thrown doubt
on this supposition.[1] Actually these laws repeat some of the
'ordinances' which have already been included in the Book of
the Covenant, with two new features. The first is the prohibition
from making a covenant with the Canaanites. In fact we know
that covenants had been made with them during the conquest
period from the story of the Gibeonites (Josh. 9), and probably
the same thing happened at Shechem and at many other places.
The prohibition is thus directed against the further spread of
Canaanite practices at a later period, presumably at one of the
reforms in the time of the monarchy. The second new feature is
the requirement that all males, who are to 'appear before the
Lord' at the three great festivals (Exod. 23: 17), should now go
up to the pilgrimage shrine, rather than the local sanctuary

---

[1] Cf. A. Weiser, *Introduction to the O.T.* (English translation, London, 1961),
p. 105; H. Kosmala, *ASTI*, I (1962), 31 ff. For the argument in this
paragraph I am indebted to the unpublished thesis of Anthony Phillips,
The Religious Background to Israel's Criminal Law (Cambridge, 1967).

(34: 23 f.—hence the promise that their land will not be molested in their absence). This may be connected with the beginnings of the centralizing policy in the reform of Hezekiah. These new regulations are not described as 'ordinances'. The only descriptive word is the verb in 34: 11: 'what I command you' (את אשר אנכי מצוך). It may be hazardous to build anything on this, but the great prominence that this word has later in Deuteronomy suggests that its occurrence here is due to a new element in the promulgation of law at the covenant renewal ceremony. This is the fact that the king has taken over the function of Judge.[1] As an absolute monarch he gives his decisions in the form of commands.[2] Moses in this context performs the part of the king, just as Yahweh does in the priestly narrative (Exod. 40: 16, etc.).

In the later codes we frequently come across another word for law, חק (D) or חקה (Ezekiel and P). These forms are not quite identical in meaning. In the early literature חק signifies an enactment by a person in authority in response to a situation which demands his decision. A good example occurs in 1 Sam. 30: 25, where David decides that those who have guarded the baggage shall have their full share of the spoils taken by the fighting men (cf. also Gen. 47: 26 (J); Judg. 11: 39). The meaning 'decision' applies equally to חק and תורה when they both occur together in Exod. 18: 16, 20 (E). חקה in the priestly legislation has become virtually a synonym of תורה. It would be reasonable to suggest that there was a distinction between them originally, חקה being an enactment made for the good

---

[1] Cf. M. Noth, 'Das Amt des "Richters Israels"', *Festschrift für A. Bertholet* (Tübingen, 1950), pp. 404–17; 'Office and Vocation in the O.T.', *The Laws in the Pentateuch, and Other Essays* (English translation, Edinburgh, 1966), pp. 229–49.

[2] Cf. Östborn, *Tōrā in the Old Testament*, pp. 55 f.: 'It is a curious fact of idiomatic usage, however, that the verb הורה, "to impart *tōrā*", is not found in the texts with any of the historical kings as subject, and that the noun תורה does not occur in the sense "direction", "instruction" proceeding from such a king.' In spite of this observation he gives elaborate arguments for the idea of the king as imparter of תורה, using, it must be confessed, an uncritical approach to the phraseology of the Deuteronomic historian. In the one place where the king's action following covenant-renewal is described, he issues commands (2 Kings 23: 4).

ordering of the cultus, and תורה being a regulation in answer to
a question about the right way of doing things. The root means
'to cut in', which implies that the original usage was in connection with carving enactments on stone slabs for the sake of
permanence. This explains why חק often carries with it the idea
of an unchangeable decree, being frequently combined with
עולם. (Compare also the creation passages, Job 38: 10, 33;
Prov. 8: 29.) In view of the ancient tradition of the stone slabs
in the covenant of Sinai, one would expect to find חק in the
early narratives of it. But in fact the writing of the Decalogue
on slabs is probably a later rationalization, and the stones were
originally the 'witnesses' of the transaction (cf. Josh. 24: 27).
In the few places where חק occurs in a covenant ceremony it
denotes the enactment of the stipulations, and it is accompanied
by משפט (Josh. 24: 25; Exod. 15: 25, referred to in Ps. 81: 5-8).
It is possible that חק ומשפט is a hendiadys, i.e. an enactment
by the שופט which has abiding force. This also suggests a reason
why the word is so rare, although it appears later to be
synonymous with other words for law. For it does not carry
with it any indication of the functionary who makes the enactment—at least no cognate noun became generally used to
describe an officer of the covenant. Three passages (Gen. 49: 10;
Judg. 5: 9, 14) suggest that מחקק or חוקק had some currency
in this sense in the north in early times (cf. also Isa. 33: 22).
But חק does not appear to have acquired a particular technical
meaning.

One more word is found as an expression for law, and that
is עֵדוֹת/עֵדֻת.[1] This is a derived meaning from the primary idea
of witness. The covenant stipulations are laws to which due
witness has been given (Josh. 24: 27), and so by a common
semantic development the word passes over from the act of
witnessing to the content of that which is witnessed, i.e. the
laws themselves. It is favoured by the priestly writer, who also
speaks of the ark as ארון העדות because it contains the objects
to which witness has been given, the slabs of the Decalogue. In

---

[1] The latter form is to be regarded as plural of עֵדוּת (contracted from עֵדְוֹת),
in spite of Ps. 132: 12, where plural should probably be read with LXX,
cf. *GK*, 91 n.

2 Kings 11 : 12 it may refer to the legal instrument or document in connection with the covenant aspect of the coronation of a king.[1]

III

We are now in a position to look at Deuteronomy, and to try to estimate the use of תורה in relation to these other terms. The most remarkable feature of the book's usage is the occurrence of all these words as synonyms, usually in combinations of two or three of them. Whatever theory is held about the origins of the book, it cannot be denied that it stands in line with the evidence we have already reviewed with regard to covenant renewal and the royal promulgation of law.[2] So we find that דברים continues to be reserved for the Ten Commandments in the historical preamble (Deut. 4: 10, 13, 36; 5: 19; 9: 10; 10: 2, 4), and they are probably referred to in the Šᵉma' (6: 6; 11: 18). Later, however, we find it used in the combination 'the words of this law' (17: 19; 27: 3, 8, 26; 28: 58; 29: 28; 31: 24; 32: 46), but these are all contexts where the later editing can be distinguished from the original code. Sometimes דברים even stands alone in this sense (12: 28; 28: 69; 31: 1). This implies that the total corpus of law is now considered to be on the same footing as the Decalogue, the divinely ordained stipulations of the covenant.

By far the most common expression in the code itself is מצוה, which, as has been suggested in connection with Exod. 34: 11, is to be connected with the function of the king in promulgating law. חקים and משפטים each occur from time to time in combination with מצות, usually in redactional or summarising contexts. It is impossible to assign any distinction of meaning to

---

[1] J. A. Montgomery–H. S. Gehman (*ICC*, Edinburgh, 1951, *ad loc.*), following the majority of older critics, emends to הצעדות = 'armlets', but J. Gray, *I and II Kings* (London, 1964), and R. de Vaux, *Ancient Israel* (English translation, London, 1961), p. 103, quote an inscription of Thothmes III for a formal protocol containing the king's obligations. This may also be referred to in Ps. 132: 12 (perhaps, then, read singular with Qimḥi). Similarly the חק in Ps. 2: 7 may be a written decree used in the ritual of coronation.

[2] Cf. E. W. Nicholson, *Deuteronomy and Tradition* (Oxford, 1967), chapter III.

them. עדות only occurs in redactional verses (4: 45; 6: 17, 20).
One can only conclude that they are selected out of a desire
for elegant variation and a liking for the fulness of synonymous
phrases. With the disappearance of any discrimination in the
use of these words, it follows that the concept of law has under-
gone a change. The predominating מצוה has assimilated to itself
the meaning of the others, bringing them into the scope of an
absolute demand exacted by the king, who speaks on behalf of
God. It is a short step from this to the position of later Judaism,
where the law is insisted on, not because of its inherent reason-
ableness, but simply because it is laid down. The notable
humanitarianism of Deuteronomy does not conflict with this
impression. For, although obedience to the law is commended
for humanitarian reasons, the code aims at a greater compre-
hensiveness than any of its predecessors, so as to bring as many
aspects of life as possible under control. Much of the introductory exhortation, in chapters 4, 5, 9 and 10, is directed to
putting the laws on to the same footing of absolute obligation
as the Decalogue, so that in the editing of the work, as we have
seen, דברים is extended to include the whole code.

This brings us to the editing of the code for publication as a
book. Though the form of it corresponds with the ceremony of
covenant renewal, the parenetic material of the introductory
and concluding chapters exceeds what would be expected in a
public recital of the law. Moreover there can be no doubt that
this material has been considerably expanded, so that it is
possible to regard it as a series of sermons.[1] It is the purpose of
these chapters to persuade the hearers to take the code of laws
seriously and to obey them willingly, not grudgingly or half-
heartedly, but with full consent. The approach is didactic in
a manner reminiscent of the Wisdom tradition. Östborn has
drawn attention to the parenetic use of the theme of the 'Way'
in the introductory historical retrospect.[2] He is surely right also
in connecting the use of תורה with the didactic character of
the editorial work. This means that the generalized notion of

---

[1] See the analysis of this material in G. von Rad, *Deuteronomy* (London, 1966).

[2] *Tōrā in the Old Testament*, p. 64; cf. 10: 12; 11: 28, etc.

'instruction', as found in the Wisdom literature, is closer to the Deuteronomic meaning than the priestly 'regulations in answer to a question', in spite of the fact that Deuteronomy is a product of priestly reformers.

This is confirmed by detailed examination of the use of תורה in Deuteronomy. It never occurs in this meaning in the code of laws as such, with the notable exception of 17: 18 f. The verb הורה is applied to the teaching office of the priests in the normal style in 17: 11 (with the cognate תורה) and 24: 8. The exception in 17: 18 f. can be discounted, because these verses undoubtedly belong to an editorial expansion. On the other hand they illustrate perfectly the didactic character of תורה. For here the editor, who at this point may even be the same writer as the historian of the Books of Kings,[1] has inserted his own comment on the ancient law of the king (verses 14 f.). The law only states that the king is to be a true-born Israelite and not a foreigner.[2] The editor then gives a thumbnail sketch of an unsuitable king, obviously modelled on his account of Solomon in 1 Kings, followed by the ideal for a king, equally obviously modelled on his hero Josiah. This king's special virtue consists in meditating on 'a copy of this law (תורה)', so that he may perform his duties with proper care and humility. The choice of תורה to designate the whole corpus is thus dictated by the fact that the code is regarded as a single and complete entity, given by God through the mediation of Moses for men to ponder and to lay to heart. It is the 'direction' or 'regulation' given in response to the question 'how may we be assured of Yahweh's blessing?'. This can even be expressed in specifically Wisdom terminology, as if the code is the instruction of a father to his sons (4: 5–8). Apart from 4: 8 (where the verb נתן should be noted), תורה only appears at 1: 5 and 4: 44 in the early part of the book. Both these passages are probably later insertions.

---

[1] Cf. G. Minette de Tillesse, 'Sections "tu" et sections "vous" dans le Deutéronome', *VT*, XII (1962), 29–87, esp. pp. 83 ff.

[2] This may be the משפט המלך referred to in 1 Sam. 10: 25. The provision was clearly essential at the time of the institution of the monarchy, if the Yahwistic basis of Israel's sacral confederacy was to be preserved; cf. A. Weiser, *Samuel, seine geschichtliche Aufgabe und religiöse Bedeutung* (Göttingen, 1962).

Leaving aside chapter 27 for the moment, the next place where we find תורה is the section on the curses that will follow disobedience (28: 58, 61), but even here it is not found in the original nucleus, which may have been no more than 28: 15–19. The same theme is continued in a series of sermons, and תורה appears in characteristic phrase in 29: 20, 28; 30: 10. G. von Rad holds that 29: 28 is modelled on a Wisdom saying. Finally the law is to be read at the feast of booths (31: 9–13), and the book is to be laid up alongside the stone tablets in the ark of the covenant (31: 24–9). The critical problems of this chapter need not concern us. The point to notice is that these provisions are intended to make the book a substitute for the Decalogue, or at least to put it on the same level.

תורה, then, is the word employed by the Deuteronomic editors to convey their concept of the code as a complete expression of the will of God, having the same binding force as the Decalogue, recorded especially for the welfare of the people, to be learnt and pondered by them. The term retains its didactic overtones, and to say 'the book of the divine instruction' might represent the real meaning better than the usual translation 'the book of the law'. The Deuteronomists use תורה to mean the code understood in this sense throughout the literature which passed through their hands. The special material describing the blessing and cursing ceremony at Mount Ebal has been edited with this in mind (Deut. 11: 26–32; 27: 1–8, 26; Josh. 8: 30–5; 24: 26). It occurs in the Deuteronomic history in Josh. 1: 7, 8; 22: 5; 23: 6; 1 Kings 2: 3; 2 Kings 10: 31; 14: 6; 17: 13, 34, 37; 21: 8; 23: 25. In many of these passages the parenetic use of הלך and דרך forms part of the same context. It must be categorically stated that, whatever be the critical opinion on the true identification of the law-book discovered by Hilkiah (2 Kings 22: 8, 11; 23: 24), the historian himself regards it as the code of Deuteronomy (cf. Deut. 17: 18 f.). The compiler of the prose portions of Jeremiah uses it in typical Deuteronomic expressions (Jer. 9: 12; 16: 11; 26: 4; 32: 23; 44: 10, 23), and even in the prophecy of the New Covenant it has the same didactic sense (31: 32). True to the Deuteronomists' desire that the law should be studied, תורה is regarded as an object of loving meditation in the Wisdom psalms (Ps. 1: 2; 19: 8; 37: 31; 40: 9; 119 *passim*).

IV

There remain, however, a few passages where תורה occurs, which do not fit easily into the line of development traced above. It is tempting to side with the older critics, and simply bracket all such verses as later additions, dependent on the Deuteronomic usage. We must, then, review them briefly, but before we do so two points are worth noticing. In the first place, the tendency to use תורה in a rather general and imprecise way for law is likely to have begun before the Deuteronomists gave it the new importance which it retained ever afterwards. Thus the references in Jeremiah just mentioned can be taken as a parallel usage in the time of the prophet himself, instead of being assigned to the later editing, without spoiling our thesis, for it was in that time that the Deuteronomic usage was evolved. Secondly, the passages to be considered are all in the poetical literature, and so do not affect the point which has been established, that the law codes themselves do not use תורה in this way.

The earliest is Hos. 8: 1: 'Because they have broken my covenant and transgressed my law' (more correctly 'rebelled against (על) my law'). Here we should give due weight to the fact that ברית and תורה are strictly parallel. Yahweh's covenant can also be referred to as his 'instruction', because it embodies his directive to the people. Although rebellion against it obviously takes the form of breaking specific commandments, this is not precisely what is said here, and תורה means law no more, and no less, than ברית does. Though it certainly anticipates the Deuteronomic usage to some extent, it does not have the Wisdom overtones. In fact it is likely to be a broader application of the priestly usage, which certainly seems to be the case in Hos. 8: 12 (where plural תורותי should probably be read).[1]

Another passage which can be held to anticipate the Deuteronomists is Ps. 78. In verse 1 תורה has the Wisdom sense, but in verses 5 and 10 it refers to the covenant law. It should be

---

[1] Is the reference in these verses to priestly explication of the covenant law, as suggested on p. 123 above?

observed that the vocabulary is didactic in both these verses. Although the psalm is likely to be pre-exilic and embodies a long-standing cultic tradition, it cannot be proved to be much older than the time of the Deuteronomists, whose work it reflects both in style and train of thought.[1]

תורה also occurs in Hab. 1:4, describing the breakdown of social order before the Josian reformation. It is here parallel to משפט, which in this context means the administration of justice. The probable meaning of the passage, then, is that both functions, of giving תורה and of administering justice, have almost completely lapsed. This is nearer to the priestly style than the Deuteronomic, even if it means secular decisions.

Similarly, Lam. 2:9 complains that 'her king and princes are among the nations; the law is no more, and her prophets obtain no vision from the Lord'. Though the Hebrew text might refer to the function of the king and the princes, most editors take the phrase separately, as an allusion to the duty of the priests (cf. Jer. 18:18). Other passages also prove on closer inspection to be irrelevant, or are doubtful on critical grounds. In Ps. 94:12 divine instruction suits the context, rather than the code of law. Ps. 89:31 belongs to a Deuteronomistic interpolation into the positive statement of the Davidic covenant. Ps. 105:45 is almost certainly a later addition. Isa. 24:5 is too uncertain, both in date and in interpretation, to be taken into consideration. Finally, in Deut. 33:4 the phrase 'Moses commanded us a law' may well be a gloss on the corrupt ישא מדברתיך of the preceding verse.[2]

---

[1] A. Weiser, *The Psalms* (English translation, London, 1962), *ad loc.*, points out that a date before the exile is required, because the psalm gives no hint of the destruction of Jerusalem and the temple, but doubts the validity of the arguments for a much earlier date.

[2] As a gloss, it should be regarded as a footnote = 'that is, the law which Moses commanded us'. In favour of this widely accepted view it may be observed that: (*a*) the verb צוה with Moses as subject is fairly common in the Deuteronomic editing, 27:1, 11; 31:23, 25, 29; (*b*) the first person suffix is out of line with the rest of the poem; (*c*) the phrase breaks the sequence of thought, which has passed on from the theophany at Sinai (verse 2) to the entry into Canaan (3*c*, 4*b*), and depends on an interpretation of 3*d* as the law-giving which is itself doubtful; (*d*) מורשה (4*b*), which is parallel to תורה, must refer to the people and the land, rather than to the covenant.

This leaves only the passages in Deutero-Isaiah where תורה occurs, and a short section of Proverbs. In spite of the exilic date of Isa. 40–55, there is no sign of direct Deuteronomic influence, and any conclusions drawn from these chapters may assist us to determine the special conditions at the time of the Deuteronomic editing. Isa. 42: 4 has תורה in parallel with משפט in a sense quite like Hab. 1: 4. The exact interpretation depends on the whole question of the identity and function of the Servant, but there is no suggestion that it means a body of statute law. On the other hand, 42: 21 gives just this impression, but the whole verse interrupts the sense of the poem so badly that it is difficult to avoid following Volz in bracketing it as a later addition. He also brackets verse 24 *cd*, though here the use of תורה is consistent with the theme of the poem. It has the didactic sense, parallel with 'his ways'. In 51: 4 תורה is again parallel with משפט, and again has the same general sense; and in verse 7 it has the connotation of interior meditation, not as a code of laws, but as the knowledge of Yahweh's will (parallel to 'know righteousness'). In all these passages the meaning is 'teaching' rather than 'law', either actualized in the divine ordering of society (42: 4), or retained in the mind as a principle of personal integrity (51: 7). It furnishes an excellent parallel to the generalized and weakened sense of תורה, with Wisdom affinities, which made it available for the new specific application to the code of law by the Deuteronomic school.

The Proverbs passages are all in the Hezekiah collection, though it cannot be asserted with assurance that they go back to his time. Prov. 28: 4 contrasts 'those who forsake the law' with 'those who keep the law'. Does this mean the statute law? The collection at this point is concerned with the ruling classes, whose wisdom and integrity are necessary for the welfare of the state, but the sayings are not closely related. The usual Wisdom sense, i.e. '(rulers) who forsake *instruction* praise the wicked, etc.', seems to me to be preferable.[1] So also 28: 7 (unless יתרה, 'wealth', is to be read here), and 28: 9 and 29: 18, are

---

[1] Those who insist on 'law' generally assign these verses to the post-exilic period. In fact, as Toy (*ICC*, Edinburgh, 1914) points out, 28: 4 would hardly be conceivable in this sense until the Greek period.

equally ambiguous, and 'instruction' is at least as probable as 'law'.

We were prepared to admit that תורה might have been established in the sense of the covenant law before the time of Deuteronomy, but the available evidence, which is in any case meagre enough, has been found to be inconclusive. It follows that the creative work of the Deuteronomists in giving תורה a new and lasting significance is not to be denied. The way was prepared by the tendency to treat all aspects of law on a single level as the commandment of the king in his capacity as the executive officer of the covenant. The consequence of this tendency was that the various words for law became more or less interchangeable synonyms. תורה was not the most obvious word for the code of law, but it was favoured by the Deuteronomic editors because of their didactic purpose. Writing most probably in the early part of the exile, they were concerned to press home the lessons of history and to promote the ideals of the Josian reformation. But deprived of the temple, which was now regarded as the one legitimate place of worship, they had to shift the focus of their religion from the institutions of the cult to the precious documents which were the title-deeds of the covenant community. The law-code has to be taught and expounded (cf. Neh. 8: 8), to be learnt and meditated on. It is sacrosanct, and nothing may be added to it or taken away from it (Deut. 4: 2).[1] In fact the work of codification of the priestly tradition was already under way, and although this may not have been intended in the first instance to replace Deuteronomy as the covenant law, the Deuteronomistic attitude to law was bound to be extended to it. Eventually it was included in the Pentateuch, which became the covenant law as a whole. תורה in the Priestly Code retained its old meaning of 'direction', but the new meaning which resulted from the work of the Deuteronomists can scarcely have been absent from the minds of the compilers. The whole law, subsumed under the didactic word תורה, is the expression of the will of God for his people for all time. From the Jewish point of view it embodies the norms of

---

[1] This was a feature of ancient law codes, e.g. Hammurabi (*ANET*, p. 178b).

human existence before God (Ecclus. 24: 23–34). It is thus not surprising that νόμος was selected as the normal translation of תורה in the Septuagint, and that the concept of law was able to enlarge its range to include further ideas from hellenistic usage in late Judaism.[1]

[1] Cf. H. Kleinknecht and W. Gutbrod, Νόμος, *TWNT*, IV, 1016–84 (English translation, *Law* (*Bible Key Words*, XI, London, 1962); *TDNT*, IV, 1022–91).

11

DIVINE FRUSTRATION
EXEGETICALLY FRUSTRATED
—NUMBERS 14: 34 תנואתי

by Raphael Loewe

Recent decades have witnessed the exploitation of new source-material, as well as older resources (especially Arabic and Accadian) for the recovery of the ancient Hebrew vocabulary; and it is a mine in which, during his long tenure of the Regius Professorship of Hebrew at Cambridge, D. Winton Thomas has proved an indefatigable worker. This linguistic burrowing would often have led to an irresponsible and unsubstantiable borrowing, had not the evidence of the ancient versions and (to a lesser extent) of early exegesis been constantly used to confirm or query a newly suggested meaning allegedly paralleled elsewhere in the semitic field. To some extent the versions might legitimately complain that they have been rummaged through, in a kind of lexical barrow-hogging typical of much nineteenth-century archaeology (and the contemporary amateur exploration of sunken wrecks): but for the purpose in hand that was, perhaps, inevitable. The study of the versions in their own right is a different task; and although the various primary translations have scarcely been neglected, they have been studied largely in isolation, i.e. with reference to the original and to parallel or secondary versions primarily for the sake of the light that each of these may shed on the version primarily under consideration. But (if the metaphor may be sustained) in addition to continued mineworking along systematic and disciplined lines, the time has now come for the study of the versions according to principles adapted from modern archaeological practice. Each several translation of, or comment on, the Hebrew text needs to be studied in the way that early Christian exegesis of the New Testament is now studied—as a *stratum*: conditioned in part by the patterns of *strata* below (which it may itself retain, destroy, modify, replace, or restore), and in part determined by the lie of the ground (i.e. the original text), as well as in the light of its own particular orientation and environment. What draughts, liable to admit air-currents bearing pollen from alien soils, was it designed to exclude? Did its windows face the sunlight at its brightest, so as to secure maximal illumination and ethical commitment regardless of the cost in physical exhaustion? Or did it, by resorting to a possibly deliberate obscurity, provide a comfortable and comforting shade that would not necessarily demand from the public concerned too rigorous an implementation of the scriptural message?

Such questions cannot be satisfactorily answered by simply arranging the versions in chronological order. The correct method is surely to study them in parallel and so formulate some ideological classification, to which (in so far as they are applicable) both chronological and confessional considerations may then be applied as a control. It is these principles that underlie the sample study that is here offered, namely, an examination of versional and exegetical treatment of the Hebrew root נוא, since at least one of its occurrences raises issues that are ideologically problematic.

נוא may be equated, with a high degree of accuracy, with the English 'frustrate'.[1] It occurs in the Hebrew bible as a verbal form in the hiph'il (including the Qre at Num. 32: 7 and יני in Ps. 141: 5, where the regular orthography is noted as a variant by *BH*), as well as in the nominal form תנואה. As a verb, it is used quite clearly of both man and of God. Ps. 141: 5, where the proposal to restore יָנָא (נאה) is endorsed by Buhl in *BH*, may probably be ignored for present purposes. Of the remaining passages, those which refer to human subjects present no problem. These deal with:

(*a*) *The overruling of women's vows* (Num. 30: 6, 9, 12, cf. also CD xvi. 10 f.).[2] The versions render by the following verbs:

---

[1] Cf. Arabic *nw'*, 3rd conj. 'contend with'; Accadian *ne'ū* = 'turn' (*KBL*, addenda p. 171 refers to von Soden § 106*w*).

[2] נוא is not otherwise recorded in Qumranic sources by A. M. Habermann's *Concordance* מגלות מדבר יהודה (Tel-Aviv, 1959), p. 98.

Divine frustration exegetically frustrated

LXX ἀνανεύειν, OL *abnuere*, Vulg. *contradicere*, Targ. O. אעדי,
Targ. Ps.-J., the Targum of MS Neofiti[1] and Pesh. בטל,
Samaritan Targum כבע,[2] Saʿad. *nhr* (chide).[3]

(*b*) *The disaffecting of morale* (Num. 32: 7, 9). Versions: LXX
διαστρέφετε, ἀπέστησαν, (OL not extant), Vulg. *subvertitis*
(*-erunt*), Targ. O. תונון, אוניאו (afflict), which may well be
interpretation rather than testimony to a variant reading from
ינה,[4] Targ. Ps.-J. בטל, Neofiti Targum and Pesh. תבר,[5] Samaritan
Targum שפל, Saʿad. *ǧbn* II (make cowardly).

All that it is necessary to note is, that in so far as concerns
Jewish exegesis of the passages to be considered below, (*a*) will
prove of some importance. The regulation and protection of
women's vows being a living concern and involving a practical
ordinance, the halakhic significance with which the text is invested renders it liable to dominate exegetical address to נוא
in non-halakhic contexts as well: so that any 'philological'
assumptions that the Jewish exegete or translator may entertain
regarding the meaning of the root in the one passage of halakhic
import may be applied by him—quite possibly without his
being fully aware of the circumstance—to its occurrence elsewhere.[6]

Before turning to instances of נוא where the Deity is immediately concerned, we may glance at the versional treatment
of תְּאָנָה, 'opportunity' [for pretext] in Judg. 14: 4, since both
the context there—its only occurrence as a noun—and the
paronomasia with תנואה may sometimes have coloured the interpretation of the latter.[7] Of the versions available to us Aquila,

---

[1] I am indebted to my friend Dr Meʾir Gertner for his courtesy in making
available to me his microfilm copy of MS Vatican Neofiti 1.

[2] E. Castell, *Lexicon Heptaglotton* (London, 1669), *s.v.*, notes Arabic derivatives
of the root meaning amputate, brand as inferior, etc.

[3] For a tentative restoration here of μετήγαγε κτλ. for Aquila see below,
p. 140, n. 2.

[4] See Nathan Adler's commentary נתינה לגר (printed in a number of
rabbinic pentateuchs since ed. Wilna, 1875), *ad loc.*

[5] So also, it may be noted in passing, in its Hebrew equivalent שבר, in Isaac
Abravanel's commentary (see p. 147, n. 5), *ad loc.*, f. 256 *b*, col. ii. line 21
תניאון ר״ל תשברו את לב בני ישראל.

[6] Cf. below, p. 149 (the case of Rashi).

[7] Cf. below, pp. 153–4.

RAPHAEL LOEWE

with προφάσιν, and the Vulgate (*occasionem*) closely represent
תאנה, as does also the Targum (תוסקפא הוא בעי לאיתגראה בפלש׳),
even though the latter—by adding לאיתגראה—elaborates so as
to make explicit the intended *aggressive exploitation* of the pretext.
The others pass proleptically to the intended *results of aggression*,
rendering by 'vengeance' or near synonyms (LXX ἐκδίκησιν,
A text ἀνταπόδομα; Pesh. *'yārtā'*, Arabic *liyantaqim*).

Three instances of נוא involve the Deity (Num. 14: 34; Ps.
33: 10; Job 33: 10). Of these, Ps. 33: 10 is—on the premisses
of most biblical thinking—unexceptionable: Job 33: 10 is
theologically equivocal; and Num. 14: 34 is theologically
problematic.

We may dispose first of Ps. 33: 10 הניא מחשבות עמים (|| ה׳ הפיר
עצת גוים). The object being the Gentiles—for the most part,
biblical anathema—no difficulty occurs to the psalmist about
God's arbitrariness in confounding their politics and frustrating
their (*ex hypothesi*) knavish tricks. The situation is not substan-
tially different from that in Num. 30: 6, etc., considered above
(the rescinding of women's vows): but whereas the Targum and
Peshiṭta render here, as there, by בטל, it is noticeable that the
other versions mostly resort to stronger language, translating
as follows: LXX ἀθετ(ησ)εῖ,[1] Aq. μετήγαγε[2] ('divert, lead
astray'), Symm. ἀνατρέπει ('turn topsy-turvy'), Quinta ἀκυροῖ
('invalidate'), Roman and Gallican psalters *reprobat*, Jerome's
(*juxta Hebraeos*) *irritas fecit*, Cassino psalter[3] *separans*,[4] Arabic
yuʿaḏḏiru ([rendered]? defective, effaced').[5]

[1] *LSJ* cite from Vettius Valens, an astrologer of the second century C.E.,
the use of ἀθ. = 'render ineffectual' (ed. W. Kroll, pp. 105 line 8; 115
line 3).
[2] Aq. also renders Ps. 91: 10 תְּאֻנֶּה by μεταχθήσεται. Possibly we may re-
construct his translation of Num. 30: 6, etc., as μετήγαγε, in which case
there would be a parallel to Rashi's treatment; p. 147, n. 2, below.
[3] MS Cas. 557, ed. A. M. Amelli, *Collectanea Biblica Latina*, 1 (Rome, 1912).
[4] It is tempting to see here the misinterpretation of בטל as בדל from some
antecedent Aramaic version: but this is open to question. Amelli held the
Cassino psalter to be a basically North African Latin text, revised with
reference to the Hebrew possibly by Rufinus (*Collectanea Biblica Latina*, 1,
pp. xxv–xxxiv, 138 f.).
[5] So Walton's *Polyglot*. I note in an Arabic psalter printed at Beyrout, 1900,
the rendering *lāša* (demolish).

Divine frustration exegetically frustrated

In Num. 14: 34 Israel are condemned to forty years' wandering, corresponding to the spies' forty days' reconnaisance of Canaan, God being represented as saying (after pronouncing sentence) וידעתם את תנואתי. I take this to mean 'and you shall [thereby] come to know my frustration'; indeed, once granted that 'frustrate' is a reasonably close equivalent of the basic concept in נוא, we have little option but to translate it thus. The noun itself, like many Hebrew abstract nouns, could be referred subjectively or objectively (conceivably, in Num. 14:27 the parallel formation תלֻנות is carefully qualified in order to make its reference unequivocal[1]—את תלנות בני ישראל אשר המה מלינים עלי). The dual possibility is of course greatly enhanced by the two constructions of which the first person possessive suffix is patient here—subjective, objective (or even, perhaps, both simultaneously). Before we turn to the surviving versions and exegesis, it might be as well to clarify our own minds as to the possible implications of each of these interpretations.

(i) *Rendered objectively*, תנואתי means 'my being frustrated [by Israel's contrariness]': a statement which clearly admits the feasibility of God being thwarted of his purpose—whether permanently so, or but temporarily, being not of ultimate theological significance.[2]

(ii) *A subjective rendering* ('my frustrating') implies an elliptical object for an act which is, of its very nature, inevitably somewhat capricious. That object is necessarily either: (*a*) 'you [Israel]' or (*b*) something of concern to the deity that affects Israel immediately.

If we assume (*a*), then 'my frustrating [you]' will mean, in the context, 'My denying you immediate entrance to Canaan'; in which case the expression is tautologous alongside the preceding

---

[1] Cf. below, p. 146, n. 2.

[2] Commenting on 'Onqelos to Num. 32: 7 Nathan Adler (see p. 139, n. 4) asserts that while נוא in Hebrew indicates either temporary or permanent annulment (of another's purpose), Aramaic בטל and אעדי refer to permanent annulment only. The argument seems to me precarious, since נוא is apparently not found (or at any rate recorded by the *lexica*) in Jewish Aramaic, Syriac or Mandaean, whilst the few biblical occurrences of Heb. בטל (Qal only) and עדה Hiph'il (Prov. 25: 20 only) are irrelevant to the issue. In the context of Num. 14: 34 any such distinction would in any case be theologically irrelevant.

condemnation to forty years' wandering as punishment for the offence detailed.

If we assume (b), the only possible objects will be either: (α) 'my frustrating [my own purpose[1] regarding you]'; or (β) 'my frustrating [my covenant with you', or 'my oath to you]'.

Of these possibilities, (i) impugns the divine omnipotence, (ii) (b) (α) infringes the divine prescience, and (ii) (b) (β) compromises the divine immutability. Each of these theological difficulties could be sensed by many of the ancient translators and medieval exegetes, even if they could not always enunciate them in what we chose to regard as articulate theological categories. Nor, indeed, were the same scholars blind to the problematic implications of (ii) (a) ('my frustrating [you]'): not merely because, on the rabbinic side at least, the presence of supererogatory tautologies in the Torah could not be admitted, but also on emotional grounds. It was not rabbinical circles alone that were reluctant, or even unwilling to contemplate the possibility of the Deity deliberately *frustrating* Israel (out of sheer obstructionist motives), rather than being compelled to *discipline* them.

The English versions translate as follows: AV 'my breach of promise'; RV 'my alienation' (margin: or, 'the revoking of my promise'); AJV and RSV 'my displeasure'; New American Jewish Version (1962) 'what it means to thwart me';[2] Jerusalem Bible 'what it means to reject me' (margin: or possibly 'know my displeasure').[3]

Of these, it is the New American Jewish Version alone ('what it means to thwart me') that unambiguously accepts the challenge of (i), and I personally regard it as conveying the real (or at all events the primary) meaning of the Hebrew. The

---

[1] Cf. Sforno's exegesis, cited below, p. 149, n. 2.

[2] Cf. N. H. Tur Sinai, who commenting on Job 33: 10 (Jerusalem, ed. 1957, p. 466) renders the present passage ('approximately') 'and ye shall know —the consequences of—obstructing me'.

[3] French original, 'ce que c'est que m'abandonner' (margin, + ou bien: 'ce que c'est que ma disgrâce'). English 'displeasure' does not quite do justice to the French 'disgrâce', which (as I am informed) is here used—somewhat archaically—to mean 'the *withdrawal* of favour'.

main text of the Jerusalem Bible hints at it while softening the expression. AV and the RV margin admit challenge (ii) (*b*) (β), the RV perhaps reluctantly and thus marginally. So also does the Jerusalem Bible—again marginally, but in its French form ('disgrâce') more forthrightly than the English, which hedges ('displeasure').¹ The remainder take refuge either in the equivocal 'alienation'² (main text of RV): subjective or objective? Most naturally, perhaps, the former, and therefore, if pressed into clarification, 'challenge' (ii) (*a*) ('my frustrating [you]'); or else in the entirely vague 'displeasure' (AJV, RSV, Jerusalem Bible, margin of English version).¹ Theology (or, more often, theological pusillanimity) apparently does its best to insist that philology and semantics, no less than philosophy, are her handmaids, and reluctance to look the Almighty squarely in the face, despite the example of Job, is of course no new exegetical *chimaera*. We may now, therefore, examine systematically some attempts to meet or to circumvent the problem, essayed by the ancient versions and within Jewish exegesis down to Isaac Abravanel (died 1508)³ and Obadiah Sforno (died 1550): since Jewish exegesis, through its living linguistic contact with the original, might be expected to have been more directly confronted by the difficulty than were the Fathers of the Church.⁴ It may, however, be observed that neither the Talmuds, nor the major midrashic collections (including the *Yalquṭ Shim'oni*) record comments on תנואתי; possibly the exponents of classical rabbinism felt embarrassed by it.

¹ See above, p. 142, n. 3.
² Possibly a blurred borrowing from Rashi; see below, p. 147, n. 2.
³ Apart from the Jewish exegetes considered below, pp. 146 f., the standard rabbinic commentaries pass in silence over תנואתי in Num. 14: 34 and have nothing to say *ad rem* on the occurrences of הניא in 30: 6, etc., and 32: 7, 9. Pseudo-Philo (*Liber Antiquitatum Biblicarum*, ed. G. Kisch (Notre Dame, 1949), pp. 154 f.) likewise has nothing on this subject.
⁴ Among the Latin Fathers listed by Migne in his relevant indexes (xliii–xliv, *PL*, 219, cols. 104, 115) none comment on the point at issue; the same applies to the Greek writers listed in the *Index* to the Greek series (col. 146). Origen (*Hom. 8 in Num.*, *PGL*, 12, col. 622 D) discusses the apparent anomaly of a good and merciful God dealing out punishment at the rate of one year per day of offence, but comes no closer to תנואתי itself. His comment is copied by Rabanus Maurus (*PL*, 108, col. 673 B) and so reaches—in catchword form—the *Glossa Ordinaria* (*PL*, 113, col. 403).

There are four ways in which, given its context, the translator or exegete can handle תנואתי. They are:

(a) *By paraphrase*, substituting for 'frustration' an alternative that is either: (i) at least as severe as the term that it replaces; or (ii) palliates it.

(b) *By retaining* 'frustration', and either: (i) accepting the *objective* force of the suffix, and thereafter either by-passing the theological difficulty or meeting its challenge; or (ii) construing the first person suffix in a *subjective* sense ('my frustrating [you]'), and then either ignoring or investigating the problematic theology implied.

We shall now proceed to classify surviving renderings and exegesis according to the foregoing scheme.

(a) (i) *Paraphrase in severe terms*

LXX τὸν θυμὸν τῆς ὀργῆς μου (OL not extant).

Josephus[1] explicitly states that the forty years' wandering was a punishment, but a punishment tempered by paternal love. Corresponding to the phrase under consideration, he declares God to have been 'moved by *hybris*' (κινηθέντα ὑπὸ τῆς ὕβρεως). He thus clearly takes the suffix of תנואתי objectively (as also (b) (ii), cf. Targums and Peshitta, below, pp. 145 f.); but his use of ὕβρις seems to be primarily intended as a hellenizing 'improvement' on the rendering of the LXX rather than as a serious attempt at rendering תנואה. (Even if Josephus had—tentatively—equated תנואה with ὕβρις, he would certainly have appreciated at once the incongruousness of any proposed use of it with an objective possessive pronoun, as τὴν ὕβριν μου, 'hybris suffered by me'. In any case, the operative word in the phrase is surely κινηθέντα, and the whole phrase is equivalent to ὀργισθέντα αὐτοῖς, = (תנואתי =) τὸν θυμὸν τῆς ὀργῆς μου.)

Vulg. *ultionem meam*.

Sa'ad. *mawḍia' 'i'nā'ati* ('the place' or 'proper application of

---

[1] *Antiquities*, III, xv, 1 (311), 2nd edition Niese I, 220, Μωϋσῆς δὲ...τὸν θεὸν ἐδήλου κινηθέντα ὑπὸ τῆς ὕβρεως αὐτῷ λήψεσθαι τιμωρίαν, οὐκ ἀξίαν μὲν τῶν ἁμαρτημάτων, οἵαν δὲ οἱ πατέρες ἐπὶ νουθεσίᾳ τοῖς τέκνοις ἐπιφέρουσι. In the *Antiquities*, as opposed to the *Jewish War* (preface, i (3)), we have presumably to reckon not with a translator from Aramaic but with Josephus' own Greek. On this question see, most recently, Abraham Schalit in the *Annual of the Swedish Theological Institute*, IV (1965), 164.

Divine frustration exegetically frustrated

my exorbitance': Walton renders *locum molestiae meae*; J. Derenbourg[1] paraphrases on the lines of Ibn Ezra's exegesis cited below, p. 151).

Since 'divine anger' and 'divine vengeance' are biblical commonplaces, the fact that they are hardly less problematic, theologically speaking, than is divine obstructionism perhaps passed unnoticed by most of these translators. But Sa'adyah, at any rate, had a formula according to which predications of such emotions as anger in the Deity are to be construed as meaning that some constituent of creation is deserving of hardship and punishment.[2]

Neofiti Targum תורעמנותי ('my murmuring') introduces a potentially severe paraphrase of תנואתי, but by exactly reproducing the Hebrew formulation by means of an abstract noun with a possessive suffix it leaves undetermined the question whether God is author or object of such murmuring. See further below, pp. 150–7.

(a) (ii) *Palliative paraphrase*

Samaritan Targum תשלמואתי ('my requital'). This virtually reduces תנואתי to a tautologous summary of the foregoing sentence of one year's wandering for each day's reconnaissance (see above, pp. 141 f.). It also, of course, implies subjective construction of the suffix.

(b) '*Frustration*' *retained*, and (i) *the suffix construed objectively*

So also Josephus, above, p. 144.

Targums 'Onqelos and Pseudo-Jonathan ית דאיתרעמתון עלי ('the fact that you murmured against me').

---

[1] *Œuvres Complètes de Saadia*, i (Paris, 1893), 214, line 19; he comments (n. 11) ר״ל וידעתם מי הוא הגורם שאני אשבור את שבועת׳ ואבטל דברי עי׳ ראב״ע ומכלל יופי. I do not understand the justification for this paraphrase; R. Dozy, *Supplément aux Dictionnaires Arabes* (1881), ii, 816, gives *exciter* as one meaning of *'wḏ'* ('*li*').

[2] *Beliefs and Opinions*, ii, 11 (8 in Judah ibn Ṭibbon's Hebrew version); Arabic text, S. Landauer (Leiden, 1880), p. 101, J. Guttmann's annotated German translation (*Die Religionsphilosophie des Saadia*, Göttingen, 1882), p. 120, English translation by S. Rosenblatt (Yale, 1948), pp. 122 f. Cf. E. I. J. Rosenthal's article in *BJRL*, xxi (1937), 168 f., and also Rosenthal's article on Sa'adyah's exegesis of the book of *Job* in the volume (*Saadya Studies*) edited by himself (Manchester, 1943), pp. 185 f., 196 f.

Peshiṭta *deʿal daréṭantòn qedāmai* ('[it is] because you murmured before me').

These translators, unlike the targumist of MS Neofiti (see above, p. 145, and below, pp. 150–1), apparently felt it to be imperative to make it clear that the first person possessive suffix in תנואתי was of indisputable objective reference, and they therefore elaborated it as עלי or *qedāmai*—'the תנואה to which I have been exposed [by you]'. But inasmuch as נוא means to 'frustrate', to have rendered as 'the frustration [to which you have subjected] me' would have been tacitly to admit the feasibility of man's obstructing the divine purpose: and this not in connection with any punitive design on the deity's part, the averting of which through penitence and prayer the rabbis could contemplate, despite its (theo)logical difficulties,[1] but in regard to the obstruction of a purpose essentially benign, i.e. the settlement of Israel in Canaan. Since no hint of successful thwarting of God in such a respect was felt by them to be tolerable, they evaded the difficulty by substituting 'frustration imposed on God' by 'murmuring' or 'grumbling against God'.[2]

Rashi's exegesis. Although Rashi does not substitute any term designed to obviate the essential meaning of תנואה as 'frustrate', his construction of the suffix as objective—albeit not with God

---

[1] Cf. my article on 'Jerome's Treatment of an Anthropopathism', *VT*, II (1952), 261–72: on נחם.

[2] Shimshon (Simon) Baruch Scheftell in his commentary to 'Onqelos (באורי אונקלוס, ed. J. Perles, Munich, 1888), p. 192, holds that it is theological scruple that has dictated the construction of the suffix in תנואתי as objective. Scheftell assumed that תנואה was equated by the targumists with תאנה, 'opportunity [for pretext]' as in Judg. 14: 4 (see above, p. 139), and that they had then advanced this semantically to mean ['opportunity for pretext for', or 'grounds of] complaint, murmuring': and that since 'murmuring' is nearly always synonymous with 'grumbling', it would have been unseemly to predicate it of the Deity. Hebrew אנה is, of course, never rendered by Aramaic רעם. But although Scheftell's argument is unacceptable as regards the relationship of 'Onqelos and Pseudo-Jonathan (as also the Peshiṭta) to the Hebrew original, it may well be that their spelling out of the (indirect) objective suffix after the finite form of the verb רעם is intended as a correction of the (?) earlier, and possibly equivocal תורעמנותי preserved in MS Neofiti. Cf. below, p. 150.

as the object—places him alongside the Targums and the
Peshiṭta. He comments:[1] '[you shall know] that you have
"disaffected" (שהניאותם) your heart from following me: תנואה
being an expression of alienation[2] (הסרה), as in Num. 30: 6.'
Here the halakhic significance of Num. 30: 6 has, so to say,
hypnotized Rashi's explanation of Num. 14: 34. On 30: 6 his
comment[3] recites the identification, by the *Siphrey, ad loc.*,[4] of
the scope of terms הניא and הפר (= 'annul' [vow]): 'one could
not tell what the hiph'il of נוא implied were it not for the fact
that in verse 9, when dealing with a husband's power of veto
over his wife's vows, the text states that "If on the day when he
learns [of it] her husband shall frustrate (יניא) her and annul
(והפר) her vow". The inescapable conclusion is that "frustration" (הנאה) indicates "annulment" (הפרה).' Thus far the
Siphrey; but Rashi himself prefaces his citation of it by paraphrasing the biblical text as follows: 'If he prevented (מנע) her
from [fulfilling] the vow, i.e. annulled (שהפר) [it] for her.' He
then quotes the *Siphrey* as authority for the equation הפר = הניא,
and continues: 'the basic meaning (ופשוטו) [of הניא] is "pre-
vention" (מניעה) and "removal" (הסרה),[5] as in Num. 32: 7,
Ps. 141: 5 and Num. 14: 34 וידעתם את תנואתי, "you shall
[come to] know the fact that you have departed from me (את
אשר סרתם מעלי)".'

---

[1] שהניאותם את לבבכם מאחרי : תנואה, לשון הסרה, כמו כי הניא אביה אותה.

[2] This may be the source of RV's 'my alienation' (see above, pp. 142f.),
with the tacit upgrading of Rashi's *indirect* object ('[of your affections from
following] me') to that of an implicitly understood *direct* object; unless
RV intends that it shall be understood subjectively, namely 'my alienation
[of you]'.

[3] ואם הניא אביה אותה . אם מנע אותה מן הנדר כלומר שהפר לה . הנאה
זו איני יודע מה היא, כשהוא אומר ואם ביום שמוע אישה יניא אותה והפר,
הוי אומר הנאה זו הפרה . ופשוטו לשון מניעה והסרה, וכן למה תניאון וכן
שמן ראש אל יניא (sic) ראשי וכן וידעתם את תנואתי, את אשר סרתם מעלי.

[4] Ed. H. S. Horovitz (Leipzig, 1917), pp. 201, lines 15 f.: איני יודע הנאה
זו...הוי אומר הנאה זו הפרה. Cf. preceding note.

[5] הסרה here clearly substantiates the reading הסרה in Rashi to 14: 34, and
there is no need to emend that passage to read הפרה. It clearly also lies
behind Abravanel's comment *ad loc.* (ed. Hanover, 1710, f. 255*a*, col. i,
line 26), אם הניא אביה אותה, כלומ' שהסיר ובטל הנדר.

Rashi's adducing of Num. 14: 34 to support his explanation of 30: 6 and vice versa does not render his argument circular, since he is able to appeal for independent support to Num. 32: 7 and Ps. 141: 5.[1] Of greater moment, however, is the effective inconsistency of Rashi's own comment with the matter from the *Siphrey* that he himself rehearses. If the *Siphrey* be disregarded, Rashi is seen to construe the suffix of תנואתי objectively indeed, but as indicating an *indirect object*, and as the equivalent of מניעתי or הסרתי, 'my [being the victim of your act of] "preventing" or "removal" [*sc.* of your loyalty]'. This exegesis, although admittedly somewhat complex, is analogous at base to the constructions recognized by the Targums and Peshiṭta (above, pp. 145 f.). But if we instead lay aside Rashi's equation of תנואה = הסרה = מניעה whilst retaining, to apply to the *Siphrey's* equation [הפר]תי = [תנוא]תי, Rashi's indirectly objective construction of the suffix, we arrive at a form of words so involved as to be almost meaningless: for if we accept the feasibility of the rendering 'my [being the victim of your act of] annulment', we are presupposing an elliptical object for 'annulment'. On no biblical premises, and probably on no premises at all, could the Deity be declared to be 'annulled'. The suffix would, as in Rashi's own explanation in terms of מניעה and הסרה, have to be construed as indirectly objective, i.e. the equivalent of לי (cf. עלי and *qᵉdāmai* in the Targums and Peshiṭta), while for the desiderated direct object we should have to presuppose an elliptical בריתי, '(my) covenant', this being the most frequent object in the Bible of the hiph'il of פרר. We should therefore arrive at the tortured rendering 'my [being the victim of your act of] annulment [of my covenant]'. The *Siphrey* itself has no comment on תנואתי in Num. 14: 34, and we need not here speculate as to whether it would have wrestled with the theological problem or would have by-passed it. But that Rashi was himself aware of the virtual impossibility of combining his own explanation of הניא, and so also of תנואתי, with the matter

---

[1] It should be noted that Menaḥem ibn Saruq, the author of Rashi's regular lexicon for biblical words, brings together under the stem נא (*art.* ii) Ps. 33: 10; Num. 30: 6; Ps. 141: 5 and Num. 32: 7 (ed. H. Filipowski, p. 121). Menaḥem does not, apparently, list תנואה itself anywhere—at least not under the stems נא, נו or תן.

quoted by him from the *Siphrey* on הניא in Num. 30: 6, is shown
by his formulation in his comment to the latter passage (see
p. 147, n. 3). The particle *waw* in ופשוטו (as Rashi's regular usage
of this term makes clear) must be construed adversatively—'*but*
the basic meaning is. . .'.

If, then, Rashi was quite clear in his own mind that the two
explanations were virtually exclusive of each other, how is it
that when he wrote his comment on Num. 14: 34 (תנואה =
הסרה) it is to Num. 30: 6 that he appeals, rather than to the
two other passages which he was to adduce (Num. 32: 7 and
Ps. 141: 5)? The answer can scarcely be that when he com-
mented on 14: 34 he did not yet appreciate that the two explanations to be offered on 30: 6 were, for practical purposes,
incompatible and that it was only when he came to scrutinize
30: 6 closely that he realized that this was so. Surely the explanation lies rather in the importance he ascribes to the sole
pentateuchal passage where נוא has halakhic implications.
Despite himself, Rashi was so dominated by these that when
he was not concerned directly with the text basic to them
he unconsciously *subsumed* his own lexical explanation
(הנאה = והסרה מניעה) within the *Siphrey's* halakhic one
(הניא = הפר), as if the two were identical, or at least re-
ciprocally complementary. When, however, he was specifically
addressing himself to the halakhic *locus classicus* at 30: 6,
Rashi's intellectual integrity led him to distinguish by an
adversative particle (ופשוטו) between two explanations which
cannot, otherwise than by a *tour de force*, be superimposed on
each other.

From Rashi we may turn to the exegesis of Obadiah Sforno[1]
(died Bologna, 1550), Reuchlin's teacher in Rome. Sforno's
comment constitutes a half-way house between side-stepping the
theological challenge and meeting it. Paraphrasing the last
words of Num. 14: 34, he writes:[2] 'you shall appreciate what
an ill thing is the annulment of my intention (בטול המכוון שלי)
through your turning aside from me (*v.l.* it), as it says (verse

---

[1] On Sforno see *Jewish Encyclopedia*, XI (New York, London, 1905), 212.
[2] תכירו מה רע בטול המכוון שלי בסורכם ממני (נ׳׳א ממנו) כאמרו
ונפלתם בחרב כי על כן שבתם מאחרי ה׳.

43), "and you shall fall by the sword, forasmuch as you turned back from [following] the Lord".' Sforno's choice of סור = 'turn aside' already reflects Rashi's (causative) הסרה = 'removal ["of loyalty"]'; and the attachment thereto of the second person suffix in a subjective sense presupposes that the first person suffix in תנואתי has been construed objectively. (בסורכם implies that, for the preceding בטול, there could be substituted בטולכם; and although המכוון שלי may indicate simple possession—'my intention'—it cannot be imagined that Sforno, or indeed anyone else, could equate the meanings of תנואה and כוונה, מכוון. Therefore תנואתי was understood by Sforno to mean "My [being subjected to the] annulment [of what had been intended by me]".) Yet if Rashi's grammatical construction of the text is paralleled by Sforno's, the theological implications of Sforno probably go considerably beyond those of Rashi. Although Rashi paraphrases תנואתי by 'your removal (הסרה) of the heart' (i.e. loyalty), Rashi does not state that the Deity has been materially affected by Israel's apostasy, nor does he hint at anything of the sort. Sforno, in substituting for Rashi's שהניאותם את לבבכם...לשון הסרה his own formulation, 'the annulment of my intention through your apostasy' (בטול המכוון שלי בסורכם), implies precisely that the possibility of frustration being imposed by man on God is a real possibility. We cannot be sure that that implication on the part of Sforno was a conscious, if guarded, one. If it was, then his exegesis (though still formally parallel to that of the Targums and of Rashi) reveals a spirit that would place it rather alongside the (differently orientated) exegesis of Ibn Ezra, considered below, pp. 151 f.

(b) (ii) '*Frustration' retained, and the suffix construed subjectively*

The Neofiti Targum renders the phrase by ותדעון ית תורעמגותי, 'and you shall come to know my murmuring', using the same Aramaic רעם to render Hebrew נוא as do 'Onqelos and Pseudo-Jonathan, although these (as seen above, p. 145) express themselves in a way that makes it clear that the suffix of תנואתי is understood objectively. In retaining the Hebrew formulation by means of noun plus 'possessive' suffix, Targum Neofiti may be avoiding the issue. Since, however, it resorts to an abstract form (otherwise unrecorded)[1] embodying a -*nuth* termination affixed to a strong root, there is at least a possibility that behind the abstract ‮ת(ו)רעמנותא‬ there loomed—at least in the mind of whoever coined it—a *nomen agentis* ending in -*ān(ā)*, i.e. ‮תרעמנ(א)‬* 'a grumbler'. In that case the suffix in ‮תורעמנותי‬ = 'my [being a] grumble[r with complaints against you]'. With this we could compare Aquila's προφάσιν for ‮תאנה‬ in Judg. 14: 4 (above, pp. 139 f.) and the various renderings of ‮תנואות‬ in Job 33: 10 (below, pp. 153 f.). Judg. 14: 4 and Job 33: 10 are, in fact, the only two passages on which the targumist could rely in order to substantiate his rendering, since 'murmur, complain' would not suit the context of ‮נוא‬ in Num. 30: 6, etc., 32: 7, etc., or Ps. 33: 10. 'My complaint [against you]' was therefore probably chosen by the targumist of MS Neofiti as a nice, vague rendering that would avoid the issues raised by ‮תנואתי‬, unless the listener paused to ponder the implications of the (underlying *nomen agentis* and the) subjective suffix (above, p. 141). If he did, he might decide that in the light of Israel's conduct it was no more than 'fair comment' on the part of the deity. But S. Scheftell's commentary on 'Onqelos *ad loc.* (see above, p. 146, n. 2), although its argument is unacceptable does indicate that in some rabbinic circles the imputation of 'grumbling' to the Deity —even grumbling that could be justified as 'fair comment'— was felt to be an impropriety; and this may have led to the inversion by the other targumists of the reference of the suffix attached to 'murmuring, grumbling'.

Abraham ibn Ezra's exegesis. Ibn Ezra comments thus: ‮את‬ ‮תנואתי, אניא דברי או מי יניאני, והטעם שישבור את שבועתי‬[2] ‮במו ואם יניא‬[3].
Presumably we should render this: 'I will [myself] frustrate my word—or [if not,] who shall frustrate me? And the meaning is "Who [else but I] shall break my[2] oath?" Cf. Num. 30: 6, "if he[3] shall frustrate, etc.".' This translation, and particularly the insertions within square brackets, bases itself on the super-

---

[1] The nearest form to be found is Syr. *mᵉra'mānā'* = 'connected with thunder' (βροντοῖος), recorded (once) by R. Payne Smith, *Thesaurus Syr.* II (Oxford, 1901), col. 3995.

[2] ‮שבועתי‬ (not ‮שבועתו‬) is the reading of some six printed editions checked by me, the earliest being Buxtorf's of 1618.

[3] ‮יניא‬ (for ‮הניא‬) through confusion with verse 9.

commentary[1] to Ibn Ezra by S. Z. Netter of Jerusalem.[2] If—as is conceivable—שבועתי ('my oath')[3] is due to the desire of printer-editors to smother the very notion of God's oath being broken, and that it stands for an original שבועתו ('his oath': compare the converse *tiqqun sopherim* of עיני > עינו at Zech. 2: 12), the effect would not be in any way to alter, but rather indeed to intensify the translation of Ibn Ezra offered above: the latter part would have to be rendered 'and the meaning is that he will [actually] break his oath [of his own initiative]'. On 30: 6, Ibn Ezra simply equates הניא with 'break, annul', referring back to the present passage.[4]

What is achieved by giving a subjective force to the suffix in תנואתי? First and foremost, נוא can be allowed its true meaning of 'frustrate' instead of being equated, by a fallacy of equivocation, with הסרה = 'alienation' [by Israel of their loyal affection, as in Rashi's exegesis]. But if God's 'frustration' (objectively, by human contrariness or opposition) is felt to be an intolerable notion, is theology any the better off if the possessive suffix is construed subjectively? At once an object for 'my frustration' is required; and if הניא is equated, as it is by Ibn Ezra, with שבר = 'break' or (on Num. 30: 6) with הפר = 'annul', the only suitable objects are—as before—(God's) 'covenant' or (his) 'oath'. 'My frustration, i.e. breaking or rescinding [of my own oath]'—have we not jumped, theologically speaking, out of the frying-pan into the fire? Ibn Ezra, apparently, contemplates without flinching the idea of God bringing his own oath to no effect: for God is, in the last resort, superior (as Creator) both to any self-imposed obligations and to any pressures or interference from any of his own creatures. If he decides to rescind and so frustrate his word, it is on his own initiative (אניא דברי), and not because he has been forced into having to do so by Israel's sinfulness or by any other agent or factor (מי יניאני).

---

[1] Printed in the Vienna pentateuch with rabbinic commentaries of 1859 (repr. Schocken, Berlin, 1937): מי הוא הגורם שאניא את דברי כמו ואם הניא (להלן ל' ו') ענין שבר דבר וביטולו.

[2] For Derenbourg's proposed interpretation of Sa'adyah's rendering on the same lines as Ibn Ezra's, see above, p. 145, n. 1.

[3] See above, p. 151, n. 2.

[4] כמו תשברון Cf. on 32: 7. כמו שבר והפר כמו את תנואתי.

Divine frustration exegetically frustrated

And so, by smuggling in an object—the divine oath—and by emphasizing the subjective force of the suffix ('my [voluntary] rescinding [of my own oath]'), Ibn Ezra has, to his own satisfaction if not quite to ours, succeeded in frustrating divine frustration. Captivity is taken captive. As far as the real theological issue is concerned it may be but guerilla warfare, but it is nevertheless magnificent.

We now deal, fairly summarily, with the other instance of נוא (Job 33: 10) which I have designated (above, p. 140) theologically equivocal rather than challenging. Here we are involved in the subtleties of a quotation which, in the context of its framework, is liable to be highly loaded with ironic exaggeration. The speaker, Elihu, is reprimanding Job for protesting his innocence to God, and he does so in terms that challenge Job to fault his argument. In verse 8 he has introduced a purported summary of Job's own assertions, which are represented as follows (verses 9 f.) : '"I am innocent, without offence ...Behold, he discovers תנואות against me, reckons me an adversary to himself"'.[1] That the third person refers to the Deity is not in question. As regards תנואות, G. Beer in *BH* endorses the emendation of G. H. B. Wright *et al.*[2] to read תאנות as in Judg. 14: 4 (see above, p. 139), i.e. 'opportunities [for quarrel]'. N. H. Tur Sinai[3] concedes the possibility that תנואות is by metathesis for תאנות (which he translates as 'pretexts'). The latter rendering underlies the English versions, which offer: 'occasions against me' (AV, RV, AJV, RSV, RV[mg] or, 'causes of alienation'). The Jerusalem Bible reads 'he is inventing grievances against me' (margin: '"grievances" Syriac; "enmities" Hebrew').[4]

The ancient versions handle the word as follows: LXX μέμψιν,[5] OL *querelam*, Vulg. *-as*, Targum תרעומתא ('murmurings'),

---

[1]

זך אני בלי פשע   חף אנכי ולא עון לי :   (9)

הן תנואות עלי ימצא   יחשבני לאויב לו :   (10)

[2] So also S. R. Driver–G. B. Gray, *ICC*, p. 241 ('highly probable').

[3] *Job* (English translation, Jerusalem, 1957), p. 466.

[4] French, '...prétextes contre moi' (margin, '"prétextes" syr.; "inimitiés" hébr.)'.

[5] H. Orlinsky has no comment on this in the section on the treatment of charges against God in his 'Studies in the Septuagint of Job', *HUCA*, xxxii (1961), 249 f.

153

Pesh. *'ellātā'* (*pl.*) ('pretexts, accusations'), = Arabic *'al'ilala* (Walton's text), Sa'ad. אלענת ('faults').[1]

Of these, the Syriac *'el^etā'* = both 'pretext' and 'accusation', and Arabic *'illatun* = 'accident', 'cause', or 'pretext' (cf. Rashi, below, p. 154). These all either presuppose תאנות or else interpret תנואות in terms of it; and the same sense ('ground of complaint') rather than 'blame' is doubtless to be recognized here in the Greek μέμψιν.[2] The Targum's תרעומתא will be based on the targumic renderings of תנואתי in Num. 14: 34 (above, pp. 145 f., 150 f.), without concern, apparently, for the reservations that there drove 'Onqelos, Pseudo-Jonathan and the Peshiṭta (but not Targum Neofiti) to eliminate possible images of a 'grumbling' Deity. Talmudic and midrashic literature apparently ignores the verse, and of the Church Fathers Gregory[3] has nothing of interest to us.

When we turn to the medieval Jewish commentators, we find that Rashi explicitly identifies the meaning of תנואות here with that of תאנות, paraphrasing the latter by עלילות—the same root which the Peshiṭta and non-Sa'adyanic Arabic here use. In biblical Hebrew עלילה means a 'wanton deed', or, if applied to the Deity, one that is not patient of human questioning, let alone remonstrance. In post-biblical Hebrew the meanings of 'pretext', 'insidious allegation' come to the fore, but neither of these quite suits the context in Rashi's comment here, which reads:[4] '[תנואות, i.e.] עלילות, viz. an expression meaning a pretext (תואנה) "to turn back" (לשוב) *from [allegiance to] God.*' The italicized words indicate the sense in which עלילות and (so תאנות and consequently also) תנואות was intended by Rashi to be understood, namely (apparent) 'provocations' to disaffection. In other words, Rashi relieves the Deity of the charge of fabricating 'pretexts' (the usual sense of תאנות) in order to

---

[1] יגד עלי אלענת, Derenbourg, *Saadia*, v, 54, 93 line 14 ('*invente contre moi des péchés*'). Sa'adyah's commentary on Job has been discussed by E. I. J. Rosenthal (above, p. 145, n. 2), who does not adduce any comment by Sa'adyah on תנואות at 33: 10.

[2] *LSJ* quote Aeschylus and Sophocles in this sense. Both the noun, and the verb μεμφέσθαι are rare in septuagintal, as in patristic Greek.

[3] *Moralia in Job*, XXIII, 16; *PL*, 76, col. 269A.

[4] עלילות לשון תואנות לשוב מן המקום.

persecute Job—a charge which, if substantiated, would convict God of an irresponsible, arbitrary and indeed capricious lack of straightforwardness. In place of this, God is represented as being (in Elihu's view) accused by Job of doing precisely what, in the prologue to the book, he is declared to authorize Satan to do—to provoke Job to the limit, as a test of his faith. This puts rather a different complexion on things: and even if the burden of Job's complaint is still God's unfairness in behaving in this way, Job's own determination not to allow himself to be provoked into abandoning God can be regarded by Rashi and others (for whom God, *ex hypothesi*, cannot be in the wrong) as neutralizing the provocation. The Deity's public face is saved by Job's reacting in a way that (in God's own foreknowledge) he was always pre-ordained to act.

Ibn Ezra's comment[1] simply refers to his explanation of תנואתי in Num. 14: 34.

Levi b. Gerson[2] (southern France, 1288–1344) is clearly influenced by Rashi's commentary both on the present passage and on Num. (14: 34 and) 30: 6; 32: 7 (above, pp. 146 f.). He begins by echoing Rashi's identification of הניא with הסיר, albeit dropping (in the first instance) the elliptical object לבב = 'heart['s affection]' there postulated by Rashi, and using the noun ('removal') not causatively, but intransitively (= 'departure, lapse'). This modification is however also implicitly combined with an interpretation of תנואות as = 'false charges', i.e. תאנות (cf. Peshiṭta and possibly LXX, above, p. 154); so that in effect תנואות receives simultaneously explanation on two levels which, though really alternatives, are not exactly mutually exclusive. Gersonides writes:[3] '[false] charges (עלילות) and [allegations of] lapses (הסרות) from his precepts, i.e. he cannot [justifiably] allege against me (שלא יעליל אותי) that I have departed (שסרתי) from his precepts.' He then proceeds to offer, but go beyond, what is in fact Rashi's explanation of

---

[1] כמו וידעתם את תנואתי.

[2] On Gersonides see *Jewish Encyclopedia*, VIII (New York, London, 1904), 26 f.

[3] תנואות, עלילות והסרות ממצוותיו ר"ל שלא יעליל אותי שסרתי ממצוותיו' או ירצה בזה שהוא ימצא בעבורי מה שיסיר אותי ממבוקשיו עד שלא אוכל לעשות אחד מהם.

תנואות in the present passage, i.e. 'provocations', but he clearly realizes that this explanation is incompatible with the foregoing. He continues:[1] 'alternatively, he [Elihu, purporting to quote Job] means that God contrives means of making me lapse from his requirements (ימצא...מה...שיסיר אותי ממבוקשיו) to such a degree that I am incapable of implementing a single one of them.' Here we have 'provocation' indeed, but something more as well. Whereas for Rashi God's seemingly arbitrary provocation of Job is cancelled out by Job's own determination not to let himself be provoked, and by God's foreknowledge of Job's determination, for Gersonides God's provocation (according to Elihu's no doubt ironically exaggerated representation of Job) is not only successful—'so that I cannot fulfil a single precept' —but is indeed *intended* to be successful. God's *métier*, then, is frustration. Gersonides is, of course, on safe ground: the speaker is Elihu, whose exaggeration of Job may be deemed a travesty, and in any case in the dénouement Elihu is both ignored by Job and shown by God's answer to Job to be irrelevant, or at any rate labouring under a misconception that has given his approach a wrong slant. In his summary of the chapter, where he paraphrases the argument, Gersonides confirms and slightly elaborates his exegesis as cited above, writing as follows:[2] 'God prevents me (ימנעני)[3] and causes me to depart (ויסירני) from all my aspirations, i.e. he hedges in my way and reckons me his adversary, so as to deny (למנוע)[3] me my desires precisely as one endeavours to deny one's enemy his objective.'

The commentary on Job edited and translated from a thirteen–fourteenth-century MS in Cambridge by W. Aldis Wright and S. A. Hirsch[4] paraphrases תנואות, as Rashi did,

[1] See above, p. 155, n. 3.
[2] הנה הש״י ימנעני ויסירני מכל מה שאני חפץ להגיע אליו ר״ל שגדר דרכי ויחשבני לאויב לו למנוע ממני מבוקשי כמו שישתדל האדם למנוע מאויבו מבוקשו.
[3] Cf. Rashi, above, p. 147, n. 3.
[4] הן תנואות שהן עלילות לחייבני . אם הניא שעל ידי עלילה הניא אביה אותה. Hirsch's translation fails to take account of the conditional construction (mistakenly) recognized by the commentator in the Hebrew text (הן תנואות עלי ימצא) of Job—probably under the (unconscious) influence of ואם הניא in Num. 30: 6.

by עלילות, but (unlike Rashi) it does not semantically extend the meaning of עלילות beyond 'pretexts': and whilst it probably presupposes Rashi's own equation *in loco* of תנואות = תאנות, it appeals explicitly to Num. 30: 6 (the 'frustrating, annulling' of women's vows) to substantiate its own exegesis: '"Behold (תנואות), does he find", i.e. pretexts (עלילות) to convict me if he [indulges in] frustrat[ing me] (אם יניא), because it is on grounds of some pretext (עלילה) that [a father is represented, Num. 30: 6] as disallowing his [daughter's vow].' This latter explanation of הניא in Num. 30: 6 is, of course, pure conjecture —in effect read into that text from the commentator's understanding of תנואות in Job 33: 10; at any rate, for the other contexts of נוא the meaning 'pretext' is either impossible (Num. 14: 34), or has to be introduced, quite arbitrarily as but an appendage to the basic meaning of the root (Num. 32:9; 33:10).

This study might be complemented by an investigation of the exegesis of פרר = 'annul', which (in the bye-form הפיר) parallels הניא in Ps. 33: 10. Where, however, the Deity is the subject, the object is either the counsels of the nations (Ps. 33: 10), liars (Isa. 44: 25), etc., or else the assertion is a negative one—God does *not* annul his covenant (e.g. Lev. 26: 44; so, effectively, Job 40: 8). In these passages, therefore, grave theological problems are unlikely to be sensed by the exegetes and translators. But it might be rewarding to investigate, on the lines that have been followed here, the versions and exegesis of Jer. 33: 21 (where God's covenant is asserted to be hypothetically capable of being annulled on his own side),[1] and Zech. 11: 10–11 (where God annuls his covenant with all peoples). But our present findings are unlikely to need modification, and in conclusion they may be summarized.

The idea that God could be permanently frustrated is obviously unacceptable to any committed translator or exegete of the Bible: because it is excluded by the very presuppositions of biblical thought itself. The notion that the Deity might be represented by the Bible as *baulked*, i.e. temporarily frustrated

---

[1] אם תפרו את בריתי...גם בריתי תפר. The passive formulation is probably itself significant here.

in carrying out its designs, is somewhat different, but has proved equally disconcerting for all but the least inhibited of modern translators: and of the versions and exegesis considered above it is the New AJV alone that is bold enough to translate Num. 14: 34 in terms of God's reaction to being 'thwarted' (above, p. 142). On the other hand the notion of a frustrator-God, to whose inscrutable purposes a measure of sheer obstructionism may be integral, is too much for the theological stomach of the average exegete—or at any rate that of his public or his ecclesiastical authorities. But honest exegesis has to take account of such a possibility and to wrestle with the problems which it entails—they were confronted, on the dramatic plane, by Aeschylus in his *Prometheus Vinctus*, and indeed by the author of the book of Job itself; 'for he is a unique one, and who can turn him aside? and what his soul desireth, that he doeth' (23: 13). The occasional spirit—of the sources here examined, only Ibn Ezra and, perhaps, Sforno—understands that unless the implications of the divine capacity to frustrate are taken seriously, God is mocked. But alongside this realization there marches, as universally within Judaism and Christianity, the unspoken conviction that obstructionism is a divine prerogative; and those who behave as if they would lay claim to it and, Pharaoh-wise, play Leviathan in their own puddles, discover that, like Leviathan, they are themselves but God's plaything.

12

THE INTERCESSION OF THE COVENANT MEDIATOR (EXODUS 33: 1a, 12–17)

by James Muilenburg

Among the many contributions Professor Winton Thomas has made to lexical studies, not a few have been devoted to the Hebrew verb יד׳, especially in those contexts where its true meaning had hitherto been uncertain or obscure.[1] It goes without saying that the verb with its congeners is one of the most important in the Old Testament. It is susceptible of many different renderings, due in part to its appearance in no fewer than eight stems, in part to its numerous syntactical constructions, and in part, also, to the variety of usages in the major classifications of Hebrew literature.[2] In several books, such as Hosea and Ezekiel, it holds a status approximating centrality.[3] It is rich in denotations and richer still in its connotations, a many-faceted word with numerous nuances and accents. Not infrequently it plays a decisive role in the composition of the *Gattungen* or literary genres, both in connection with the terminology characteristic of the particular genre in question and as a keyword in climactic or strategic collocations. One thinks, for example, of its usages in the hymns and royal hymns or

---

[1] For references see the Bibliography.

[2] Such as the legal, cultic, historical, prophetic, and sapiential literatures. There is much semantic overlapping, to be sure, but there is also much that is characteristic of the general type of speech within each classification.

[3] H.W.Wolff, '"Wissen um Gott" bei Hosea als Urform von Theologie', *Evangelische Theologie*, xii (Munich, 1952/53), 533–52 = *Gesammelte Studien zum Alten Testament, Theologische Bücherei*, xxii (Munich, 1964), 182–205; W. Zimmerli, *Erkenntnis Gottes nach dem Buche Ezechiel. Eine theologische Studie (Abhandlungen zur Theologie des alten und neuen Testaments*, xxvii, Zürich, 1954) = *Gottes Offenbarung. Gesam. Aufsätze (Theologische Bücherei*, xix, Munich, 1963), pp. 41–119; James M. Ward, *Hosea: a Theological Commentary* (New York, 1966), pp. 83–9 and *passim*.

liturgies, in confessions and laments, in the divine self-disclosures and, for want of a better term, the *confessiones fidei*, in prophetic calls and in the several types of covenant formulations. It is our wont to render the verb by *to know*. But knowing is of many kinds and dispositions, depending not only upon the particular context in which it appears, but also upon the particular attitude or frame of mind that is intended in the context. So if we are to attempt to define the precise meaning of the word, we may find ourselves at times at a loss to discover *le mot juste* for the English equivalent, but, what is more, we shall be compelled by the very nature of the case to resort to well over a score of words in order to do justice to the wide range of meaning that the word covers in the original Hebrew.

It was our original design, therefore, to scrutinize a number of representative *Gattungen* or literary types in order to call attention to the precise meaning that the verb bears in its linguistic and literary settings and in relation to the *Sitz im Leben* of the genre, and then to describe, as well as one is able, the function that the verb performs in the pericope under inspection. Such an undertaking is of course too wide-ranging and spacious for an essay of the present length. We shall content ourselves, therefore, with examining a passage of very limited scope, the impassioned and fateful dialogical encounter between Moses and Yahweh on Mount Sinai, as it is reported to us in Exod. 33: 12–17, with a view first of all to pointing out the features which mark its composition and then to determining the different meanings of the verb ידע, which appears no fewer than six times within a literary unit of fewer than one hundred words, and always in striking collocations.

If we are to assess with any degree of confidence the particular function and intention of our pericope, then it is essential, first of all, to establish its setting within the complex of traditions in which it finds its place. We observe at once that it appears in a *covenant* context, indeed within the *locus classicus* of the Sinaitic covenant (Exod. 19–24, 32–4). The two major blocs of tradition define the limits of the section. While they are separated by a substantial insertion from the Priestly source (Exod. 25–31), there can be no question that at some stage in the history of transmission they were continuous, although not in the present ordering of materials in chapters 32–4. The old Pentateuchal sources, the Yahwist and the Elohist, are present in both, albeit with accretions and elaborations in chapters 32–4, and in somewhat different guise and certainly in different types of formulation. The first complex (Exod. 19–24) is quite generally recognized today as a unified and coherent whole and as representing a particular *Gattung*, whether one thinks of it as reflecting the structure and component parts of the suzerainty treaties such as we find among other peoples of the Near East, notably the Hittites, Accadians, and Assyrians,[1] or as the *Festlegende* or liturgy employed in connection with the annual celebrations of the covenant renewal festival.[2] The traditions in our second complex (Exod. 32–4) have clear affinities with the first (Exod. 19–24). They are, in the first place, *covenant* traditions and presuppose the conclusion of the covenant between Yahweh and Israel. The *mise en scène* is still Sinai, the mountain of God. Moses continues to serve as mediator of the covenant (cf. Exod. 20: 18–20). The motif of the liberation from Egyptian slavery which forms the historical preamble to the covenant in Exod. 19–24 appears again and again as a major motif and always in the same rhetorical and stylistic form (32: 1, 4, 8, 11, 23; 33: 1; 34: 18), and the giving of the law recounted in the first section may be said to constitute the framework of the whole complex of tradition preserved in the second (Exod. 32–4), since it opens with the breaking of the tablets in chapter 32 and concludes

[1] V. Kurošec, *Hethitische Staatsverträge* (*Leipziger Rechtswissenschaftliche Studien*, IX, 1931); G. E. Mendenhall, *Law and Covenant in Israel and the Ancient Near East* (Pittsburgh, 1955); Julien Harvey, S.J., 'Le "Rîb-pattern" réquisitoire prophétique sur la rupture de l'alliance', *Biblica*, XIV (1962), 172–96; R. Frankena, 'The vassal-treaties of Esarhaddon and the dating of Deuteronomy', *Oudtestamentische Studiën*, XIV (1965), 122–54. For a full bibliography on the treaties, see Dennis J. McCarthy, S.J., *Treaty and Covenant* (*Analecta Biblica*, XXI, Rome, 1963), pp. xiii–xxiv.

[2] G. von Rad, *The Problem of the Hexateuch and Other Essays*, trans. by E. W. Truman Dicken (Edinburgh and London, 1966), pp. 27 ff.; *Old Testament Theology*, I, trans. by D. M. G. Stalker (Edinburgh and London, 1962), pp. 188 f.; Murray Newman, *The People of the Covenant: a Study of Israel from Moses to the Monarchy* (New York and Nashville, 1962); Walter Beyerlin, *Origins and History of the Oldest Sinaitic Traditions*, trans. by S. Rudman (Oxford, 1965).

with their renewal and the restoration of the covenant bond in chapter 34.

But such similarities as we have pointed to must not obscure the striking differences between the two sections, for, whereas the first is a recognizable unity, the second has every appearance of being a catena of originally separate pieces which originally had little or nothing to do with each other. They are more perhaps than a *disiecta membra*, but the several parts do not cohere well with each other. This impression of disunity is confirmed when one undertakes the difficult task of source analysis.[1] Chapter 33 is a case in point.[2] To begin with, it interrupts the

[1] The most important discussions are the following: S. R. Driver, *An Introduction to the Literature of the Old Testament* (Edinburgh, twelfth edition, 1906); A. H. McNeile, *The Book of Exodus* (*WC*, London, 1908); Gustav Westphal, *Jahwes Wohnstätten nach den Anschauungen der Alten Hebräer* (*BZAW*, xv, 1908); Hugo Gressmann, *Mose und seine Zeit. Ein Kommentar zu den Mose-Sagen* (Göttingen, 1913); Otto Eissfeldt, *Hexateuch-Synopse* (Leipzig, 1922); W. Rudolph, 'Der Aufbau von Exodus 19–34', *Werden und Wesen des Alten Testaments*, edited by Paul Volz, Friedrich Stummer, and Johannes Hempel (*BZAW*, lxvi, 1936); Gerhard von Rad, *The Problem of the Hexateuch and Other Essays*, especially 'The Form-critical Problem of the Hexateuch', pp. 1–78 (English translation, 1966. Original German edition published in *BWANT*, xxvi, 1938); Walter Beyerlin, *Origins and History of the Oldest Sinaitic Traditions*, trans. by S. Rudman (Oxford, 1965. Original German edition published in 1961); Martin Noth, *Überlieferungsgeschichte des Pentateuch* (Stuttgart, 1948) and *Exodus: a Commentary* (English translation, London, 1962).

While the area of disagreement is considerable, perhaps the following conclusions would commend themselves to at least the majority of the foregoing scholars: (1) While chapter 32 belongs with the complex of materials in chapters 32–4, it nevertheless represents a later insertion designed to form the introduction or background for chapter 34. Driver and Beyerlin assign most of the chapter to E; others like Rudolph and Noth argue for J. (2) Chapter 33 is composed of several independent pieces; the opening section (verses 1–6) is certainly composite and contains a substratum of J, which joins well with verses 12–17. Verses 7–11 are an intrusion into the context and may well have originally displaced a pericope on the ark. The remainder of the chapter (verses 12–17 and 18–23) represents a later redaction of J. (3) Our pericope (verses 12–17) connects well with Exod. 24: 3–11, which was very likely its original locus (see Rudolph, *BZAW*, lxvi, 46 and Eissfeldt, *Hexateuch-Synopse*, pp. 53 ff.).

[2] Cf. Noth, *Überlieferungsgeschichte des Pentateuch*, p. 33 n. 113: 'Auf eine literarkritische Analyse von Ex. 33 muss man wohl verzichten. Es handelt sich hier anscheinend um ein Konglomerat von sekundären Wucherungen

natural sequence of chapters 32 and 34, despite the excellent transition provided by 32: 34 a. On the face of it, we have before us here four separate literary units (33: 1–6, 7–11, 12–17, 18–23), but upon closer examination it becomes apparent that verses 1–6 are composite. Verses 3 b–6 contradict what is said in their immediate context. It is generally recognized that verses 7–11 constitute a unit by itself, and have nothing to do with what precedes or follows, although the editor or compiler may have considered verse 11 as a fitting context for verses 12–17: 'Thus Yahweh used to speak to Moses face to face, as a man speaks to his friend.' Perhaps the majority of scholars hold verses 12–17 to be composite also,[1] but their unity is supported by more recent studies.[2] Nor is there any agreement as to the precise scope of the literary unit since verse 17 is assigned by many to the following pericope (33: 18–23), a view that fails to do justice to the form and structure of the passage. It is in contexts such as these that stylistic and rhetorical criticism proves a great boon, for it helps us to see what the methodologies of literary and historical criticism taken by themselves cannot disclose.

With Rudolph and Beyerlin and others we hold 33: 12–17 to be a self-contained unity. But it is without a satisfactory introduction. This, by itself, need not be taken too seriously for it is the manner of many of Israel's literary compositions to begin quite *in medias res*, but the situation here requires some sort of preliminary statement in view of the opening words of Moses, 'Consider! you say to me, "Lead forward this people!"' Now

in Anschluss an Ex. 32, 34 a*ª*, das vielleicht schon innerhalb der noch gesonderte J-Erzählung entstand (in vv. 1 ff. begegnen wir sogleich wieder deuteronomische Stil). Für E spricht nichts in diesem Kapitel; als Gottesname kommt — und zwar sehr häufig — nur יהוה vor.' On the other hand, Noth recognizes the motivation that lies behind all the literary units: 'The varied pieces of Ex. 33 are held together by the theme of the presence of God in the midst of his people, which plays some part in all of them. This common theme was evidently also the reason for the collection of all the passages.' See his commentary on *Exodus*, p. 253. See also von Rad, *The Problem of the Hexateuch*, pp. 17 ff.

[1] S. R. Driver, A. H. McNeile, A. Westphal, H. Gressmann, and Curt Rylaarsdam in *IB*, 1 (1952).

[2] W. Rudolph, M. Beyerlin, and Noth. Eissfeldt apparently takes the whole of verses 12–23 as a unit. See *Hexateuch-Synopse*, p. 157.

it is only in the opening verse of the chapter that we have such a word from Yahweh: 'Yahweh said to Moses "Depart, lead forward this people".' Rudolph contends rightly that this must form the beginning of our pericope. Beyerlin would add verse 3 to 1 a and Westphal would include 3 b–4 also. But this runs counter to the style of the words which follow in verses 12–17, and, moreover, it is doubtful whether the words belong to the same source. It is to be observed that the keyword עלה is strategically placed not only in Yahweh's command to Moses, but in Moses' immediate reply (12 a) and then, later, in the climactic and concentrated plea preceding the long motivation of verse 16: 'if your Presence will not go, do not cause us to press forward (תַּעֲלֵנוּ) from this (place).' The qal imperative of the verb in verse 1 a is followed appropriately by the twofold hiph'il imperative at the beginning (12) and close (15 c) of the discourse proper. Though we shall return to the point again, it is well to notice that the ambulatory terminology, so frequent and so revealing in other Old Testament contexts, is stressed by the close relation between leading forward (עלה) and going (הלך, note especially the moving contexts of verses 14 a and 15 a). There are other connections between verse 1 a and verses 12–17. The phrase 'from here' (מִזֶּה, 1 a) is repeated in connection with the same verb עלה in the same dramatic climax of verse 15 c. Even more significant is the phrase 'you and the people' (1 c) which is taken up and stressed by Moses twice in the final words of his impassioned plea: 'I and your people' (16 c and 16 e). The opening directive of Yahweh in 33: 1 a is certainly very brief, but this comports well with the compressed style of the words that follow. On the other hand, one must always reckon with the possibility that in contexts such as these the tradition may well have been telescoped. Subtractions are fully as important as additions in the history of transmission.

In the translation which follows I have attempted to articulate the wording and forms of the successive predications, but without strict adherence to their possible poetic structure[1]

---

[1] Compare J. Arvid Bruno, *Die Bücher Genesis–Exodus. Eine rhythmische Untersuchung* (Stockholm, 1953). While most scholars will have their reservations concerning the poetic guise of these books, Bruno's rendering

and have retained the usage of the verb *to know* for the time being.[1]

33: 1 *a.*
 And Yahweh said to Moses:
  'Go, depart from here,
   you and the people.'
12. And Moses said to Yahweh:
  'Consider! you (אתה) say to me,
   "Lead forth this people!"
  Yet you (אתה) have not let me know[a]
   whom you will send with me,
  But you (אתה) have said:
   "I know you by name[b]
    and you have indeed (וגם) found favour in my eyes."[c]
13. And now (ועתה)[d] if I have truly (אם־נא) found favour in your eyes,[e]
   Pray (נא) make me to know your ways[f] that I may know you[g]
   in order that (למען) I may find favour in your eyes.
  Consider! that (כי) this nation is your people.'[h]
14. And he said:
  'My Presence will go (פני ילכו)[i]
   and I will give you rest.'[j]
15. And he said to him:
  'If (אם־אין) your Presence will not go[k]
   do not lead us forth from here!
16. For in what way (ובמה) will it ever (אפוא) be known that
   (כי) I have found favour in your eyes,
   I and your people?

does call attention to the rhythms that may well lie behind our present text; moreover it has the advantage of revealing the way in which the predications are articulated and related to each other. Compare Martin Buber, *Die Fünf Bücher der Weisung*. Verdeutscht in Gemeinschaft mit Franz Rosenzweig (Cologne, 1954). For the rendering of our pericope, see pp. 246 f.

[1] The merit of preserving the English word 'know' is that it calls attention to the presence of the same word. As we shall see, the word bears different connotations in different contexts.

Is it not (הלוא) in your going with us
that we may be distinct,[1] I and your people,
from every people on the face of the earth?'
17. And Yahweh said to Moses:
'This very word (גם את הדבר הזה) that you have spoken
I will do,
for you have found favour in my eyes,
and I know you by name.'

TEXTUAL COMMENTARY

[a] The Greek renders MT the second person singular hiph'il of ידע
by ἐδήλωσας, 'revealed, made manifest or visible'. Vulg. *et non
indicas mihi.*

[b] MT 'by name'. Greek παρὰ πάντας, 'above all'. So also in verse
17. Vulg. *novi te ex nomine.*

[c] Greek παρ' ἐμοί.

[d] MT 'and now if'. Greek εἰ οὖν. Vulg. *si ergo.*

[e] MT 'in your eyes'. Greek ἐναντίον σου. Vulg. *in conspectu tuo.*

[f] Greek ἐμφάνισόν μοι σεαυτόν 'reveal yourself to me'.

[g] Greek has γνωστῶς ἴδω σε 'that I may see Thee clearly'.

[h] The Greek seeks to overcome the awkwardness of MT by 'in order
that I may know that this great nation is your people'.

[i] Greek Αὐτὸς προπορεύσομαι.

[j] Arnold B. Ehrlich, *Randglossen zur Hebräischen Bibel*, I (Leipzig,
1908), p. 405, finds the Hebrew here 'impossible', and proposes the
emendation והנחיתיך 'and I will lead you'. Cf. W. Eichrodt,
Theology of the Old Testament, II (English translation, London, 1967),
p. 38 n. 1.

[k] Greek Εἰ μὴ αὐτὸς σὺ πορεύῃ. Vulg. *si non tu ipse praecedes.*

[l] For MT 'be distinct' or 'be distinguished' Greek has ἐνδοξασ-
θήσομαι. So too Vulg. *glorificemur.*

It is of the first importance for our understanding of the
passage to recognize the *kind* of speaking that is going on and
to delineate as well as one may where the major accents lie.
Such an endeavour is the more important because of the presence of several leading motifs. We may begin by stressing that
the participants in the encounter are Moses and Yahweh:
Moses, the covenant mediator, and Yahweh, the Lord of the
covenant. Hugo Gressman subsumes the pericope under the

theophanic rubric of the פְּנֵי יהוה (פָּנִים) (Exod. 23: 20–33; 33: 1–6, 12–23; 34: 5*b*–9; Num. 10: 29–36).[1] There can be no doubt that the פָּנִים (lit. 'face') does indeed play a central role in all of these texts, but, surprisingly, Gressman draws no inference from this circumstance as to the nature of the literary genre. Nils Johansson classifies the passage among the intercessions of Moses (Exod. 8: 8–14 (Heb. 4–10); 8: 28–32 (Heb. 8: 24–8); 9: 27–9; 10: 16–19; 32: 11–14, 30–6; 33: 12–17; 34: 8 f.; Num. 12: 9–16; 14: 13–19 (especially verses 17–19); 21: 4–7).[2] P. A. H. de Boer in his thorough study recognizes the affinities of our text with the intercessions, but does not devote any separate treatment to it.[3] H. H. Rowley counts the following among the intercessory prayers of Moses: Exod. 32: 11 ff., 31 f.; 33: 12 ff.; 34: 9; Num. 11: 11 ff.; 14: 13 ff.; 21: 7; Deut. 9: 18 ff.; 10: 10.[4] Martin Buber characterizes the pericope simply as one of the conversations of Moses with Yahweh (Exod. 32: 7–14, 31–4; 33: 1–5, 12–23; 34: 1–10).[5] They are reminiscent of the dialogical engagements at the Burning Bush (J; 3: 1–4*a*, 5, 7–8, 16–22; 4: 1–9 with additions. E: 3: 4*b*, 6, 9–15; 4: 17. Cf. Noth, *Überlieferungsgeschichte des Pentateuch*), although the formulation and style are quite different.

If we take into account the history of tradition and raise the question as to the place and function of this intercession in

---

[1] *Mose und seine Zeit*, p. 218. Gressmann's comment on the difficulties of source analysis is quite revealing here. 'Die Bezeichnung der Varianten mit J und E ist hier, wie gleich zu Anfang betont sei, völlig willkürlich; dennoch ist sie aus praktischen Gründen beibehalten worden, besonders des bequemeren Zitierens wegen.' He recognizes that verses 12–17 form a single complex, but views it as highly composite.

[2] *PARAKLETOI: Vorstellungen von Fürsprechern für die Menschen vor Gott in der alttestamentlichen Religion, im Spätjudentum und Urchristentum* (Lund, 1940), pp. 5 ff., 181 f.

[3] *De Voorbede in het Oude Testament* (Leiden, 1943), pp. 42–121. De Boer does not include our text among the intercessions strictly speaking, but he clearly recognizes the primary relationship between Moses and Yahweh: 'Zijn verzoeningsdaad geschiedt niet, doordat hij in zulk een nauwe relatie met zijn volk staat, maar doordat hij in biezonderen dienst van Jhwh staat' (p. 57).

[4] *Worship in Ancient Israel* (London, 1967), p. 163 n. 6.

[5] Martin Buber and Franz Rosenzweig, 'Das Leitwort und der Formtypus der Rede', in *Die Schrift und ihre Verdeutschung* (Berlin, 1936), pp. 262 ff.

Israel's life, then it seems to the writer that we must conclude that it is cultic in intent and design. Its original position immediately following the covenant liturgy of Exod. 19–24, its dialogical character, and, above all, the significance of the פנים for Israel's worship and faith would suggest as much. We may think of our passage at least tentatively as a liturgy. It is much more than a legendary memory; more, too, than a 'historical' episode or a scrap of ancient tradition. It is the plea or intercession of the mediator of the covenant, the representative of Yahweh, Israel's Lord and Suzerain, on behalf of the people and Yahweh's answering assurance. In the encounter a momentous issue is at stake. The style is correspondingly elevated and solemn, without any historical or geographical or descriptive reference or concrete detail. It is the kind of speech that is congenial to and suited for the worship of the covenant community. It is shrouded in holy awe, freighted with urgency and passion, and burdened with the sense of destiny.

The most striking feature of the passage is its extraordinary concentration into the very minimum of speech. The composition is superbly fashioned. The keywords and key-sentences and dominant motifs (and there are several) are interwoven into the linguistic and literary fabric with consummate skill; the architectonics of rhetoric, the interior structure of the succeeding lines, and their movement towards their consummation is the work of someone more than a diligent craftsman; in actuality it is the product of extraordinary literary sensitivity.[1] Yet there is nothing contrived or aesthetic here, no striving after effect, no description or self-conscious rhetoric. It has the stamp of authenticity marked upon it.

Observe, first of all, the speaking quality (*Sprachlichkeit*) of

[1] Cf. *ibid.* p. 262: 'Das immer wieder aufgenommene Zwiegespräch Gottes mit Moses nach der Sünde des Volkes, 2M. 32: 7–14, 31–34; 33: 1–5, 12–23; 34: 1–10, ist, im Zusammenhang gefasst, von unerhörter Gebautheit, unerhörter tektonischer Dichtigkeit. Ich kenne kein andres Werk rednerischen Charakters, in dem die Beredtheit, in deren Wesen es zu liegen scheint dem Geheimnis abzusagen, so geheimnistreu bleibt, aber auch keins, wo so wie hier immer wieder die festen Wortbrücken, Leitwortbrücken geschlagen werden, um den zitternden Fuss über die Abgründe zu tragen.'

the pericope. The *formulae citandi* are well contrived and in chiastic form: 'Moses said to Yahweh' (12 a), 'and he said' (14 a), 'and he said to him' (15 a), 'and Yahweh said to Moses' (17 a; cf. 33:1 a!). But the *verba dicendi* penetrate into the citations themselves: 'Consider! you say to me' (12 b), 'you have not informed me' (12 d), 'but you have said' (12 f). These rhetorical phenomena are accented by the way in which Moses quotes Yahweh's own words (12 c and 12 gh) and by the way he enters into engagement with them (12 de and 13). Yahweh's concluding words, 'you have found favour in my eyes', is immediately taken up on the lips of Moses, 'And now, if I have really found favour in your eyes' (13 a). Similarly, Yahweh's momentous assurance, 'My Presence will go' is forthwith taken up in Moses' rejoinder, 'If your Presence will not go', which is immediately followed by harking back to the opening crucial line (12 c): 'do not lead us forth from here' (15 c). Repeatedly, throughout the little liturgy, we listen again and again to the motif, 'find favour in...eyes' (12 h, 13 a, 13 c and then again in 16 b and finally in the climactic close, 17 c).[1] This literary device is frequent in the Ugaritic texts as well as within the Old Testament, most notably in Jeremiah and the Psalter. It is, of course, particularly characteristic of cultic contexts.

But we turn to another illustration of the oral or spoken character of our passage. It fairly teems with particles of many different sorts, each performing its own particular function in its particular context, as our translation has attempted to indicate. No translation can reproduce the nuances and effects of these particles in the original Hebrew. It is unfortunate that it should be so, for it is precisely these vocables and sounds that serve to articulate the interior sequences of the successive lines and to reveal the texture of the linguistic fabric. Observe, for example, the function that is served by the deictic and climactic particle *ki* in 13 d, 16 b, and 17 c and the related word of motivation

[1] For the favourable disposition of the suzerain to his vassal and the vassal's love of his suzerain, see William L. Moran, S.J., 'The Ancient Near Eastern Background of the Love of God in Deuteronomy', *CBQ*, xxv (1963), 77–87. While the stress upon the mutuality of love is pronounced in Deuteronomy, it would seem to be implied here in the gracious gift of 'finding favour in his eyes'. See below, p. 177, n. 1.

למען in 13*c*; also the function played by גם in the opening
and closing speeches (12*h* and 17*b*) and by the conditions אם
נא and אם אין in 13*a* and 15*b*. A closely related feature of the
first consequence is the presence of assonance; what the eye
may often fail to discern, the ear can grasp at once. If the
passage is to be 'understood', it must be heard. The repetitions
of key-words and key-sentences produce their own euphony or
sonorous effect, but, more than that, they reveal where the
stresses lie. Finally, it is the pervasive stress upon the speaking
that is going on line after line which gives special force to the
final assurance of Yahweh to his mediator: 'This very word that
you have spoken I will perform.'

We turn now to a somewhat closer scrutiny of our text. It is
surely a continuing and unbroken dialogue from beginning to
end. Yet, despite this continuity and brevity, it falls into two
divisions with two subdivisions each. In each the plea of the
mediator is followed by a divine assurance or promise (12–13
and 14, 15–16 and 17). The pleas are of about the same length
and also contain two parts, as is clear in the first plea from the
striking and significant ועתה (13*a*) and in the second by the
direct and climactic question introduced by הלוא (16*d*), which
should not be emended. The divine responses are very short
as we should expect from such cultic and oracular formulations. We may articulate the structure, then, somewhat
as follows:

Introduction: Depart from here!   33: 1*a*
1. The mediator's plea and the divine response: 33: 12–14
   a. The mediator's plea: 12–13
     (1) 'You have not let me know the one who will lead us.'   12
     (2) 'Let me know your ways.'   13
   b. The divine response: My Presence will go.   14
2. The mediator's plea and the divine response: 33: 15–17
   a. The mediator's plea: 15–16
     (1) 'How will it ever be known?'   15
     (2) 'Is it not in your going with us?'   16
   b. The divine response: the Word fulfilled.   17

The opening plea of verses 12–13 begins and ends impressively.
The initiating call to attention expressed by the imperative of

the verb ראה[1] is followed dramatically by the motif which lies within and behind all the words of the pericope: 'Consider! [or Realize!] you say to me, "Bring forth this people"' (12 *bc*). The concluding line (13 *c*) returns superbly to the opening motif and is fashioned in much the same way: by the repetition of the imperative, by bringing its focus to bear again upon the people, thus echoing the central affirmation of the old covenant credos and confessions: 'Consider that this nation is your own people.' It should occasion no surprise that the major motif of the people is repeated three times in the second plea and in a singularly effective manner (16 *c*, *e*, *f*).

Particularly revealing is the threefold use of the second person singular pronoun in addressing Yahweh: אתה אתה אתה. Then follows at once at the turning point of the plea the adverbial ועתה. The assonance is striking, both because of the threefold repetition of the personal pronoun, and more especially because of the assonant ועתה at the opening of the second part of the plea (13 *a*).[2] It is in this manner that the crucial issue is brought home and with remarkable effect. Further, the function of the conditional formulations in each division, i.e. within the pleas, deserves special notice. The first appears immediately after the ועתה, אם נא (13 *a*), the second at the very beginning אם אין (15 *b*). These conditional formulations are noteworthy because they

---

[1] Compare Gen. 27: 27; 41: 41; Exod. 7: 1; 31: 2; 33: 12; and especially Deut. 1: 8, 21; 2: 24; 3: 27; 11: 26; 30: 15 and often.

[2] See André Laurentin, 'Wᵉ'attah-Kai nun. Formule caractéristique des textes juridiques et liturgiques (à propos de Jean 17, 5)', *Biblica*, XLV (1964), 168–97. Note the observation on p. 174: '*Kai nun* est une formule presque technique dans la langue d'Israël; or cela apparaît très tôt, peut-être même avant l'écriture.' While I am somewhat dubious about the connection between 33: 7–11 and 12–17, which Laurentin stresses, I am in accord with his understanding of the nature of the speech as liturgical (p. 184). Note his concluding comment concerning the importance of the word 'and now': 'c'est une expression très forte, avec des résonnances émotives qui la porte aux extrêmes, enthousiasme ou détresse, acceptation ou refus, autorité ou indignation' (p. 194). See also the valuable treatment by H. A. Brongers in *VT*, XV (1965), 289–99. Both Laurentin and Brongers recognize the strategic role the word plays in biblical compositions: 'Innerhalb der Rede bildet es den Wendepunkt' (Brongers, p. 298). See too the writer's discussion in 'The Form and Structure of the Covenantal Formulations', *VT*, IX (1959), 347–65 and Klaus Baltzer's *Das Bundesformular* (Neukirchen, 1960).

appear in profusion not only in the Old Testament legal and covenant texts, but also in the treaties and laws of the peoples of the ancient Near East.[1] One may query, further, whether the apodoses of the two conditionals are not meant to bear some connection with each other since Moses' request to know Yahweh's ways that he may know him (13b) may possibly refer specifically to the question uppermost in his mind, the leading forth from Mount Sinai (15c).

The response of Yahweh to the earnest plea of Moses (14) is in the manner of early oracular and theophanic utterance:[2]

פני ילכו

והנחתי לך

'My Presence will go,[3] and I will give you rest.'[4] Despite the

---

[1] See the writer's discussion in the essay referred to above. The importance of the conditionals in treaty or covenant formulations has received much attention since then, most notably in R. Frankena, 'The vassal-treaties of Esarhaddon and the dating of Deuteronomy', *Oudtestamentische Studiën*, XIV (Leiden, 1965), 189–200.

[2] Hermann Gunkel, *Die Kultur der Gegenwart*, Teil I, Abteilung VII. *Die orientalischen Literaturen*, 'Die israelitische Literatur', pp. 83 f. See also Claus Westermann, *Basic Forms of Prophetic Speech*, trans. by Hugh Clayton White (Philadelphia, 1967), pp. 24 f.: 'Prophetic speech begins chiefly with short utterances.' 'The basic unit of prophetic speech is the short saying, the short single saying which is in itself independent.' This would apply *mutatis mutandis* to all early oracular utterances.

[3] The nuance of פנים as literally 'face' or 'countenance' should not be lost. It indeed signifies Yahweh himself and is thus employed as synecdoche. See A. R. Johnson, 'Aspects of the use of the term פנים in the Old Testament', *Festschrift Otto Eissfeldt* (Halle, 1947), pp. 155–60. See *Textual Comments* above for LXX and Vulgate. Luther retains the anthropomorphism 'Angesicht' as does Martin Buber 'Antlitz'. But see his *Moses* (London, 1946), p. 155: 'That God's "face" goes with means... that Yhvh goes ahead of the people in order to overthrow foes who meet them on the way; for which reason Moses also talks in this connection of the impression on the world.' AV and RSV both render פנים by 'presence', which seems to the writer the best way to preserve the original denotation of the word and its use in the theophanic or covenant cult.

[4] The promise of 'rest' does not refer so much to 'resting places' (*contra* KBL, p. 602 and Beyerlin, *Origins and History of the Oldest Sinaitic Traditions*, p. 109) as protection from annihilation. Cf. von Rad, *Old Testament Theology*, I, 288: 'Jahweh himself protects his people from this annihilating encounter, and takes precautions in order that his design to "give Israel rest" (Exod. 30: 14) may achieve its end.'

admitted awkwardness, it is doubtful whether we should resort to emendation or addition. The words are meant as oracular (note 2'2' metre! cf. 33: 1). Moses replies:

אם אין פניך הלכים
אל תעלנו מזה

'If your Presence will not go, do not make us go forth from here.' The repetition of Yahweh's words is characteristic of dialogical cultic style and argues for the retention of the Massoretic Text in both instances. Be that as it may, the words of Yahweh and the reply of Moses, the one at the close of the first division, the other at the beginning of the second, appear in the middle of the pericope and strike its dominant keynote. The issue at stake here, as we have been at pains to point out, is of supreme moment. This accounts for the passionate urgency of the mediator's plea.[1] Will Yahweh indeed leave his holy habitation on Mount Sinai and accompany his people to Canaan and remain with them there as their God? That would seem on the face of it to be utterly impossible and unprecedented according to the prevailingly spatial mentality of the peoples of the ancient Near East for whom the gods have their own provinces and holy places and for whom land and people are psychically related.[2]

[1] Noth in his commentary on *Exodus* says, 'The demanding and forceful tone in which Moses speaks to Yahweh is striking' (p. 256). That it is forceful and striking is certainly true, but it is hardly demanding. It is rather urgent and passionate. On the other hand Noth is one of the few scholars to recognize the true force of Yahweh's words in verse 14, which is quite generally understood as a question (cf. *GK*, §150a). Cf. Noth, *ad loc.*: 'The present wording does not favour this conception. The text rather means that the first, brief promise of Yahweh, which is to give Moses "rest" (verse 14b should be understood in this simple way) is still not a sufficient reply to Moses' urgent request and that he requires a specific confirmation over and above this.'

[2] Beyerlin, *Origins and History of the Oldest Sinaitic Traditions*, pp. 101 f.: 'The passion with which the argument is conducted and with which the narrative of the Midianite Ḥobab ben Reʿuel is abruptly set aside is only intelligible against the background of a burning, existing problem. Obviously this consisted in establishing and getting recognition for the conviction that the God who once revealed himself fully and for the first time on *Sinai* was now present with his people in *Canaan* also.' Cf. also pp. 161 f.: 'Accordingly, the tradition of Exod. 33: 12b–17, the nucleus

It was precisely Yahweh's deed of deliverance in the alien land of Egypt that had evoked Jethro's great confession: 'Now I know that Yahweh is greater than all gods because he delivered the people from under the power of the Egyptians' (Exod. 18: 11). But for him to leave Sinai to accompany them to Canaan and to establish his residence there was quite another matter (cf. Judg. 5: 4; Hab. 3: 3 ff.). It is indeed probable that for a long time throughout the pre-exilic period pilgrimages were made to Sinai, as we see most clearly in the case of Elijah (1 Kings 19: 3 ff.).[1] The momentousness of Yahweh's words to Moses, 'My Presence will go', is clearly reflected in Deut. 4: 32–40 (especially verse 37; cf. Isa. 63: 9). It is no wonder that Moses as the mediator of the covenant should press the issue 'If your Presence will not go, do not make us go forth from here' (15).

The pulsebeat of destiny throbs through the words. The future of Israel lies in the balances of the divine decision. That this is by no means an overstatement is conclusively demonstrated by the powerful lines that follow. The solemnity and portentousness of the conditional are to be discerned in the extraordinary

of which certainly goes back to the early history of Israel and which strives to establish that the God of Sinai did, in fact, go up in person with his people to Canaan (pp. 99–112), remained alive right up to the period of the monarchy, and indeed it was first given literary expression in the later Yahwistic source (pp. 100 f.). In connection with Exod. 33: 12 b–17, and 33: 3 b–4, 5–6, the Jehovistic redaction has been at pains to establish that Yahweh did not only then appear at Sinai (34: 5 f.) but thanks to Moses' prayer of intercession (pp. 92 f.), appears even now in the midst of a stiff-necked people in Canaan and shows himself as Israel's living God' (pp. 90–8, 110 f.). For the wider implications of the פנים or Face of God in the history of religions, see especially Mircea Eliade, *Cosmos and History: the Myth of the Eternal Return* (New York, 1924), pp. 102 ff. on 'History Regarded as Theophany'.

[1] Martin Noth, 'Der Wallfahrtsweg zum Sinai (Num. 33)', *PJB*, xxxvi (1940), 5–28. Cf. R. E. Clements, *God and Temple: the Idea of the Divine Presence in Israel* (Oxford, 1965), p. 27: 'Perhaps there were some in Israel who had thought of Yahweh as bound in some way to Sinai, so that the migration to Canaan was a departing from him. Consequently, it was out of a certain religious tension and struggle that the belief gained firm hold that Yahweh had given his word to Moses that his presence (Heb. *panim*) would be with his people. The way in which this word was fulfilled was given outward expression in the cult and worship of Israel.'

terseness of the protasis and apodosis. The crucial significance of the words is further confirmed by the immediately following extended motivation in two parts of three cola each (16*abc* and 16*def*). Even more important, each part contains an urgent question directed to Yahweh. The first is formulated in an unusual, though by no means unprecedented fashion: 'in what way will it ever be known?' Then follows the election motif, the choosing of Moses as mediator and of the people as the people of the covenant. It is precisely the interrogative form spoken in this way to Yahweh that gives the line its weight. But the second question is even more direct. Moses is reminding Yahweh of the supreme meaning of this holy hour: 'Is it not in your going with us (here explicitly for the first time and surely intentionally so!) that we shall be distinguished from every people on the face of the earth.' We have encountered this same boldness of the mediator before in Moses' reply to Yahweh's demand in 33: 12. The ambulatory motif, so pregnantly stated in Yahweh's two words in 14*b*, so urgently repeated in Moses' laconic response (15*b*), here turns into a breathless climax. Israel here emerges upon the stage of world history as the people whose God is Yahweh, the One who will go to the Land of Promise. The same motif is in all probability present in Abram's migration (Gen. 12: 1–3) and on the occasion when David the King wishes to build a temple to Yahweh (2 Sam. 7: 4 ff.).

But surely this is not our finale. The intercession demands an answer. Yahweh will set his seal on the fateful words that have been spoken by his mediator, his imprimatur on his words, his confirmation of his assurance. Again, as in verse 14, he takes to himself Moses' perplexity and bafflement and transmutes them into decision and promise. The opening *formula citandi* is particularly impressive here: 'And Yahweh said to Moses' (cf. 33: 1*a* and 12*a*). But, what is more, Yahweh has been entering into the encounter of spoken speech from the very beginning, and now brings it to its culmination: 'This very word you have spoken will I perform.' That would seem to be sufficient for Moses and for the people, but, again, as so frequently in many different types of divine pronouncements in the Old Testament, the words are followed by a weighty motivation, all the more moving because we have listened to the mediator's long motivations immediately preceding, and the words are fashioned out of the citations in the first plea (12–13).

In the foregoing discussion we have attempted to demonstrate that the composition of Exod. 33: 1 a, 12–17 has been meticulously wrought, that the major motifs and keywords have been so carefully woven into the literary fabric that it is difficult to believe that it represents anything less than a unified and coherent whole. Moreover, we need have no doubt that the stress upon the divine presence accompanying Israel was responsible for its inclusion within the complex of materials centring in the covenant at Sinai. But, more than that, it was preserved because its content focused upon the motif that is central to all worship, namely, the presence of God, for worship is only possible when and where God is believed to be present. It was not a motif that could be cavalierly taken for granted because Yahweh belonged to Sinai, it was there that he surely was present, there that he had revealed himself to his people, there that Moses had served as mediator, there that the covenant had been concluded and its stipulations set forth.

Nevertheless, if we are to penetrate more deeply into our pericope, discern the interior nature of its dialectic, gain a synoptic view of its contents, we shall see that there is a word which holds a position of pre-eminence throughout, a word to which we have heretofore done less than justice. We referred at the beginning of our discussion to the importance of the verb ידע in the Old Testament and more particularly in our present passage. In the Book of Exodus it appears frequently and often in crucial contexts, but, so far as I am aware, we shall look in vain for any passage to rival this. Within the compass of five verses, it appears six times and always, let it be remembered, in significant collocations.

How are we to explain this terminology? It is surely more than fortuitous that it should appear so profusely in so small a literary unit and always in striking contexts. We have already stressed the centrality of the covenant relationship in the large literary complexes of which our passage forms a part. The covenant associations of the word have long been recognized, not only here but frequently elsewhere in the Old Testament. In recent years, however, we have come to see more clearly than before the function that the word plays in the treaty formulations of the peoples of the ancient Near East and the close relationships they reveal to the biblical formulations. To the divine command to go forth from Sinai Moses replies, 'You have not let me know the one you will send with me'. That knowledge is necessary, but it remains undisclosed. Unless Moses knows who the leader will be, the future remains dark and ominous. But Moses presses on to another kind of knowing of which Yahweh has already given him assurance, 'I know you by name'. Here we arrive at an important juncture. Nothing is more clear than that here again, as so often in the Old Testament, knowing implies a personal relationship, indeed a very personal inward relation.[1] It is a freely-offered gift of grace on the part of the divine Suzerain to his representative and mediator. So we may render the verb best perhaps by the verb

---

[1] Eberhard Baumann, 'ידע und seine Derivate im Hebräischen', *ZAW*, XXVIII (1908), 22–41, 110–43. See especially, p. 30: 'Danach bezeichnet ידע hier im Grunde eine persönliche Verbindung, auf Grund deren ein enger Verkehr stattfindet, ein Austausch nicht nur von Wissen, sondern mehr noch von Achtung, Liebe, Fürsorge, Wohltaten, Diensten u.s.f., weshalb der ידוע eigentlich der jemand Zugehörige, danach nicht nur der Vertraute, sondern ebenso sehr der Geachtete, Geliebte, Ersehnte, Gepflegte etc. sein kann.' See further, p. 33: 'Der Sinn wäre demnach: Jahwe hat Mose mit Namen genannt und damit dokumentiert, dass Mose zu seiner Verfügung wie unter seinem Schutze steht, dass Mose von ihm erwählt und berufen sei zu ganz bestimmten Beruf. Genaueres lässt sich nicht ausmachen.' This interior understanding of the verb is supported in an illuminating way by the call of Jeremiah where the verb stands in close relation to the verb יצר, on the one hand, and to the verb הקדשתיך, on the other. We have an excellent parallel from Egypt from the stele of king Pianchi (25th dynasty, c. 751–730 B.C.), in the speech of Amun to the king: 'It was in the belly of your mother that I said concerning you that you were to be ruler of Egypt; it was as seed and while you were in the egg, that I knew you, that I knew you were to be Lord.' (M. Gilula, *VT*, XVII (1967), 114.) E. A. Speiser suggests that ידע in such contexts as ours means 'to single out', and this is surely involved in the meaning here. See his commentary on *Genesis* (Anchor Bible series, New York, 1962), p. 133 and note on Gen. 18: 19.

'to choose'.[1] Moses is to know who he is in relation to Yahweh and his people by being given the word of grace and of responsibility implied in the appointment. While we do not have exact parallels to this particular formulation, 'I know you by name', the meaning is clear. He has been singled out as a person, given his identity, released from bondage to his own knowing by the prior divine knowing. The roots of such knowing by name doubtless lie in the field of magic where the name plays a crucial role. But to be known of God is to be liberated from the coercions of magical techniques. For Yahweh to know Moses is a demonstration to him that he has found favour with him. That should be sufficient to dispel all doubt and anxiety. But Moses asks for more, and he presses his intercession on the frontiers of the divine knowing in order that he may himself live in the reciprocity and mutuality of knowing. So immediately following the decisive ועתה he seeks to clarify his situation in relationship to the momentous demand upon his life: 'And now, if I have truly found favour in your eyes, please let me know your ways that I may know you.' The human-divine dialectic is very striking. The relevant predications of the first major section of the pericope are so closely linked, indeed so closely interwoven and interlaced, that they form a remarkable sequence. But what is more, the verb appears twice in each subsection, and each pair is related to the other:

You have not let me know the one you will send with me (12 *de*)
But you have said, 'I know you by name' (12 *fg*)
Please let me know your ways (13 *b*)
that I may know you (13 *b*)

The second and fourth predications are connected with the first and third, and it is the relation of the second and fourth (where

[1] So perhaps the great majority of scholars. Compare Gen. 18: 19 (RSV): 'No, for I have chosen him (Hebrew ידע), that he may charge his children and his household after him to keep the way of the Lord by doing righteousness and justice; so that the Lord may bring to Abraham what he has promised him (Hebrew אשר דבר עליו).' Cf. also Amos 3: 2. For the expression, 'I have called you by name', cf. especially Isa. 43: 1; 45: 3–4; 49: 1 and their contexts. In this connection, see also the important discussion by William L. Moran, 'The Ancient Near Eastern Background of the Love of God in Deuteronomy', *CBQ*, xxv (1963), 77–87.

the accents surely lie) which is crucial for our interpretation. What is involved is the mutuality of the knowing relationship between Yahweh and Moses. It is a *covenantal* knowing, a knowing between Lord and servant, between King and subject, between Suzerain and vassal.[1] It is clear that Moses is the mediator here, for the climax of verse 13 *d* brings this out in a most impressive way: 'Consider that this nation is your people.'

In the second division of the pericope the word 'to know' likewise plays a central role. This is apparent again from the *precise* context of the word. After receiving the divine assurance of his accompanying Presence, Moses repeats the crucial words and makes an issue of them. First the conditional in the manner of the covenant and treaty formulations with the decisive apodosis, 'do not lead us forth from here' (cf. 33: 1 *a*^b, 12 *c*) which is followed by the moving and climactic motivation: ובמה יודע אפוא: 'For in what way will it ever be known?' (cf. Gen. 15: 8). How will it ever be 'realized' or 'recognized' that Moses is indeed Yahweh's chosen instrument, that he is indeed Yahweh's mediator? This meaning of the verb ידע is of course frequent in the Old Testament, notably in Second Isaiah and the Psalms. It may be observed in passing that it is very close to the verb ראה (cf. 12 *b* and 13 *d*) and is not infrequently used in conjunction with ראה to form a hendiadys. The following question is rather awkward, but should not for that reason be simply connected with the preceding words by such a conjunction as 'unless', for this is to dissipate the force of the interrogation. No, what we have here is a word of the deepest import and consequence. It must, therefore, retain its own independence. 'Is it not in your going with us that we will be distinguished from all other peoples on the face of the earth?' Nothing is said about a human guide, about the ark or tent of meeting, of the pillar of cloud by day and pillar of fire by night. It is in this

---

[1] As often in Hosea. H. W. Wolff, '"Wissen um Gott" bei Hosea als Urform von Theologie', *Evangelische Theologie*, xii (Munich, 1952–3), 116–68 = *Gesam. Stud. zum A.T.* (*Theologische Bücherei*, 1964), pp. 182–205, esp. pp. 193–9. On p. 197 Wolff writes of the knowledge of God as 'a summa summarum of the covenant relation'. For Baumann's criticism, see *Evangelische Theologie*, xv (Munich, 1955), 416–25 and Wolff's reply, *ibid.* 426–31.

event of the Leader going on before, the theophanic פנים present, Yahweh in his self-manifestation, that Israel will recognize her distinction from all other peoples and confess it in her holy rituals and celebrations.[1]

We have confined our study thus far to a single Old Testament passage, although we have had occasion from time to time to point to the affinities between the covenant formulations in the Old Testament, notably Exod. 19–24 (cf. also the Book of Deuteronomy), and the suzerainty treaties of the peoples of the ancient Near East. It has long been recognized by scholars that the terminology of knowing finds its parallels in not a few of the royal texts from these peoples.[2] More recently, however, H. B. Huffmon of Johns Hopkins University has demonstrated that the nature of the relationship between suzerain and vassal in the treaties is described in terms of the mutuality of knowing much as we encounter it in a substantial number of Old Testament contexts.[3] 'The most obvious technical usage of "know" is that

---

[1] This is not to deny that the presence of Yahweh is related to the ark. Some scholars believe that our pericope was at one time preceded by one of the ark, and it is also contended that our text was at one time followed immediately by the ark songs in Num. 10: 29 ff. This may well be right, but it is significant that no such reference is suggested in the pericope itself. This is, of course, what we should expect in a cultic formulation of this kind. Yahweh is *invisibly* present. See the excellent comment by Buber, *The Prophetic Faith*, p. 49: 'The paradox on which the sanctity of the ark is based (every "holy" thing is founded on a paradox) is this, that an invisible deity becomes perceptible as One Who comes and goes.'

[2] A. Zimmern in E. Schrader's *Keilinschriften und das Alte Testament* (Berlin, 1903), p. 403, and S. Mowinckel, 'Motiver og stilformer i profeten Jeremias diktning', *Nordisk Tidsskrift for Litteraturforskning* (Oslo, 1926), 257.

[3] 'The Treaty Background of Hebrew YĀDA'', *BASOR*, clxxxi (1966), 31–7. Note, for example, his citation of the treaty between the Hittite king, Suppiluliumas and Haqqanas from eastern Asia Minor: 'And you, Huqqanas, know only the Sun regarding lordship; also my son (of) whom I, the Sun, say, "This one everyone should know (*sakdu*)...you, Huqqanas know him (*apun sa[k]*)! Moreover (those) who are my sons, his brothers (or) my brothers...know (*sak*) as brother and associate. Moreover, another lord...do not...know".' In the Amarna letter from Abdi-Asirta, king of Amurri, to his suzerain Amenophis III, we have the same usage: 'may the king, my lord, know me and put me under the charge of Paha(m)nate, my (royal) governor' (p. 32). See also H. B. Huffmon and Simon D. Parker, 'A Further Note on the Treaty Background of Hebrew YĀDA'', *BASOR*, clxxxiv (1966), 36–8.

with reference to mutual legal recognition on the part of suzerain and vassal' (*op. cit.*, p. 180, n. 3 above). We have the requests of the vassal and the promises and assurances of the suzerain, just as we have with Moses on behalf of Israel. Father Moran has also called attention to the motif of the mutuality of love in the treaties and the Book of Deuteronomy (*CBQ*, xxv (1963), 77–87), and it is apparent that the knowing relationship both in our text and in other biblical passages[1] carries with it the same connotation (see p. 177, n. 1 above). It is only to be expected that we should encounter the verb in the lawsuits for breach of treaty (Isa. 1: 3; Jer. 2: 8; Hos. 4: 1 ff.) and in the prophet's call (Jer. 1: 5). It may not be without significance that some of the most illuminating parallels are associated with Abraham (Gen. 18: 19), Moses (Deut. 34: 10), and David (2 Sam. 7: 20).

In the light of the intimate associations of our text with the covenant and more especially with the mediator of the covenant, and in the light, too, of the many striking parallels from the Near Eastern treaties with their emphasis upon the relations between suzerain and vassal, it was only natural that our little liturgy should be preserved. It was not confined to the archives of Israel as among the other Near Eastern peoples, nor yet to her treasured memorabilia in the manner of antiquarians, nor to the fickle winds of time. Rather it was probably employed in the ancient sanctuaries, such as the amphictyonic centres at Gilgal, Shiloh, and Shechem, and each time the words were heard Israel could rejoice that Yahweh had indeed come from Sinai, his Presence had accompanied them on their way to Canaan, the Land of Promise, and had made his abode at some point in the history of the tradition upon Zion's holy hill. But more than that, they made contemporary the awesome event in which Yahweh had spoken the formula of ordination and induction, 'I know you by name' and the mediator had come as no other to know him and his ways.

[1] Amos 3: 2; Hos. 2: 20 (Heb. 22); 6: 3, 6; 8: 2; 13: 4, cf. 4: 1, 6; Jer. 1: 5; 15: 15 (?), etc.

13

THE ECSTATICS' FATHER

by Anthony Phillips

In searching for his father's asses, Saul left his native land of
Benjamin and entered the land of Zuph (1 Sam. 9: 3 ff.). There
he encountered the seer, Samuel, who anointed him king over
Israel (1 Sam. 10: 1). In order to confirm to Saul that this
anointing had been performed in accordance with Yahweh's
will, Samuel gave Saul a sign by forecasting three things which
would occur to him on his return to his homeland (1 Sam.
10: 2 ff.): at Rachel's tomb he would be told that the asses had
been found, at the oak of Tabor he would be given two loaves
of bread, and at Gibeah he would encounter a band of ecstatic
prophets coming down from the high place, and would join
them in their ravings, being 'turned into another man'.

1 Sam. 10: 10 ff. records the fulfilment of this last forecast. Saul
met the troop of ecstatics, and proceeded to prophesy with them.
His friends were not unnaturally astounded at his action of which
they had had no previous hint. 'What has come over the son of
Kish? Is Saul also among the prophets?', they asked. And one
of the locals added, 'And who is their father?'. It is the task of
this essay to establish to whom the word 'father' referred, and
why the questioner used this particular term to describe him.

אב ('father') is, of course, most commonly used to describe
the male parent. But even if the LXX's rendering of the local's
question 'And who is his father?' is read, there is no question
of any such meaning here. Saul's father, Kish, was well known,
and indeed reference had already been made to him by Saul's
friends (1 Sam. 10: 11). Nor if we accept the MT's rendering
of the question need we suppose that a parent is referred to, for
there is no indication that these ecstatics were natural brothers
descended from a common father. Clearly the word father is
being used in an extended sense.

In addition to one's actual father, אב can be used quite

generally of any male ancestor (Gen. 28: 13; 32: 10; 1 Kings 15: 3, 11, 24, etc.). Further, working from the analogy of a human family, it can also denote a founder of a sect or the patron or originator of a profession. Thus some two centuries after his death the Rechabites describe their founder Jonadab as their father (Jer. 35: 6), and in Gen. 4: 20 f. we read that Jabal was the father of those who dwelt in tents and had cattle, while his brother Jubal was the father of all those who played the lyre and pipe. We might then suppose that in 1 Sam. 10: 12 אב simply referred to the founder of this particular ecstatic band. In other words the local was asking whose band of ecstatics these were. But while I shall argue that אב does in fact refer to the leader of the ecstatic band, I believe that the term is here used for a different purpose. If all the local wanted to know was the identity of the ecstatics' leader, he could have waited until they had finished prophesying, and then asked them direct. In my view the local's question arises out of an urgent situation: the אב must be ascertained while the ecstatics are still raving.

In a recent discussion P. A. H. de Boer has recognized that both אב ('father') and אם ('mother') can be used as technical terms to denote a guide or counsellor.[1] But when אב and אם are used in this way they are not to be understood in the general sense of adviser, but refer to a person who is capable of performing a specialized type of counselling, namely the disclosure of information hidden from normal men. The אב does not just rely on his human intelligence to give his counsel: he possesses certain supernatural gifts which enable him to have access to information not available to others. Let us examine some occurrences of אב and אם used in this way in the Old Testament, many of which were in fact considered by de Boer in his discussion.

It is recorded that when Joseph declared his identity to his brothers, he said that God had made him 'father to Pharaoh, and lord of all his house and ruler over all the land of Egypt' (Gen. 45: 8). The event which had led to Joseph's elevation as viceroy of Egypt was his ability to interpret Pharaoh's dream

[1] 'The Counsellor', *Wisdom in Israel and in the Ancient Near East* (*VTS*, III, 1955), pp. 57 ff.

(Gen. 41: 25 ff.), an ability which was denied to everyone else
(Gen. 41: 8). It was this capacity of being able to disclose
hidden information which resulted in his designation as אב
לפרעה.[1] Thus this expression is not to be understood as a mere title
of honour, nor does it have anything to do with Joseph's age,
but it refers to the special office of royal counsellor which Joseph
held by virtue of this unique gift.[2]

In Judg. 17: 7 ff. Micah encounters a young Levite from
Bethlehem and asks him to remain with him and be to him 'a father
and a priest'. The apparent contradiction between verse 10 in
which the Levite is asked to be a father to Micah and verses 7 and
11 in which he is described as a young man whom Micah is led
to treat as if he were one of his own sons has lent support to
the theory that Judg. 17–18 is the combination of two similar
sources.[3] But in fact the passage is a unit, for the term אב does
not refer to the age of the Levite, nor is it a title of honour, but
it denotes part of the Levite's office. Besides carrying out the
sacrificial duties inherent in his role as priest, he is also to be an
אב, that is a person who can reveal information not accessible
to ordinary people.[4] To enable him to do this, Micah has had
installed in his shrine the necessary oracular instruments, the
'*ephod* (1 Sam. 23: 6 ff.; 30: 7 ff.)[5] and the *teraphim* (1 Sam.
15: 23; Ezek. 21: 26; Zech. 10: 2). Thus the Danite spies can
ask the Levite for information about the future which they could
obtain in no other way (Judg. 18: 5), and when the Danites

---

[1] de Boer, *ibid.* p. 57 points out that the phrase 'father to Pharaoh' is
unknown in Egyptian, though 'father of god' occurs with reference to a
priest. Cf. our discussion of Judg. 17: 10; 18: 19 below.

[2] de Boer, *ibid.* p. 58 refers to the Targumim which in Gen. 41: 43 sub-
stitutes for the problematic אברך the phrase אבא למלכא ('father to the
king').

[3] C. F. Burney, *The Book of Judges* (London, 1918), pp. 409 f.; C. A. Simpson,
Composition of the Book of Judges (Oxford, 1957), p. 66.

[4] This distinction is not brought out by de Boer, *Wisdom in Israel*, p. 57.

[5] In the pre-exilic period '*ephod* only refers to a garment where the verb
חגר ('gird') is used (1 Sam. 2: 18; 2 Sam. 6: 14). Thus בד ('linen')
should be omitted from 1 Sam. 22: 18 as in the LXX. It seems to the
present writer probable that the linen '*ephod* does not denote a special
cultic garment, but a small loin cloth which one would expect a child to
wear (1 Sam. 2: 18), but which was unsuitable for an adult (2 Sam. 6: 14).

took away the contents of Micah's shrine, it was only natural that they should persuade the Levite to go with them in order that he might continue in his office as both father and priest (Judg. 18: 19). Micah's *'ephod* and *teraphim* would have been no use to them without an אב to use them.[1]

Whether we are to render the title אבי־עד Isa. 9: 5 as father 'in perpetuity'[2] or as father 'about the future',[3] it would seem that we should again understand אב in the technical sense already outlined. Indeed we should note that the child whose birth is forecast had already been described as פלא יועץ ('wonder of a counsellor'). Thus these titles indicate that he is to be endowed both with an extraordinary amount of natural wisdom and also with the supernatural ability to determine things which no amount of natural intelligence however abundant could discover (cf. 1 Macc. 2: 65).

Further instances of this use of אב are probably to be found in Isa. 22: 21 where Eliakim is described as 'father to the inhabitants of Jerusalem and to the house of Judah';[4] and in the LXX version of Esther 3: 13, where the title δευτέρου πατρὸς ἡμῶν ('our second father') is applied by King Ahasuerus to his trusted counsellor Haman.

Similarly אם ('mother') can be used as a technical term to

---

[1] At first sight the phrase והוא גר־שם ('and he was a resident alien there') in Judg. 17: 7 seems to indicate that the Levite was already living in Ephraim in contradiction of the following verses, and therefore regardless of my interpretation of the term אב, the passage could still not be a unit. But it is probable that the letters of this phrase disclose the identity of the Levite which we would have expected to have been introduced into the narrative before Judg. 18: 30. Thus we would read והוא בֶּן גֵּרְשֹׁם ('and he a son of Gershom'). Cf. J. Bewer, 'The Composition of Judges, 17, 18', *AJSL*, xxix (1912/13), 271 ff.; Burney, *Judges*, p. 422. In my view Judg. 17–18 originally described the origin of the legitimate Danite sanctuary which only contained the recognized oracular instruments of the *'ephod* and *teraphim*. Later, in order to discredit this sanctuary at which Jeroboam I placed one of his golden calves, the graven image (פסל) was introduced into the story, and the account of its origin added (Judg. 17: 1–4). In this way it was shown that even the original Danite sanctuary was apostate.

[2] R. H. Kennett, 'The Prophecy in Isaiah 9: 1–7', *JTS*, vii (1906), 340.

[3] de Boer, *Wisdom in Israel*, p. 58.

[4] Cf. Elisha's role as royal counsellor to successive kings of Israel as outlined below.

denote a woman capable of obtaining information not available to ordinary persons. Thus Deborah is described as 'a mother in Israel' (Judg. 5: 7). This refers to the fact that she alone knew what the future held, and could organize appropriate action to meet it (Judg. 4: 6 ff.). Thus she could determine when to rally the troops to meet Sisera in battle, and the precise moment for the attack to begin (Judg. 4: 14).

Another instance of אם being used in this sense is preserved in 2 Sam. 20: 14 ff. Here Joab is accused of being about to destroy the town of Abel described by an inhabitant (a wise woman) as an ancient place renowned for the seeking of information not readily available—clearly an oracle town. Because knowledge which could not be ascertained normally could be gained at Abel, this town can be called אם בישראל ('a mother in Israel') (2 Sam. 20: 19).

Further, it is probable that אם can even be used in this way of a thing. Thus in Ezek. 21: 26 the phrase אם הדרך ('the mother of the way') has been interpreted as referring to a signpost which the king of Babylon had to consult.[1] Before he could be certain which way to go, he had to ascertain the special information which 'the mother of the way' possessed. The signpost was a counsellor to him in his journey. But since considerable skill was needed to interpret such signposts in the ancient Orient, the king resorted to recognized forms of divination in order to discover its hidden message.

The term אב is also used of the prophets Elijah (2 Kings 2: 12) and Elisha (2 Kings 6: 21; 13: 14). As far as Elisha is concerned we have no reason to doubt that אב is again used as a technical term. Proof of this is provided by 2 Kings 6: 12, where it is specifically stated that Elisha was able to tell the king of Israel everything which the king of Syria spoke in his bedchamber. Elisha was, therefore, much more than a clever royal adviser, for through his extraordinary powers he was able to obtain knowledge which no one else could get. This entitled him to occupy the special position of royal אב to successive kings of Israel (2 Kings 6: 21; 13: 14) to whom he was freely available for consultation, although, unlike Joseph at Pharaoh's court,

[1] de Boer, *Wisdom in Israel*, pp. 59 f.

he does not appear to have occupied any defined political post. Thus there can have been no doubt of Elisha's value to the royal house, and it is therefore not to be wondered at that Joash should regard the death of his counsellor as a major disaster for Israel (2 Kings 13: 14). It was indeed as if Elisha represented 'the chariotry of Israel and the horsemen thereof', for he could supply the king with information which would be decisive in any military encounter (2 Kings 13: 17).

Further, it appears from 2 Kings 8: 7 ff. that even Benhadad, king of Syria, recognized Elisha's supernatural power to reveal information otherwise unobtainable. Thus when he was critically ill and wanted to know whether or not he would live, he sent his envoy Hazael to inquire of Elisha whether he would recover. In other words he used Elisha as his אב. This is confirmed by Hazael's use of the term בן ('son') when he described his master to Elisha as 'your son, Benhadad, king of Syria' (2 Kings 8: 9).

2 Kings 2: 12 records that at the disappearance of Elijah, Elisha uttered the same despairing cry as that used by Joash (2 Kings 13: 14). There is, however, considerable doubt as to whether we should accept this utterance as authentic in the mouth of Elisha. Elijah was never involved in external politics in the way in which Elisha was, and, therefore, the description of him as 'the chariotry of Israel and the horsemen thereof' seems inappropriate. The title fits admirably into the context of 2 Kings 13: 14, concerned as this is with the Syrian war (2 Kings 13: 15 ff.), and accords with the position which I have shown Elisha enjoyed under successive kings of Israel, but which Elijah never held owing to the hostility of Ahab and Jezebel. It would, therefore, seem to me that since Elijah had been specifically instructed to anoint Elisha to take over his office of prophet (1 Kings 19: 16), it was evidently thought appropriate by a later compiler to transfer Joash's description of Elisha to his predecessor. Indeed this transferred exclamation may very well have been used as the basis for the introduction of the chariot of fire drawn by the horses of fire in the story of Elijah's translation (2 Kings 2: 11).[1]

It is at this point that we must introduce into the discussion

[1] Cf. J. Gray, *I and II Kings* (London, 1964), pp. 421 ff., 542.

the בני הנביאים ('sons of the prophets') referred to in 1 Kings
20: 35; 2 Kings 2: 3, 5, 7, 15; 4: 1, 38; 5: 22; 6: 1; 9: 1; Amos
7: 14. Now it is clear from this last reference that these persons
fulfilled a role distinct from that of the ordinary נביא ('prophet')
for Amos was able to deny that he was a member of either
prophetic group. The clue to their identity is to be found in
2 Kings 9: 1 ff. There Elisha orders one of the בני הנביאים to
anoint Jehu king, which anointing takes place in private. When
Jehu goes out to his fellow officers they ask him, 'Is all well?
Why did this madman come to you?' By referring to this
emissary from Elisha as a madman, the officers clearly indicate
that these בני הנביאים were in fact the ecstatic prophets (cf. Jer.
29: 26).[1] This is confirmed by Jehu's evasive answer to his
officers, 'You know this fellow and his talk', by which Jehu
intended them to understand that the ecstatic only spoke in
gibberish to him. In this way he hoped to side-step an awkward
question while he weighed up the situation.

Now it is clear that the word 'son' can only be used in relation
to the word 'father'. Thus the ecstatics would never have been
called בני הנביאים if there were not another prophetic personage
who acted as their 'father'. It is my belief that it is in 1 Sam.
10: 12 that we find a reference to the prophetic father, and in
the light of the foregoing discussion can answer the questions
which I posed at the beginning of my essay.[2]

Although the band of prophets coming down from the high
place of Gibeah are not described as בני הנביאים, they are
undoubtedly ecstatics who have whipped themselves up into
a prophetic ecstasy through their music. To the crowd who
watched them, their ravings were pure gibberish and of no
direct value save that they showed that divine power had fallen
upon them. An interpreter was needed if any sense were to be
made of their inspired ravings. But only a man who himself
possessed supernatural powers could fulfil this function, for as
Jehu implies (2 Kings 9: 11), no ordinary person could have
understood the ecstatic gibberish. In fact the person who was

[1] Cf. *ibid.* p. 488.
[2] de Boer, *Wisdom in Israel*, pp. 57 ff., does not consider 1 Sam. 10: 12 in
his discussion.

wanted was none other than an אב. Just as we have recognized that an אב was needed to interpret dreams (Gen. 45: 8) and to consult the oracular instruments of the *'ephod* and *teraphim* (Judg. 17: 10; 18: 19), so an אב was required to interpret the gibberish talk of the ecstatics who, as a result of their relationship to such men, came to be known collectively as בני הנביאים ('sons of the prophets') or individually as בן־נביא ('son of a prophet').[1] Thus it is my contention that the terms בני הנביאים and אב denote two prophetic offices, that of speaking in tongues, and that of interpreting them, a distinction still to be found in New Testament times (1 Cor. 14: 5, 13). The אב is not only the leader of the ecstatic group responsible for their organization (2 Kings 6: 1 f.), but is also the person through whom their ecstatic utterances, which were clearly understood to be divinely inspired, were rendered intelligible both to the ecstatics themselves, who were quite unaware of what they had uttered, and also to others who witnessed their prophesying. Here again we see the אב fulfilling his role of counsellor.

The meaning and relevance of the local's question in 1 Sam. 10: 12 now becomes apparent. Saul's friends were astonished to find him in the company of a wandering band of ecstatic prophets, and apparently acting as if he were one of them. 'Is Saul also among the prophets?', they asked. They wanted to know if the gibberish which he was uttering really showed that he had become an ecstatic. The onlookers knew that the fact that Saul was joining in the ravings of the prophetic band was by no means proof that he was himself one of them for ecstatic fervour was infectious. Bystanders in the excitement of watching ecstatics prophesying could themselves temporarily become delirious and join them in their ravings. Thus in 1 Sam. 19: 20 f. we read how three successive batches of Saul's messengers were so overwhelmed at seeing a company of ecstatics prophesying that they themselves joined in the group's activity. Yet there is no suggestion that these men thenceforth became ecstatics. Their prophesying was only a temporary phenomenon. It was this situation which was in the minds of Saul's friends: had Saul

---

[1] On the plural form בני הנביאים, see J. G. Williams, 'The Prophetic "Father"', *JBL*, LXXXV (1966), 348.

really become a genuine ecstatic, or had he just been temporarily overcome with ecstatic fervour? Only one person could determine this, namely the group's אב, for only he could interpret the gibberish which Saul was uttering and judge its significance. Hence the importance and urgency of the local's question, 'And who is their father?' The group's אב must be found while the ecstatics and Saul were still raving. But their אב was not found (1 Sam. 10: 13). Saul's ecstatic experience was not intended for his friends' benefit but for his own, for through it he knew that Yahweh had confirmed Samuel's act in anointing him king.

Thus the local's question cannot be understood as a contemptuous aside indicating that the ecstatics ancestry was unknown or lowly.[1] It is an integral part of the narrative and provides us with another instance of אב used as a technical term to denote someone with supernatural powers of interpretation. Indeed there is nothing at all in 1 Sam. 10: 10 ff. to indicate that at this time the ecstatics were held in contempt. Their ravings were a recognized form of divine manifestation, though they needed an interpreter if their utterance was to be comprehended.[2]

Further, there is no ground at all for the view that the בני הנביאים were the sons of prophetic fathers, and that therefore their office was hereditary.[3] Anyone could become a member of an ecstatic band regardless of his ancestry, though in doing so he would acquire a new אב, the leader of the group who was able to interpret their ecstatic utterances.

It would seem from the local's question in 1 Sam. 10: 12 that the ecstatic troop which Saul encountered was not resident at Gibeah, but had evidently come there to take part in some cultic function at the sanctuary, for otherwise their אב would

---

[1] Cf. A. Bentzen, *Introduction to the Old Testament*, 1 (Copenhagen, 1958), 168; J. Lindblom, *Prophecy in Ancient Israel* (Oxford, 1962), p. 74; A. R. Johnson, *The Cultic Prophet in Ancient Israel* (Cardiff, 1962), p. 16; L. H. Brockington, 'I and II Samuel', *Peake's Commentary on the Bible* (rev. ed., London, 1962), p. 322*b*; W. McKane, *I and II Samuel* (London, 1963), pp. 75 f., 122; H. W. Hertzberg, *I and II Samuel* (English translation, London, 1964), p. 86.

[2] But cf. below our discussion of Jehoshaphat's question in 1 Kings 22: 7, and consider 2 Kings 9: 11.

[3] A. Guillaume, *Prophecy and Divination among the Hebrews and other Semites* (London, 1938), p. 124.

have been known. However, we can reasonably conjecture that since Samuel evidently organized the encounter between Saul and the ecstatic band, he was in fact their אב, as he certainly seems to have been to the ecstatics gathered at Naioth in Ramah over whom he presided (1 Sam. 19: 20).[1]

It is impossible to be dogmatic about the organization of these ecstatic groups. The local's question in 1 Sam. 10: 12 'And who is their father?' would seem to indicate that at this time there were a number of such groups each organized under their own אב.[2] But in 2 Kings 4: 38 ff. and 6: 1 ff. we find Elisha apparently acting as אב to two different groups, unless we are to understand the Gilgal of 2 Kings 4: 38 to refer to Gilgal near Jericho.[3] But it has, however, been argued that under Elijah the ecstatic prophets became organized on a national basis under a single אב.[4] The evidence for this is contained in 1 Kings 19: 15 f. where Elijah is commanded to anoint Hazael to be king over Syria, Jehu to be king over Israel and Elisha to be prophet in his stead, which must, it is felt, also refer to the transfer of leadership over an organized group.[5]

We know very little about the lives of these ecstatic groups, though it would seem probable that they had some association with the more important shrines (2 Kings 2: 3, 5; 4: 38). Evidently these ecstatics lived together (2 Kings 6: 1 f.), and ate at a common table (2 Kings 4: 38), though they could be married (2 Kings 4: 1). While the ecstatic group dwelt together under the leadership of its אב (2 Kings 6: 1), it would seem that the latter was by no means obliged to remain with them, but could come and go as he pleased (2 Kings 4: 38).[6]

[1] In this case Saul seems to have been overcome with ecstatic fervour even before he encountered the ecstatic group (1 Sam. 19: 23). 1 Sam. 19: 24 b may in fact be a later addition to the narrative, the purpose of which would seem to have been to show that Saul was still subject to Samuel (cf. 1 Sam. 13: 8 ff.; 15: 17 ff.) rather than to account for the origin of the proverb. However, Saul's moods no doubt encouraged its repetition. Cf. above our discussion of the same cry in 2 Kings 2: 12 and 13: 14.

[2] It is possible that the sons of the old prophet at Bethel (1 Kings 13: 11 ff.) were not his natural sons, but members of his ecstatic group.

[3] Cf. Gray, I and II Kings, p. 448.   [4] Williams, JBL, LXXXV, 344 ff.

[5] Cf. our discussion of 1 Kings 22: 10 ff. below.

[6] Cf. Gray, I and II Kings, p. 459.

In my view the Old Testament does contain one example of
an אב actually interpreting the delirious ravings of an ecstatic
group. Thus in 1 Kings 22: 10 ff. (2 Chron. 18: 9 ff.) we read
that about four hundred ecstatics were prophesying before the
kings of Israel and Judah when Zedekiah the son of Chenaanah
came forward and interpreted their ravings both for the kings
and for the ecstatics themselves. Their utterances had indicated
quite unequivocally that Ramoth-gilead should be attacked.
Once the ecstatics knew what it was that they had been crying
in their delirious ravings (1 Kings 22: 10), they gave specific
voice to it (1 Kings 22: 12).[1]

That Zedekiah acted as an אב to these ecstatics is confirmed
by 1 Kings 22: 24, for when the content of their message was
challenged by Micaiah, it fell to Zedekiah to defend it, since
he was responsible for its interpretation. Through the special
gift of the spirit he had been able to act in his role of אב and
ascertain the meaning of the ecstatic gibberish. How dare
Micaiah question his competence: was he not recognized as the
group's אב?[2] But in fact Micaiah does not deny that Zedekiah's
interpretation was correct: it is the ecstatics who have let him
down for, through divine intervention, 'a lying spirit' has been
put into their mouths (1 Kings 22: 22 f.)—in other words they
gave him the wrong information.

Thus Jehoshaphat asked his question about another prophet
(1 Kings 22: 7) because he wanted a second opinion as to
whether or not the kings ought to attack—and not a four
hundred and first! Perhaps we see reflected here a different
appreciation of the value of the ecstatics. While Ahab was content to rely on the interpretation of their ravings for guidance,
Jehoshaphat, at least by implication, seems to seek a prophet
who can give a direct revelation of God's will.[3]

Finally, we must consider how אב and אם came to be used as
technical terms for the counsellor who could reveal information

---

[1] It would seem to me that verses 10–12 are to be understood as an expansion
of verse 6, and properly belong before verses 7–9, which latter verses lead
directly to verse 13.

[2] Zedekiah certainly seems to have been sole אב to all the ecstatics of Israel
(see above).

[3] Cf. Gray, *I and II Kings*, pp. 399 f., and note 2 Kings 3: 11 ff.

not obtainable by ordinary men. It would seem to me that ultimately this must derive from the role of Hebrew parents in educating their children (Prov. 1: 8; 6: 20). Now as the Book of Proverbs shows this education was not concerned with the 'three Rs': indeed in ancient Israel it is probable that the ability to read and write did not extend outside the professional scribes and ruling class. Rather the Hebrew parents sought to teach their children the means whereby they might lead an ordered life—in other words that knowledge which the Hebrews called wisdom. This was not something which the child could learn naturally by observation, like picking up his father's trade: it had to be specially revealed to him. The parents were not just instructors or advisers: they were interpreters of the hidden things of life which any child needed to know if he was going to find happiness.

Similarly the Hebrew sage, like a wise parent, fulfilled the same educative role in relation to his pupils, whom he termed his sons, by passing on to them that wisdom which had been specially entrusted to him, but had been hidden from other men.

In my view it follows from this that any person who possessed special powers of wisdom in being able to reveal information which was hidden to ordinary men came to be known as אב or אם—whether he was the interpreter of a dream, could consult the oracular instruments, knew facts about the future, or could interpret ecstatic utterances.[1]

---

[1] I propose to leave open for discussion the question of a possible relationship between this technical use of אב and the magical term אוב ('necromancer'). If we are to understand אוב as referring to the medium who could obtain information from the spirits of the dead, then clearly this term is being used in a manner analogous to the technical use of אב outlined in this essay. It would seem that the necromancer was able to describe the spirit (אלהים) whom he conjured up, but who was invisible to others (1 Sam. 28: 13 f.), and then made the spirit appear to speak through the art of ventriloquism (1 Sam. 28: 15 ff.; Isa. 8: 19; 29: 4). Cf. W. Robertson Smith, 'On the forms of divination and magic enumerated in Deut. 18: 10, 11', *JPhil*, xiv (1886), 127 f.; S. R. Driver, *Deuteronomy* (Edinburgh, 1902), pp. 225 f.; H. Schmidt, 'אוב' (*Marti Festschrift*), *ZAW*, xli (1925), 253 ff.; M. Vieyra, 'Les noms du "mundus" en hittite et en assyrien et la pythonisse d'Endor', *Revue Hittite et Asianique*, xix (Paris, 1961), 47 ff.; H. A. Hoffner, 'Second Millennium Antecedents to the Hebrew 'ÔB', *JBL*, lxxxvi (1967), 385 ff.

14

BIBLE EXEGESIS AND FULFILMENT IN QUMRAN

by Bleddyn J. Roberts

Despite the abundant literature of the scrolls, there are still aspects of their study which repay fresh investigation, and in the present article an attempt is made to examine the extent to which the acknowledged preoccupation of Qumranites with scripture influenced the life and history of the Community. It is contended that an unusual aspect of biblical interpretation emerges which makes 'exegesis' appear in a form rather unfamiliar to us, but which, because it is historically authentic, needs to be considered anew alongside the more conventional forms of biblical interpretation. As a by-product, it will be suggested here that in the New Testament, too, traces of a similar exegesis are to be found which might influence our understanding of the gospel story, or at least draw attention to an unusual dimension in exegesis. It is an interpretation essentially different from what is sometimes known as *eisegesis*, where the Old Testament is regarded, frequently by forced symbolism, as illustrating the New. Our concern is to show that the Old Testament, again sometimes by forced exegesis, has directly influenced the New.

The basis of the argument, however, lies in the Qumran Community, and the commonly recognized fact that its history and teaching were developed on an essentially biblical basis. It is a feature which implies a far-reaching control by Scripture, and even limits our reconstruction of the Qumran way of life, especially in that our definition of the Community rests on the basic fact that they were 'Bible people'. The Bible was their concern and constituted their whole being.

One immediate effect was that as a community they were self-sufficient and self-contained, and this is the aspect which emerges forcibly when we look—as we should more often than is customary—at the ruins of the settlement at Qumran. The thousands of visitors to the site immediately comment on the thick and well-constructed walls, the long conduit and the substantial cisterns for the water supply, the orderly layout of the rooms, the farmstead and the cemetery nearby—all these features point to a well-organized and successful community. It is suggested here that such an establishment is quite consistent with a community who deliberately formed themselves into 'the people of God' and regarded themselves as the embodiment of a unique identification with the divine oracle. The large number of coins found at Qumran testify to an active commercial life, but the members simply used the currency for their normal needs, just as they used their strongly fortified settlement for normal defensive purposes and their well-planned rooms for normal living and the practice of piety. There was a normality about their circumstances that accounts for the fact that the scrolls dwell only on the abnormally high spiritual level of their way of life. But it also means that as a community they were wholly turned in on themselves, and it was their preoccupation with the Bible that alone saved them from becoming absorbed in themselves. The Bible had taught them to live vicariously; and they achieved this by concentrating on their own holiness. And it is this feature that made them an abnormal people.

Our concern is to examine the way in which the Community used the Bible as a basis for their whole way of life, and to consider how the application inevitably introduces a unique approach to the understanding of Scripture. Three features in the scrolls will serve to illustrate the point.

First, the titles given to the officials reveal that the Community was completely Bible controlled. All the officers were known by biblical titles; not once is any officer referred to by his personal name. משכיל (the Interpreter), it has been suggested,[1] was used in a professional sense even in the Old Testament writings of the post-exilic period. In the book of

[1] Cf. G. Vermes, *The Dead Sea Scrolls in English* (Pelican, London, 1962), pp. 22 ff. The idea had also occurred to the present writer quite independently.

Daniel it seems to have a technical usage, for example when Daniel was pondering on the meaning of Jeremiah's prophecy of seventy years, 'the man Gabriel' came to give him the interpretation להשכיל.[1] Likewise in chapters 11–12[2] the משכילים evidently form a professional class, albeit vulnerable to flattery. The Chronicler's usage[3] again reminds us of the same technical explanation; and the משכיל Psalms likewise. Whether the usage in Proverbs can be included is a moot point. The obvious gloss in Amos 5: 13 provides a further good instance of the way the משכיל functioned.

Other titles in the Community demonstrate more clearly their biblical derivation. מבקר, as the lexica show, was always a priestly officer, and its attribute of 'discerning between good and evil' in Lev. 27: 33 is almost parallel with the main trends of the long description of the office in the Zadoqite Documents.[4] Likewise, the פקיד of the scrolls is seemingly indistinguishable from the מבקר, just as in the Old Testament. Finally, the scrolls' דרש התורה, 'the Seeker of the Law', does not lack antecedents in the Old Testament.

Despite the basic similarity, however, it would be misleading to assume that the offices in the two literatures are to be thought of as identical, or that there was even a historical continuity between them. The fact that the scrolls describe the functions of each office at some length suggests that there was a deliberate departure from the traditional roles. The titles were derived from the Old Testament, and the function was largely similar, but this might mean simply that the title and role etymologically fitted each other. The character of each office (and consequently the nature of the exegesis) was defined according to the special requirements of the Community itself. Consequently, we conclude that just as the actual home of the Community at Qumran indicates self-containment, the Community, too, regarded itself as independent of the contemporary situation and trends in Judaism.

Two further titles, of particular importance to the scrolls,

---

[1] Dan. 9: 1–2, 21 ff. [2] Dan. 11: 33–5; 12: 3, 10.
[3] Cf. Vermes, *The Dead Sea Scrolls, loc. cit.*
[4] CD 13: 7 ff.

need to be introduced into the survey, namely the Zadoqites and the Teacher of Righteousness.

The Community called themselves בני צדוק, and the title has caused considerable controversy mainly because of the obvious differences between them and the Sadducees. It is here suggested that by dealing with this title in the same way as the others mentioned above a possible solution might be achieved. First, the title is an Old Testament one, and Ezek. 40: 46[1] immediately springs to mind. Such an appelation would suit the Community quite admirably. Further than this, however, we cannot go in pursuit of any speculation about a historical association with any בני צדוק known from any other source, because the Community thought of itself, and only itself, as the Elect of God. It was quite immaterial to them that another body of people in Judaism claimed descent from Zadoq; they interpreted the Bible according to their own canons.

Likewise, the Teacher of Righteousness, the founder of the Community, derives his title from the Old Testament. מורה as teacher is attested in Prov. 5: 13, and the whole context of Isa. 30: 20 fits in well with the Teacher of the scrolls. Regarding צדק this is not the first time that the suggestion is made that by means of the title the connection between the Teacher of Righteousness, the founder of the Community, and the בני צדוק, is stressed. Against the background of the whole corpus of Qumran writings, however, it must be urged that מורה הצדק was a title in which the personality of the founder had been wholly absorbed, and consequently the seemingly endless speculation about his identity is misguided, or, at least, irrelevant for the real understanding of the Qumran story. As with all other Qumran officials, the Teacher of Righteousness was no individual in our sense but a functionary who filled a role presaged by Scriptures. Anonymity, in this context, was the result of complete surrender to the control of Scripture, and is basic to our understanding of the scrolls.

By the same token, the enemies of the Community were, to them, not historical people or peoples, but the actual per-

---

[1] 'Who alone among the sons of Levi may approach the Lord to minister to him.' Cf. also Ezek. 44: 15, which is actually quoted in CD 4: 1.

sonifications of their biblical prototypes. We have become obsessed with the desire to identify the Kittim, the Wicked Priest and the other wicked ones with historical figures, but to the Community they were enemies because their wickedness had been predicted by the divine oracles, and it was important that they should be dealt with according to the oracles, so that the word of God should be fulfilled. By becoming over-concerned about their 'historicity' we might be losing sight of the real significance of the scrolls. What we have here is the literature, the actual self-expression, of a people who regarded themselves, and everything surrounding them, as the embodiment of the fulfillable Word of God. It is this that explains the essential and inevitable anonymity of everyone who figures in the scrolls.

Secondly, just as personalities were swallowed up in biblical identification, so were events and happenings. Two of the scrolls contain passages capable of being called historical, but the fact that they are so widely debated again suggests that they are hardly 'historical' in any conventional sense. The passages form parts of the Zadoqite Documents and the פשר scrolls, particularly the Habakkuk scroll.

The Zadoqite Documents begin with a brief account of what might be called the origins of the Community.[1] It refers to 'the period of wrath, three hundred and ninety years after he had given them into the hand of King Nebuchadnezzar of Babylon'. There is general agreement that the basis of this passage is the 390 days referred to in Ezek. 4: 5. But the text proceeds to say[2] that 'for twenty years they were like blind men groping for the way' and thereafter God raised for them a Teacher of Righteousness. It has been suggested that the number is 'historical', adduced by the author of the scroll who was contemporary. But this argument suits only one particular interpretation of the historical background, and cannot suit any other. But a further difficulty lies in the fact that such 'historicity' is out of keeping with the general character of the scrolls, and it would appear strange that the author should abruptly change from a 'schematic' calculation to actual history in one and the same passage. The alternative view is that here again the calculation is

---

[1] CD 1: 1 ff. [2] CD 1: 9.

schematic, though not specifically indicated. Out of a fairly large choice, two possible biblical sources might be mentioned. From Chronicles[1] we learn that Levites functioned from the age of twenty—and therefore twenty years of 'groping' must elapse before the Minister takes up his duties. Again from Chronicles[2] we learn that Solomon took twenty years to build the temple, which might likewise symbolize twenty years of 'groping'. The following paragraph in the scroll,[3] which describes 'the generation of the congregation of the faithless' clearly brings us back to Bible fulfilment, for 'it is the time about which it was written' and there follows a quotation from Hos. 4: 16. The biblical text provides the basis for the verdict, not an illustration of it.

We are frequently told in the Zadoqite Documents that the Community sojourned in Damascus, and, again, speculation about the 'historical context' has been rife. As far back as 1952 Professor H. H. Rowley[4] outlined a variety of diverging views put forward by scholars since the first publication of the Documents in 1910, which had been further complicated by the advent of the Qumran scrolls. But it is suggested here that once more the key to the problem lies in the Community's use of Scripture. 'Damascus' as such does not figure in any other scroll as yet published, nor is there even an indirect hint of any sojourn, or expulsion of the Community to Damascus at any stage in its history. But in the Zadoqite Documents,[5] a whole section seems to form a crux to the problem. In a discussion based on Isa. 7: 17 the text deals with apostates and believers, and this leads to a conclusion based on a passage quoted from Amos 5: 26–7. It is this quotation which actually concerns us at present. According to the scroll the verse in Amos reads 'I have exiled (or "shall exile" reading a prophetic perfect) the Sikkuth (tabernacle) of your king and the Kiyyun (bases) of your statues from my tent to Damascus'.[6] The key-terms in the

---

[1] E.g. 1 Chron. 23: 27.   [2] 2 Chron. 8: 1.   [3] CD 1: 13 ff.
[4] *The Zadokite Fragments and the Dead Sea Scrolls* (Oxford, 1952), cf. especially pp. 75 ff.
[5] CD 7: 1–8: 21.
[6] There are significant variations from the MT which show that the Interpreters, although they accepted the authority of Scripture, did not cavil at textual changes in order to make the text suit their needs.

passage, namely סֻכּוּת and כִּיּוּן are interpreted symbolically (and very artificially) in the following lines, where the whole passage is stripped of its originally condemnatory meaning. Damascus, too, is no longer a place of exile and punishment, but has become a place of refuge, where the דורש התורה functions, and ultimately brings victory. In other words, Damascus, in this particular scroll, is the biblical basis for Qumran.

One final 'historical' point. The period from the death of the Teacher, says the Document,[1] lasts until the end of all the men of war '...and will be about forty years'. In vain do scholars seek for a satisfactory historical solution to the term 'forty years' but the context of the scroll passage, provided we accept the standpoint advocated here, shows they are clearly those of Deut. 2: 14 with its tragic verdict on the wilderness period.

The next class of 'historical' scrolls is the פשר documents, particularly the Habakkuk and Nahum scrolls. The latter has gained great favour because, for once in the scrolls, there is an actual reference to a historical person, namely, Demetrius, king of Greece.[2] In view of the general anonymity of the scrolls it might appear that the occurrence is an unfortunate one for the present thesis, but in fact it does little to change the general emphasis that to the author of the פשר the Bible is a source book which has immediate relevance to the experiences and circumstances of the Community. And the present exception does not appear to require any drastic modification of the general conclusions concerning anonymity in the scrolls, for it is nowhere suggested that wherever the word 'lion' occurs in the scrolls it must necessarily refer to Demetrius, king of Greece.

The Habakkuk scroll confirms even more strongly than the other scrolls the view that פשר, both in this type of scroll and in other Qumran passages where the term is used, is concerned with a technique of interpretation rather than the provision of historical references. A good example, and, for the present purpose an important one, is provided by the פשר on Hab. 2: 1–2.[3] It says that the prophet himself did not understand his message,

---

[1] CD 20: 14 ff. [2] 1QpNah. 1: 2 f.
[3] 1QpHab, 6. 13 f.; 7: 1–4.

which had relevance for 'the last generation', but the meaning is revealed to the Teacher of Righteousness 'to whom God made known all the mysteries of the words of His servants the Prophets'. Some of the 'revelations' have a bearing on events experienced by the Teacher himself, others by the Community, and yet others are purely apocalyptic, where, e.g. the interpretation of Hab. 2: 9–11[1] relates to the 'House of Judgement', with the threat of 'fire of sulphur for the wicked'.

The historical allusions, however, often serve to show the principles of interpretation. For instance a fairly long section of the Habakkuk scroll[2] is largely devoted to a discussion of the Chaldeans (Hab. 1: 6b–13a), who are identified with the Kittim (also an old biblical title). The equating is superficial, and generally dependent on incidental verbal similarities without any consideration for the original contexts. Sometimes the equation is given an artificial twist, to include a circumstance obviously recognizable by the Community but otherwise unknown. But the point to be made here is that the equation of Chaldeans with Kittim is not consistently observed, for, where the oracle in 1: 12–13a still refers to the wicked Chaldeans, the פשר makes it an encouraging promise to the Community, who will make atonement for the wicked. There appears to be no end to the freedom which the Interpreter adopts with the original contexts, as witness the next comment which, in the Massoretic text, says of God 'Thou who art of purer eyes than to behold evil'; in the scroll it is made to refer to the Community which 'do not let themselves be led astray into lewdness during the time of wickedness'.[3]

The third part of the present argument is concerned with the extent to which the organization of the Community reveals a scriptural foundation. In one sense it is a development of the first part in which the office-bearers have scriptural titles, but the point to be made here is that the whole organization reflects the application of major biblical concepts or whole sections of Scripture to the everyday life of the community. The main source of the evidence lies in the Community Rule (1QS).

---

[1] 1QpHab. 10: 2–4.   [2] 1QpHab. 3–5.
[3] 1QpHab. 5: 7–8.

Bible exegesis and fulfilment in Qumran

The scroll obviously represents a mature stage in the history of the Community, but the impression remains that developments within it had occurred consistently, in accordance with well-established principles and there is no indication of major changes or innovations in the spiritual or historical growth of the Community.

The opening section of the Community Rule[1] adequately illustrates the point, for in it the annual admission ritual seems to be wholly explained by the Torah account of the preparation for the entry into Canaan. The משכיל instructs the members according to clearly-defined Deuteronomic principles, the admission rite reflects Deut. 27–30, and the details of the procession are according to those given in Deut. 1: 15. Within the Community, the main emphasis is on the authority of the Priests and Levites, and on the segregation of the Community from the 'wicked', both of which are again pre-eminently Deuteronomic. The pooling of property and wages seems also to reflect the Levitical prohibition to hold property (cf. Deut. 14: 29 and often). Membership of the community was prohibited until the age of twenty, as in the case of the Levites (cf. 1 Chron. 23: 27). Precedence in the assemblies, with the Priests at the head, elders second and then the rest of the people reflects Num. 11: 16–17.

A further point needs to be mentioned here. In the Zadoqite Documents and the Warfare scroll the word 'Camp' (מחנה) is commonly used for the Community, whereas in the Community Rule and the פשר scrolls the term used is Congregation (יחד). The threefold occurrence of יחד in close proximity in the Zadoqite Documents might be accounted for by the source-criticism of the manuscript, with its obvious mixture of sources.

The presence of two titles in the scrolls, מחנה and יחד, has given rise to divergent views among scholars, who insist that they refer to a variety of activities or different types of Covenanters. For instance it is argued that יחד denotes the people at Qumran whereas מחנה describes their activities outside. The theories, however, fail to satisfy an examination of the general contents of the respective scrolls, and rather reflect a desire to make the scrolls fit in with what Josephus and Philo

[1] 1QS. 1: 16; 2: 18.

say about the Essenes. But it is surely more relevant to note that the usage of the two terms, with the exception of the above-mentioned passage in the Zadoqite Documents, is mutually exclusive, and that מחנה derives immediately from the Torah designation of the people of Israel. Consequently we again find evidence of the biblical basis for Qumran terminology. The corresponding term, יחד, does not seem to be biblical, but, in view of its obvious affinities with the Greek κοινωνία, it might be set aside as a topic lying outside the scope of the present article.

The mention of מחנה draws our attention to the scroll which has special relevance for the discussion, namely the Warfare scroll, in which the term figures very prominently. As we examine the scroll the general conclusion of the present article seems to be even more strongly established than in the preceding instances, for the Scriptures provide the basis that runs throughout the document. A suggestion by Professor Yadin in his masterly treatment of the scroll[1] that 'in the light of these conclusions (concerning military service) we must re-examine the description of the "courses" in the Davidic period, as set out in I Chron. 27: 1–5', can be widened to include many other Old Testament topics. We can well re-examine, in the light of this scroll, the Old Testament teaching on the Holy War, and, extending the examination still further, the teaching of apocalyptic writing generally on the concept of Armageddon in the setting of the Holy War. Obviously, it is too large a topic to be included in the present survey, but it might well be that it could provide one of the most fruitful aspects of Qumran studies. Furthermore, throughout the scrolls as a whole we are seldom far from the concept of conflict between the Community and the wicked outside world, and any attempt to resolve the tension by means of semi-philosophical and gnostic associations will only result in explaining away the uniqueness of Qumran. The Warfare scroll teaches us about the true nature of the Community, and, of all the scrolls, it is the one most closely associated with the Old Testament. It is unfortunate that

[1] *The Scroll of the War of the Sons of Light against the Sons of Darkness* (English translation by B. and C. Rabin, Oxford, 1962), p. 83.

scholars have been side-tracked to emphasize the enigma of this
scroll and to debate whether it is actual history or apocalyptic
vision. Actually, of course, like all apocalyptic writing of this
nature, it is neither 'actual history' nor vision. Its patent affinities
with Roman military history have been established, but any
'historical situation' which might fulfil the descriptions contained in the scroll can hardly be conceived.

In general, the present survey shows that the Community's
piety was essentially based on its self-identification with the
'people of God' of the Old Testament. Every aspect, even every
detail of its order and teaching, is derived from it. Its hymns
and meditations are full of biblical phrases woven into a patch-
work more impressive in its intricate construction than in its
direct teaching. But the one element that characterizes the super-
structure to which Scripture provides the base, is the apocalyptic element. Because of the apocalyptic preoccupation, Scripture,
though a basis, is also a 'mystery' whose solution and application always need to be established along apocalyptic lines. Consequently, interpretation is concerned with the consummation
of the Holy Word, and not with its direct meaning derived from
its proper context. Scripture was oracle, and always the object
of research into its 'hidden' meaning. דרש, which in the Old
Testament is normally used for consulting the deity, or, as in
Wisdom writing for the examination of the religious virtues,
now becomes the technical term for the study of Scriptures to
discover its apocalyptic 'secrets'. And because the Community
embodied and realized the 'secrets', everything contained in
Scripture has relevance for them, and for them alone. As
already mentioned, in the Habakkuk פשר scroll,[1] it was to the
Teacher of Righteousness alone that God had made known the
real message of the Prophet, because it was he who was to
inaugurate the Community, and thereby bring about the consummation. Likewise the Community was 'the camp' of Torah
Israel, because they were the Elect of God. They were in the
wilderness to prepare the way[2] in accord with Isa. 40: 3, but
the relevance of the passage, as the context shows clearly,

[1] 1QpHab. 7: 1–2.
[2] 1QS. 8: 14.

applies not so much to Qumran and the surrounding wilderness, but to the fact that there was a 'preparation', an examination (דרש) of the Torah, for the people to observe 'according to all that is revealed from time to time...'.

Under the stress of acute apocalyptic realization and anticipation, with its tensions and terrifying immediacy, the Teacher of Righteousness instituted and probably developed a technique of biblical 'research' whereby his followers and later the Community were able to identify themselves, in all aspects of their way of life, with the fulfilment of the Scriptures.

Of course, this technique of interpretation does not exhaust all aspects of Qumran teaching, and some important elements lie outside the scope of the present article, such as the use of a divergent calendar, the significance of the few ritual exercises which were practised, and the general question of relationship with Essenism. And it is not at all clear why the Qumran scribes should have been so diligent in copying the Scriptures, and why so many of these texts varied so much. But these and other problems do not seem to invalidate the central emphasis of the present survey.

In one respect, however, it is felt that the discussion opens up further lines of study. If the case is made, then it is right to ask whether a further application to apocalyptic writings might not be justified, particularly in the New Testament which has some striking parallels with the Qumran use of the Bible. Almost at random, the following points may be chosen where the Gospel story shows a similar process of interpretation to that of Qumran. Jesus had to be conceived by the Virgin, because of the Immanuel prophecy of Isa. 7: 14,[1] and had to be born in Bethlehem because the prophet Micah (5: 2) had said so. The flight to Egypt and the return took place in order 'to fulfil what the Lord had spoken by the prophet' (Hos. 11: 1). The story of the slaughter of the Innocents is followed by the statement, 'then was fulfilled what was spoken by the prophet Jeremiah' (31: 15). Again, Jesus dwelt in Nazareth in order to fulfil the prophecy (Isa.

---

[1] Whether this parallel with Qumran suggests that, after all, it is not the LXX that is responsible for the equation is a question I would not be prepared to answer.

11: 1), 'He shall be called a Nazarene' (with a disastrously artificial exegesis). The parallel with Qumran exegesis is striking, and naturally has been exploited by New Testament scholars. But the parallel is also far-reaching, and could well constitute a problem of faith for the Christian if the Qumran-type really has its counterpart at least in part in the Gospels. The Passion story stands out as a challenge. During the Gethsemane scene, when one of the disciples drew his sword to strike the slave of the high-priest, Jesus said to him, 'Put up your sword...How then could the scriptures be fulfilled, which say that this must be?' Was Jesus setting out deliberately to 'fulfil the Scriptures' by each step he took towards and on the Cross on Calvary? It was thus that Qumran understood and applied the Scriptures. And we are repeatedly told in the Gospels that this or that event, even in the Passion story, provided fulfilment of the prophets. In the Gospel discourses we are told that Jesus had to suffer because the prophets had foretold it. He was to be raised from the dead because the prophets had taught so. Hosea (6: 2) had said, 'After two days he will revive us; on the third day he will raise us up, that we may live before him'. Is this why Christ was resurrected on the third day?

15

הוצאתיך IN GENESIS 15: 7

by J. Weingreen

It may be a platitude, though it is quite true, to say that one of the primary aims of the Old Testament scholar, in his constant study of Hebrew biblical texts, is to discover the sense which strange Hebrew words and phrases would have conveyed to the Israelites to whom these texts are claimed to have been addressed and to the later generations who read them. In attempting to ascertain the meanings of problematic Hebrew words and phrases in biblical texts scholars are now able to apply the developed technique of reference to comparative Semitic roots. In this way an impressive number of lost meanings of hitherto enigmatic Hebrew words and phrases have been restored and many textual difficulties which confronted earlier generations of scholars have been satisfactorily resolved, without having recourse to textual emendation.[1] Yet, even where this scholarly process is successfully employed, the precise sense of Hebrew words and expressions in Old Testament passages is often determined by the contexts in which they occur. In a spoken language the meanings of words are often modified by the phrasing in which they are embodied or by other words with which they are directly and immediately associated, though such fluctuations in meaning may stem from a parent root notion.

The purpose of this exercise is to go beyond the stage of noting the impact of a context upon the specific meanings of words and phrases appropriate to that context. Its aim is to demonstrate that, in special instances, a word or phrase in an Old Testament passage may have been deliberately selected by

---

[1] Though written thirty years ago the article by D. Winton Thomas on 'The Language of the Old Testament', *Record and Revelation*, ed. H. Wheeler Robinson (Oxford, 1938), pp. 374 ff., seems, to the present writer, an excellent presentation of modern scholarly methods, which still holds good today.

the writer to hint implicitly at some well-known item of information not immediately apparent from the sense, as determined by impeccable scholarly methods. Such implications,
though they may elude us, would have been immediately appre-
hended by an ancient Israelite to whom, of course, Hebrew was
the vernacular. To illustrate this kind of literary phenomenon,
whereby an allusion was meant to be conveyed by the writer
by implication, the special case of the choice of the word הוֹצֵאתִיךָ
in Gen. 15: 7 will be examined.

To prepare the way for the consideration of the theme of this
essay, it will be useful to demonstrate, very briefly, some of the
fluctuations in meaning of the verbal root יָצָא (וַיֵּצֵא) 'went out,
departed', as determined by the close association of this verb,
in both its basic Qal and its derived Hiph'il form, with nouns or
prepositions in various contexts. (1) The expression יָצָא לִפְנֵי
(lit. 'went out before') can have the meaning 'led', often in a
military sense. In 1 Sam. 8: 20 the Israelites inform the prophet
that they are determined to have a king who would govern
them and, they add, וְיָצָא לְפָנֵינוּ, which means 'and who will
lead us'. (2) The expression כָּל יֹצֵא צָבָא 'all who (were able to)
go forth to war' (RSV rendering, but the brackets are mine)
in Num. 1: 20, 22, 24, etc., simply means 'all men of military
age' and is usually applied when a census of the population is
ordered. (3) In connection with the regulations dealing with
slavery this verb, when referring to the serf, has the sense of his
being given his freedom. In Exod. 21: 2 the law lays down that
an 'Ibrî slave[1] has to serve his Israelite master for six years, but
in the seventh he is to be freed וּבַשְּׁבִיעִת יֵצֵא לַחָפְשִׁי. (4) When
this verb is used in connection with the noun שֵׁם 'name, reputation', then the sense is of a reputation being spread abroad. In
2 Chron. 26: 15 we find the expression וַיֵּצֵא שְׁמוֹ עַד לְמֵרָחוֹק—
'his fame (was) spread afar'. The Hiph'il of this verb in association with the noun שֵׁם produces, as we would expect, the meaning of a reputation spread abroad by someone. It is found, for
example, in Deut. 22: 14, in which a bridegroom who falsely

---

[1] In an article on 'Saul and the Ḥabiru', published in the *Transactions of the
World Congress of Jewish Studies, Jerusalem* (1967), I endorsed the view that
this refers to a Ḥabiru slave.

accuses his bride of pre-marital shameful conduct, is described
as one who והוציא עליה שם רע 'he brings an evil name upon
her' (RSV) or, rather, he gives her an evil reputation. (5) In
connection with trade, the Qal of this verb 'came out' (from
another country) is used to mean, in our terms, 'was imported'
and the Hiph'il 'caused to go out', 'brought out' (from the
writers' country) produces the sense 'was exported'. Both
forms of this verb are found in these senses in 1 Kings 10:
29, with reference to the importation of chariots and horses
from Egypt and their export to the Hittites and Syrians
by traders.

When this verb is used in a context of personal distress or
danger, the qal has the meaning of escaping or being delivered
from a painful situation. In Prov. 12: 13 we find the expression
ויצא מצרה צדיק, which the RSV rightly renders 'a righteous
man escapes from trouble'. The Hiph'il of this verb in such
associations has the active sense of saving, rescuing. In Ps. 18: 20
we find the line ויוציאני למרחב יחלצני, of which the literal
translation 'he brought me forth into a broad place, he delivered
me' should be modified, in view of the indication, from the
parallelism of the verse, that the first verb, like the second, conveys the notion of deliverance. However, perhaps more conclusive proof is provided by the parallel versions of Ps. 18: 49
and the same verse in 2 Sam. 22. The expression מפלטי מאיבי
'who delivered me from my enemies' in the Psalm is represented
by the variant textual reading ומוציאי מאיבי in the Samuel text.
The RSV rendering 'who brought me out from my enemies' is
surely, too literal and does not make sense. The meaning,
clearly, is the same as in the parallel text in Psalm 18. Though
the textual tradition may be different in the two versions of
this expression, the sense is the same in each. The Hiph'il
participle of the verb, describing God's practical intervention
in a dangerous situation has the meaning of saving. This
was recognized by the Targum on the Samuel version, which
rendered the Hebrew ומוציאי by the Aramaic וּפָרְקִי—'and
my deliverer'.

One of the most dramatic lines in which our verb occurs in
the Hiph'il is the introduction to the Decalogue in Exod. 20: 2

and Deut. 5: 6—אנכי יהוה אלהיך אשר הוצאתיך מארץ מצרים,
which is usually rendered: 'I am the LORD, your God, who
brought you out of the land of Egypt.' This phrasing is ideally
suited to the public recital of a sacred text in the celebration
of a special event in the history of Israel. This opening line would
have had an impressive quality in the ears of the Israelites, for
the statement of their deliverance from the Egyptian bondage
was inherent in the word הוצאתיך.

I find it curious that this very formula should have been used
in Gen. 15: 7. The scene for the formal making of a covenant
between God and Abraham opens with the statement made by
God in the following words: אני יהוה אשר הוצאתיך מאור כשדים,
which is generally translated: 'I am the Lord, who brought you
out of Ur of the Chaldeans.' One may ask whether this English
rendering conveys any sensible information at all. If this is
taken to refer to Abraham's call, then one is forced to the conclusion that the stay in Haran was an intermediate stage on his
journey, following upon his obeying the divine call and that
there is some dislocation of texts at the end of Gen. 11 and the
beginning of chapter 12. However, my impression is that this
dramatic statement does not refer to the call of Abraham at all
and that it conveyed something of a totally different nature:
first, by the correct understanding of the meaning of the verb
in this connection and, secondly, by the implication of an
allusion to a well-established story about the adventures of
Abraham. We noted earlier that this formula was used to introduce the Decalogue and that it conveyed the idea of divine
deliverance from oppression. It seems to me that the employment of this same formula to set into motion the scene of
covenant making between God and Abraham in Gen. 15: 7
was by deliberate choice and was meant to have the same
meaning. That is to say that this dramatic statement contains
the inherent allusion that Abraham had been saved from some
peril by divine intervention. The recital of this introductory line
would have reminded the Israelites of a folk tale of this theme
which, though not included in the Abrahamic saga in Genesis,
nevertheless circulated among the people.

In this connection I should like to quote an extract of an

הוצאתיך *in Genesis 15: 7*

article on Abraham, written by the late Professor Cassuto, in the first volume of *Encyclopaedia Miḵrā'it* (*The Biblical Encyclopaedia in Hebrew*).[1] He wrote:

From Scriptural writings it becomes clear that, apart from what is narrated in the Book of Genesis, there still existed an early tradition about Abraham and his family. Certainly it must have told much about Terah, about his wanderings from Ur Kasdim to Haran... References in the Old Testament point to specific traditions which had not been accepted (for inclusion) in the Torah. It is also possible that, in the later legends about Abraham which are known to us from non-sacred writings, from the Rabbinic Midrashim and from Christian and Islamic literature, are preserved the foundations of earlier traditions. Such, for example, would be the saving of Abraham from the hands of Nimrod and his title as the friend of God, which have an important place in other legends.[2]

We should test the validity of Cassuto's assertion that there are indications in scriptural passages of the currency in ancient Israel of heroic legends about Abraham which found their full literary expression and permanency in the rabbinic Midrashim.

It is remarkable that, in contrast to the elaborate accounts of the perils faced by later Old Testament heroes because of their steadfast faith and their deliverance by direct divine intervention, nothing of this nature is recorded about Abraham in Genesis. Since he is designated, not only as the father of the Israelite race, but also as the founder of their religion, one might have expected to find some reference in Genesis to the conflict between him as the champion of the true faith and a hostile heathen population. His trials at their hands and his ultimate vindication by miraculous divine deliverance would have provided the right kind of material for the theme that fortitude in one's faith, in the face of personal danger, must ultimately triumph. It may be that the compiler of Genesis considered that this theme of steadfastness in faith was amply and dramatically demonstrated in the graphic account of the patriarch's unhesitating arrangements for the sacrifice of Isaac, in unquestioning obedience to God's command. There may be a more plausible explanation for the absence of such legends in

[1] *Encyclopaedia Miḵrā'it*, ed. M. D. Cassuto (Jerusalem, 1950), p. 62.
[2] The translation from the Hebrew is mine.

Genesis, but there is reason to hold that the Midrashic account of such an experience goes back to biblical times and that this is hinted at in Gen. 15: 7.

The Midrashic account[1] describes a ruse adopted by Abraham to prove conclusively to his idol worshipping father Terah and his contemporaries the futility of worshipping idols. This involved him in the smashing of all the idols in his father's store, except the largest. This incident was urgently reported to the great King Nimrod, who ordered that Abraham be cast into a fiery furnace. The sentence was duly carried out but, to everyone's amazement, Abraham walked about in the fire unscathed. This legend is reminiscent of the trials of Daniel and his companions and also of the theme in the apocryphal account of Daniel and Bel and the Dragon. The Midrash, in its own inimitable fashion, states that the scriptural reference to this incident is to be found in the statement made by God to Abraham in Gen. 15: 7 under discussion. First, the choice of the word הוצאתיך is rightly taken to mean 'I saved you' and the word אור, found on several occasions in the Old Testament with the meaning 'fire',[2] is taken to have this meaning here, as the Targum J. indicates by rendering the Hebrew מאור כשדים in the Aramaic מֵאַתּוּן נוּרָא דְכַסְדָּאֵי, 'From the fiery furnace of the Chaldeans'.

Let us now examine this Midrashic interpretation of Gen. 15: 7 to see whether, in spite of its fanciful character, it does not, in fact, contain the germs of a realistic understanding of the text. We begin with the view that the choice of the word הוצאתיך conveyed the notion of divine deliverance from peril. Then it is to be noted that the same formula was used in Nehemiah where, in the introduction to a summary of the early history of Israel, this statement is made (9: 7): אתה הוא יהוה האלהים אשר בחרת באברם והוצאתו מאור כשדים, which, when taken literally, is rendered: 'You are the Lord, the God, who chose Abram and brought him out of Ur of the Chaldeans.' The persistent tradition of God's 'bringing Abraham out of Ur of the Chaldeans' which we find preserved in Nehemiah and the

---

[1] Genesis Rabbah 38; Koran XXI, 58 ff.
[2] E.g. Isa. 31: 9; 44: 16, etc.

adoption of the Genesis form of this statement in public recital suggests that reference is made to some positive divine action, rather than to the issuing of a command to Abraham that he should proceed to the land of Canaan. I find myself drawn to the conclusion that there is an allusion, both in the Genesis and Nehemiah texts, to Abraham's fortitude in his faith and to his deliverance by divine grace.

We may find confirmation of this conclusion from a reference to Abraham in Isa. 29: 22. In his conviction of the ultimate redemption of Israel the prophet says: 'Thus says the Lord, who redeemed Abraham, concerning the house of Jacob.' The Hebrew אשר פדה את אברהם surely suggests an occasion of the divine deliverance of Abraham. We note also that, though the verb פדה is generally translated 'redeemed', it is used in several Old Testament passages in the sense of saving as, for example, in 2 Sam. 4: 9 where David swears by God אשר פדה את נפשי מכל־צרה. The sense is, surely, 'who saved me from all adversity'. It is contended that the reference in Isa. 29: 22 would have reminded the prophet's audience or his readers of a legend which was in general circulation telling of God's special care of Abraham and of his deliverance from personal danger in an incident in which he became involved. Curiously enough, the medieval Jewish commentator Rashi comments on this phrase by adding to the words 'from Ur of the Chaldeans'. Whether or not the legend alluded to refers to the Midrashic story of Abraham and the idols, what seems to emerge is some such folk tale, which was well known in Israel.

The general conclusion of this discussion is that, in ancient Israel, folk stories about the adventures of Abraham, other than those recorded in Genesis, were in circulation and that indirect references to them are sometimes implied in biblical texts. This view suggests, furthermore, that the Midrash has a long tradition, stretching back into biblical times and that there was much Midrashic material in existence in, what we would call, the Oral Torah. Such extra-biblical folklore persisted and was ultimately given fixed literary form, with accretions and embellishments, in the Midrash.

BIBLIOGRAPHY OF THE
WRITINGS OF
DAVID WINTON THOMAS

compiled by Anthony Phillips

1932

'A Note on מחלצות in Zechariah 3: 4', *JTS*, xxxiii, 279 f.

1933

'Job's "Comforters"', *Durham University Journal*, xxviii, 276 f.
'A Note on the Hebrew Root נחם', *ET*, xliv, 191 f.
'A Note on חליצותם in Judges 14: 19', *JTS*, xxxiv, 165.
'En-dor: A Sacred Spring?', *PEFQS*, lxv, 205 f.

1934

'The Root ידע in Hebrew', *JTS*, xxxv, 298–306.
'The Meaning of the Name Hammoth-dor', *PEFQS*, lxvi, 147 f.
'The Root שנה = *saniya* in Hebrew', *ZAW*, N.F. xi, 236–8.
Review: *Myth and Ritual. Essays on the Myth and Ritual of the Hebrews in relation to the Cultural Pattern of the Ancient East* (ed. S. H. Hooke), *Journal of Egyptian Archaeology*, xx (London), 125 f.

1935

'A Note on the Hebrew Text of Judges 16: 20', *Archiv für Orientforschung*, x (Berlin), 162 f.
'The Word רבע in Numbers 23: 10', *ET*, xlvi, 285.
'The Root ידע in Hebrew, ii', *JTS*, xxxvi, 409–12.
'Naphath-dor: A Hill Sanctuary?', *PEFQS*, lxvii, 89 f.
'A Study in Hebrew Synonyms: Verbs Signifying "to breathe"', *Zeitschrift für Semitistik und verwandte Gebiete*, x (Leipzig), 311–14.
Review: *An Introduction to the Books of the Old Testament* (W. O. E. Oesterley and T. H. Robinson), *JTS*, xxxvi, 78–80.

1936

'Until the day break, and the shadows flee away', *ET*, xlvii, 431 f.
'A note on לא תדע in Proverbs 5: 6', *JTS*, xxxvii, 59 f.

Bibliography

'The Root מכר in Hebrew', *ibid.* pp. 388 f.

'The Meaning of the Name Mishal', *PEFQS*, LXVIII, 39 f.

Review: *The Old Testament: A Reinterpretation* (S. A. Cook), *The Hibbert Journal*, XXXIV, 634–8.

Review: *Le Judaïsme Palestinien au temps de Jésus-Christ* (J. Bonsirven), *JTS*, XXXVII, 85–7.

1937

'A Note on Exodus 15: 2', *ET*, XLVIII, 478.

'Notes on Some Passages in the Book of Proverbs', *JTS*, XXXVIII, 400–3.

'More Notes on the Root ידע in Hebrew', *ibid.* pp. 404 f.

'The Root שנה = *saniya* in Hebrew, II', *ZAW*, N.F. XIV, 174–6.

1938

'The Language of the Old Testament', *Record and Revelation*, ed. H. Wheeler Robinson (Oxford), pp. 374–402.

'A Note on ולא ידעו in Jeremiah 14: 18', *JTS*, XXXIX, 273 f.

Review: *Ancient Hebrew Poems* (W. O. E. Oesterley), *ibid.* pp. 422 f.

1939

The Recovery of the Ancient Hebrew Language (Cambridge).

'The Lachish Letters', *JTS*, XL, 1–15.

'A Note on לְבִי סְחַרְחַר in Psalm 38: 11', *ibid.* pp. 390 f.

'The Root אָהֵב "love" in Hebrew', *ZAW*, N.F. XVI, 57–64.

1940

'A Note on the Meaning of מתנחם in Genesis 27: 42', *ET*, LI, 252.

'A Note on the Meaning of ידי in Hosea 9: 7 and Isaiah 9: 8', *JTS*, XLI, 43 f.

'The Site of Ancient Lachish: the Evidence of Ostrakon IV from Tell ed-Duweir', *PEQ*, LXXII, 148 f.

'Some Recent Books on the Old Testament', *Theology*, XLI (London), 175–9.

Review: *Catalogue of the Samaritan Manuscripts in the John Rylands Library at Manchester* (E. Robertson), *JTS*, XLI, 58 f.

Review: *Das Hebräische bei den Samaritanern. Ein Beitrag zur vormasoretischen Grammatik des Hebräischen* (F. Diening), *ibid.* p. 60.

Review: *Das Buch Job* (F. Wutz), *ibid.* pp. 288 f.

Bibliography

Reviews: *The Psalms, Translated with Text-critical and Exegetical Notes*
(W. O. E. Oesterley) and *Psalterium ex Hebraeo Latinum* (F.
Zorell), *ibid.* pp. 289–92.
Obituary: Mr H. M. J. Loewe, *Cambridge Review*, 1 November,
pp. 78 f.

1941

'Julius Fürst and the Hebrew Root ידע', *JTS*, XLII, 64 f.
'A Note on לִיקְהַת in Proverbs 30: 17', *ibid.* pp. 154 f.
Review: *The Bible and Archaeology* (Sir Frederick Kenyon), *PEQ*,
LXXIII 30 f.
Review: *Al-Ašʿarī's Al-Ibānah 'an Uṣūl Ad-Diyānah* (*The Elucidation
of Islam's Foundation*) (W. C. Klein), *Theology*, XLII, 304 f.

1945

'Jeremiah 5: 28', *ET*, LVII, 54 f.

1946

' *The Prophet*' in the Lachish Ostraca (London).
'The Interpretation of בְּסוֹד in Job 29: 4', *JBL*, LXV, 63–6.
'Some Rabbinic Evidence for a Hebrew Root ידע = *waduʿa*', *JQR*,
N.S. XXXVII, 177 f.
'The Lachish Ostraca: Professor Torczyner's Latest Views', *PEQ*,
LXXVIII, 38–42.
'Jerusalem in the Lachish Ostraca', *ibid.* pp. 86–91.

1947

Review: *Histoire Sainte, le Peuple de la Bible* (D. Rops), *Erasmus*, 1
(Amsterdam), cols. 77 f.
Review: *The Rediscovery of the Old Testament* (H. H. Rowley), *PEQ*,
LXXIX, 56–9.

1948

'The Interpretation of Proverbs 29: 5', *ET*, LIX, 112.
'Job 37: 22', *JJS*, 1, 116 f.
'A Note on וַיֵּדַע אֱלֹהִים in Exod. 2: 25', *JTS*, XLIX, 143 f.
'Ostracon III: 13–18 from Tell ed-Duweir', *PEQ*, LXXX, 131–6.
Review: *The Legend of King Keret, a Canaanite Epic of the Bronze Age*
(H. L. Ginsberg), *JJS*, 1, 63 f.
Review: *Studies in the Book of Nahum* (A. Haldar), *ibid.* pp. 122–4.

219

Bibliography

Review: *The Alphabet: A Key to the History of Mankind* (D. Diringer), *PEQ*, LXXX, 137–45.

Reviews: *Prophecy and Tradition: The Prophetic Books in the Light of the Study of the Growth and History of the Tradition* and *Zur Frage nach Dokumentarischen Quellen in Josua xiii–xix* (S. Mowinckel), *Theology*, LI (London), 36–8.

1949

'The Root צוע in Hebrew, and the meaning of קדרנית in Malachi 3: 14', *JJS*, I, 182–8.

'A Reply to Professor H. Tur-Sinai (Torczyner)', *JQR*, N.S. XL, 192.

'A Note on בְּמַדָּעֲךָ in Eccles. 10: 20', *JTS*, L, 177.

Review: *Le Nouveau Psautier Latin* (A. Bea), *Erasmus*, II (Amsterdam), cols. 451–4.

Review: *Tōrā in the Old Testament: A Semantic Study* (G. Östborn), *JJS*, I, 159 f.

Review: *Word and Wisdom: Studies in the Hypostatization of Divine Qualities and Functions in the Ancient Near East* (H. Ringgren), *ibid.* pp. 200 f.

Review: *Storia e Civiltà dei Semiti* (S. Moscati), *ibid.* p. 201.

Review: *Introduction to the Old Testament*, I (A. Bentzen), *ibid.* pp. 201 f.

1950

Editor: *Essays and Studies Presented to Stanley Arthur Cook* (*Cambridge Oriental Series*, no. 2, London).

'Select Bibliography of the Writings of Stanley Arthur Cook', *ibid.* pp. 1–13.

'Ostraca XIX–XXI from Tell ed-Duweir (Lachish)', *ibid.* pp. 51–8.

'לוחות לכיש', *Melilah*, III–IV, 55–66.

'The Age of Jeremiah in the Light of Recent Archaeological Discovery', *PEQ*, LXXXII, 1–15.

'Stanley Arthur Cook 1873–1949', *Proceedings of the British Academy*, XXXVI, 261–76.

Review: *Le prophète Isaïe* (J. Steinmann), *Erasmus*, III (Amsterdam), cols. 678–80.

Review: *Hebrew Union College Annual*, XXII, *JC*, 24 March, pp. 15, 23.

Review: *Studies in Old Testament Prophecy presented to Professor Theodore H. Robinson* (ed. H. H. Rowley), *ibid.* 16 June, pp. 15, 18.

Review: *Bulletin I of the Louis M. Rabinowitz Fund for the Exploration of Ancient Synagogues*, *ibid.* 3 November, p. 12.

Bibliography

1951

'The Textual Criticism of the Old Testament', *The Old Testament and Modern Study*, ed. H. H. Rowley (Oxford), pp. 238–63.

'Hebrew Language', *Oxford Junior Encyclopaedia*, IV, 183 f.

'Semitic Languages', *ibid.* p. 403.

'Mount Tabor: The Meaning of the Name', *VT*, I, 229 f.

Review: *Die Nachtgesichte des Sacharja* (L. G. Rignell), *JBL*, LXX, 337–9.

Review: *Joshua and Judges* (H. Freedman and J. J. Slotki), *JC*, 2 March, p. 10.

Review: *Studies in Koheleth* (H. L. Ginsberg), *JJS*, II, 159 f.

1952

'מלאו in Jeremiah 4: 5: A Military Term', *JJS*, III, 47–52.

'A Note on מוּעָדִים in Jeremiah 24: 1', *JTS*, N.S. III, 55.

'A Further Note on the Root מכר in Hebrew', *ibid.* p. 214.

'The Dead Sea Scrolls', *Theology*, LV, 321–4.

Review: *Chronicles* (I. W. Slotki), *JC*, 1 February, p. 12.

Review: *Cult and Canon: A Study in the Canonisation of the Old Testament* (G. Östborn), *JJS*, III, 91 f.

Review: *Théorie de l'emphase hébraïque* (E. Lemoine), *ibid.* pp. 136–8.

Review: *The Dead Sea Manual of Discipline* (W. H. Brownlee), *Theology*, LV (London), 115 f.

1953

'Ancient Hebrew Literature', *Literatures of the East, an Appreciation* (ed. E. B. Ceadel, Wisdom of the East Series, London), pp. 1–21.

'Note on בַּל־יָדְעָה in Proverbs 9: 13', *JTS*, N.S. IV, 23 f.

'A Consideration of Some Unusual Ways of Expressing the Superlative in Hebrew', *VT*, III, 209–24.

Review: *Text, Wortschatz und Begriffswelt des Buches Amos* (V. Maag), *JJS*, IV, 136–8.

Review: *The Zadokite Fragments and the Dead Sea Scrolls* (H. H. Rowley), *Theology*, LVI (London), 185 f.

Review: '*Gott erkennen*' im *Sprachgebrauch des Alten Testamentes* (G. J. Botterweck), *TLZ*, LXXVIII, cols. 97 f.

1954

'Bible Languages of the Old Testament', *The Bible* (June Supplement to *The Times*), p. 2.

'Note on לָדַעַת in Job 37: 7', *JTS*, N.S. v, 56 f.

Bibliography

Review: *Le prophète Jérémie* (J. Steinmann), *Erasmus*, VII (Amsterdam), cols. 8–10.

Review: *Le Cantique des Cantiques* (A. Feuillet), *ibid.* cols. 135–7.

Reviews: *Archaeology and the Religion of Israel* (3rd ed.) (W. F. Albright) and *The Zadokite Documents: (i) The Admonition; (ii) The Laws* (ed. C. Rabin), *JC*, 3 September, p. 16.

Review: *Australian Biblical Review*, I, II, *JJS*, V, 42–4.

Review: *Hebrew University Garland: A Silver Jubilee Symposium* (ed. N. Bentwich), *ibid.* pp. 90–2.

Review: *The Song of Songs: A Study, Modern Translation and Commentary* (R. Gordis), *JTS*, N.S. V, 234 f.

Review: *Der Traum im Alten Testament* (E. L. Ehrlich), *ibid.* pp. 236 f.

Review: *Babylonian and Assyrian Religion* (S. H. Hooke), *PEQ*, LXXXVI, 36 f.

Review: *Oudtestamentische Studiën*, X, *VT*, IV, 333–5.

1955

Editor (with M. Noth): *Wisdom in Israel and in the Ancient Near East presented to Professor Harold Henry Rowley* (*VTS*, III).

'Textual and Philological Notes on Some Passages in the Book of Proverbs', *ibid.* pp. 280–92.

'Zechariah 10: 11 a', *ET*, LXVI, 272 f.

'Some Remarks on the Hebrew Root ידע', *JJS*, VI, 50–2.

'Note on הַדָּעַת in Daniel 12: 4', *JTS*, N.S. VI, 226.

'The Language of the Old Testament', *The Teacher's Commentary* (rev. ed.), ed. G. Henton Davies and A. Richardson (London), pp. 98–104.

Review: אוצר המגילות הגנוזות (E. L. Subenik), *JC*, 9 September, p. 22.

Review: *The Universal Bible: The Pentateuchal Texts at First Addressed to All Nations* (*Torat B'nei No'ach*) (S. Schonfeld), *ibid.* 4 November, p. 16.

Review: *The Scrolls from the Dead Sea* (E. Wilson), *ibid.* 9 December, p. 20.

Review: *Australian Biblical Review*, III, *JJS*, VI, 56 f.

Review: *Opuscules d'un hébraïsant* (P. Humbert), *JSS*, IV, 382–4.

Review: *Die Klagelieder, übersetzt und erklärt* (H. Wiesmann), *JTS*, N.S. VI, 126–8.

Review: *Studies in the Book of Lamentations* (N. K. Gottwald), *ibid.* pp. 262–5.

1956

'Haggai', *The Interpreter's Bible*, VI (New York), pp. 1037–49.

Bibliography

'Zechariah 1–8', *ibid.* pp. 1053–88.

'The Use of נֶצַח as a Superlative in Hebrew', *JSS*, I, 106–9.

'Note on נוֹעֲדוּ in Amos 3: 3', *JTS*, N.S. VII, 69 f.

Review: *Journal of Semitic Studies*, I, 1, *ET*, LXVII, 203.

Review: *Canaanite Myths and Legends* (G. R. Driver), *ibid.* pp. 358 f.

Review: *A Striking Hymn from the Dead Sea Scrolls* (M. Wallenstein), *JC*, 31 August, p. 16.

Reviews: *The Dead Sea Scrolls* (M. Burrows), *The Qumran Community: its History and Scrolls* (C. T. Fritsch), *The Dead Sea Scrolls* (J. M. Allegro), *The Meaning of the Dead Sea Scrolls* (A. P. Davies), *ibid.* 5 October, p. 16.

Review: *Australian Biblical Review*, IV, *JJS*, VII, 128–30.

Review: *Chronikbücher* (W. Rudolph), *JSS*, I, 72–4.

Review: *Hebrew Grammar and Grammarians Throughout the Ages* (D. Mierowsky), *ibid.* pp. 174 f.

Review: *Studies in the Traditions of the Hebrew Language* (Z. Ben-Ḥayyim), *ibid.* pp. 175 f.

Review: *Teach Yourself Hebrew* (R. K. Harrison), *ibid.* p. 176.

Review: *Cinquante années de recherches linguistiques, ethnographiques, sociologiques, critiques et pédagogiques* (M. Cohen), *ibid.* pp. 279 f.

Review: *Discoveries in the Judaean Desert*, I (D. Barthélemy and J. T. Milik), *ibid.* pp. 280–3.

Review: Hollenberg-Budde's *Hebräisches Schulbuch* (21st ed.: W. Baumgartner), *ibid.* p. 404.

Review: *A Study of the Language of the Biblical Psalms* (M. Tsevat), *JTS*, N.S. VII, 88–90.

1957

'Some Observations on the Hebrew Root חדל', *VTS*, IV, 8–16.

Review: *The Hebrew Scripts* (S. A. Birnbaum), *BSOAS*, XIX, 169 f.

Review: *The Scriptures of the Dead Sea Sect* (T. H. Gaster), *JC*, 14 June, p. 21.

Review: *Australian Biblical Review*, V, nos. 1–2, *JJS*, VIII, 126 f.

Review: *Saadia Gaon, The Earliest Hebrew Grammarian* (S. L. Skoss), *JSS*, II, 211 f.

Review: *Atlas of the Bible* (L. H. Grollenberg), *ibid.* pp. 281–3.

Review: *Hebräische Syntax* (C. Brockelmann), *ibid.* pp. 389–91.

Review: *Étude descriptive et comparative du Gafat (Éthiopien méridional)* (W. Leslau), *ibid.* pp. 391 f.

Review: *Hebrew Union College Annual*, XXVII, *ibid.* pp. 404–7.

Review: *Klagelieder (Threni)* (H.-J. Kraus), *JTS*, N.S. VIII, 138–40.

Bibliography

1958

The Hebrew Bible since Claude Montefiore (Claude Montefiore Centenary Lecture, London).

Editor: *Documents from Old Testament Times* (London).

'Letters from Lachish', *ibid.* pp. 212–17.

'Again "The Prophet" in the Lachish Ostraca', *Von Ugarit nach Qumran (Festschrift für Otto Eissfeldt)*, eds. J. Hempel and L. Rost (Berlin), pp. 244–9.

Review: *Samaria: The Capital of the Kingdom of Israel* and *Babylon and the Old Testament* (A. Parrot), *The Excavations at Qumrân: A Survey of the Judaean Brotherhood and its Ideas* (J. van der Ploeg), *JC*, 22 August, p. 22.

Review: *Scripta Hierosolymitana*, IV (eds. C. Rabin and Y. Yadin), *ibid.* 31 October, p. 28.

Review: *Australian Biblical Review*, VI, *JJS*, IX, 193 f.

Review: *Classical Hebrew Composition* (J. Weingreen), *JSS*, III, 178f.

Review: *L'Ancien Testament et L'Orient. Études présentées aux VIes Journées Bibliques de Louvain (11–13 Septembre 1954)*, *ibid.* pp. 186–9.

Review: *Chi furono i Semiti?* (S. Moscati), *ibid.* pp. 215–17.

Review: *Ancient Semitic Civilisations* (S. Moscati), *ibid.* p. 390.

Shorter Notice: *Australian Biblical Review*, V, nos. 3–4, *JJS*, IX, 110.

1959

'The Dead Sea Scrolls', *Antiquity*, XXXIII (Cambridge), 189–94.

'Cook, Stanley Arthur', *The Dictionary of National Biography*, pp. 174f.

Review: *The Dead Sea Community: Its Origin and Teaching* (K. Schubert), *The Church of England Newspaper*, 27 November, p. 15.

Review: *Hebrew Bible* (N. H. Snaith), *ET*, LXX, 234 f.

Review: *Ten Years of Discovery in the Wilderness of Judaea* (J. T. Milik), *JC*, 13 March, p. 27.

Review: *The People of the Dead Sea Scrolls* (J. M. Allegro), *ibid.* 29 May, p. 24.

1960

'A Note on וְנוֹדַע לָכֶם in 1 Samuel 6: 3', *JTS*, N.S. XI, 52.

'The Worship of God', *The Listener*, 4 August, pp. 179 f.

'*Kelebh* "Dog": its Origin and Some Usages of it in the Old Testament', *VT*, X, 410–27.

'The LXX's Rendering of שנות לב טוב in Ecclus. 33: 13', *ibid.* p. 456.

Bibliography

Review: *Light from the Ancient Past* (2nd. ed.) (J. Finegan), *JC,*
16 September, p. 16.
Review: *The Treasure of the Copper Scroll* (J. M. Allegro), *ibid.* 18
November, p. 25.
Review: *Australian Biblical Review,* VII, *JJS,* XI, 79 f.
Review: *Text and Language in Bible and Qumran* (M. H. Goshen-
Gottstein), *ibid.* pp. 187–90.
Review: *Les Inscriptions araméennes de Sifré (Stèles I et II)* (A. Dupont-
Sommer), *JSS,* V, 281–4.
Review: *The Bible in Aramaic.* i. *The Pentateuch according to Targum
Onkelos* (ed. A. Sperber), *ibid.* pp. 286–8.
Review: *The Bible in Aramaic.* ii. *The Former Prophets according to
Targum Jonathan* (ed. A. Sperber), *ibid.* pp. 430 f.
Review: *Festschrift Friedrich Baumgärtel zum 70. Gerburtstag 14. Januar
1958 gewidmet von den Mitarbeitern am Kommentar zum Alten
Testament* (J. Herrmann and L. Rost), *JTS,* N.S. XI, 356–60.

1961

'The Sixth Century B.C.: A Creative Epoch in the History of Israel',
JSS, VI, 33–46.
'Psalm 35: 15 f.', *JTS,* N.S. XII, 50 f.
'Robinson, Theodore Henry', *RGG,* V, cols. 1131 f.
'Rowley, Harold Henry', *ibid.* col. 1204.
Review: *The Dead Sea Scrolls* (R. K. Harrison), *JC,* 28 July, p. 18.
Review: *Cyrus the Great* (H. Lamb), *ibid.* 1 December (Quarterly
Supplement), p. iii.
Review: *The Cairo Geniza* (2nd ed.) (P. E. Kahle), *JSS,* VI, 116–18.
Review: *Materials for a Non-Masoretic Hebrew Grammar. II. An
Etymological Vocabulary to the Samaritan Pentateuch* (A. Murtonen),
ibid. pp. 273–5.
Review: *Le Cantique des Cantiques: Poème d'amour mué en écrit de sagesse*
(J. Winandy), *JTS,* N.S. XII, 312.

1962

'Micah', *Peake's Commentary on the Bible* (revised), eds. M. Black and
H. H. Rowley (London), pp. 630–4.
'ḤDL-II in Hebrew', *CBQ,* XXIV, 154.
'A Pun on the Name Ashdod in Zephaniah 2: 4', *ET,* LXXIV, 63
'צַלְמָ֫וֶת in the Old Testament', *JSS,* VII, 191–200.
'A Lost Hebrew Word in Isaiah 2: 6', *JTS,* N.S. XIII, 323 f.
'Tetragramm', *RGG,* VI, col. 703.
'אַ֫י in Proverbs 31: 4', *VT,* XII, 499 f.

Bibliography

Review: *Introduction to the Law of the Aramaic Papyri* (R. Yaron), *JC*, 9 March, p. 26.

Review: *Scripta Hierosolymitana*, VIII (ed. C. Rabin), *ibid.* 4 May, p. 24.

Review: *The Crescent and the Bull* (E. Zehren), *ibid.* 23 November, p. 24.

Review: *Discoveries in the Judaean Desert*, II (P. Benoit, J. T. Milik and R. de Vaux), *JSS*, VII, 129–31.

Review: *Linguistica Semitica: Presente e Futuro* (ed. G. Levi Della Vida), *ibid.* pp. 142 f.

1963

The Text of the Revised Psalter (London).

Editor (with W. D. McHardy): *Hebrew and Semitic Studies presented to Godfrey Rolles Driver* (Oxford).

'בְּלִיַּעַל in the Old Testament', *Biblical and Patristic Studies in memory of Robert Pierce Casey*, eds. J. N. Birdsall and R. W. Thomson (Fredburg), pp. 11–19.

'A Note on דַּעַת in Proverbs 22: 12', *JTS*, N.S. XIV, 93 f.

'Translating the Psalms', *St Catharine's Society Magazine* (Cambridge), pp. 69–73.

'The Revised Psalter', *Theology*, LXVI (London), 504–7.

'The Text of Jesaia 2: 6 and the Word שׂפק', *ZAW*, N.F. XXXIV, 88–90.

Review: *The Hebrew Passover from the Earliest Times to A.D. 70* (J. B. Segal), *BSOAS*, XXVI, 652 f.

Review: *L'Ancien Testament dans L'Eglise* (S. Amsler), *Erasmus*, XV (Amsterdam), cols. 707–11.

Review: *Moses and Monarchy: A Study in the Biblical Tradition of Moses* (J. R. Porter), *ET*, LXXIV, 365.

Review: *The Torah: The Five First Books of Moses*, *ibid.* LXXV, 10.

Review: *An Introductory Hebrew Grammar* (A. B. Davidson: revised J. Mauchline), *Modern Churchman*, VI (Oxford), 251 f.

Review: *The Judean Scrolls and Karaism* (N. Wieder), *JC*, 7 June, p. 19.

Review: *Before the Bible: The Common Background of Greek and Hebrew Civilisations* (C. H. Gordon), *ibid.* 11 January, p. 20.

Review: *Discoveries in the Judaean Desert*, III (M. Baillet, J. T. Milik and R. de Vaux), *JSS*, VIII, 268–71.

1964

'נִצָּב in Psalm 39: 6', *Studies in the Bible presented to Professor M. H. Segal*, eds. J. M. Grintz and J. Liver (Jerusalem), pp. 10*–16*.

'Proverbs 20: 26', *JJS*, XV, 155 f.

Bibliography

'Additional Notes on the Root ידע in Hebrew', *JTS*, N.S. xv, 54–7.
'The Meaning of חַטָּאת in Proverbs 10: 16', *ibid.* pp. 295 f.
'Job 40: 29 b: Text and Translation', *VT*, xiv, 114–16.
'Driver, Samuel Rolles', *EB*, vii, 696.
'Smith, William Robertson', *ibid.* xx, 836.
Review: *The Theology of the Samaritans* (J. Macdonald), *ET*, lxxvi, 79 f.
Review: *The Problem of 'Curse' in the Hebrew Bible* (H. C. Brichto), *JJS*, xv, 161–3.
Review: *The Bible in Aramaic.* iii. *The Latter Prophets according to Targum Jonathan* (ed. A. Sperber), *JSS*, ix, 379.
Short Notice: *Sprüche Salomos* (B. Gemser), *JTS*, N.S. xv, 241.

1965

'The Meaning of זִיז in Psalm 80: 14', *ET*, lxxvi, 385.
'Hebrew עֲנִי "Captivity"', *JTS*, N.S. xvi, 444 f.
'Notes on Some Passages in the Book of Proverbs', *VT*, xv, 271–9.
Review: *The Canaanites* (J. Gray), *ET*, lxxvi, 117.
Review: *Shechem, The Biography of a Biblical City* (G. E. Wright), *ibid.* pp. 385 f.
Review: *Men of God: Studies in Old Testament History and Prophecy* (H. H. Rowley), *JSS*, x, 86–8.
Review: *Der Prediger, Hebräisch und Deutsch* (R. Kroeber), *JTS*, N.S. xvi, 151–3.

1966

'Translating Hebrew 'ĀSĀH', *The Bible Translator*, xvii (London), 190–3.
'The Dead Sea Scrolls', *St Catharine's Society Magazine* (Cambridge), pp. 63–6.
'Sgroliau'r Mor Marw', *Y Cymro*, 13 October, p. 19.
Review: *Illustrations of Old Testament History* (R. D. Barnett), *JC*, 15 July, p. 20.
Review: *Irony in the Old Testament* (E. M. Good), *ibid.* 2 September, p. 23.
Review: *Israel unter den Völkern. Die Stellung der klassischen Propheten des 8. Jahrhunderts v. Chr. zur Aussenpolitik der Könige von Israel und Juda* (H. Donner) (*VTS*, xi), *JSS*, xi, 107–9.
Review: *Mélanges Eugène Tisserant*, *JTS*, N.S. xvi, 115–17.

Bibliography

1967

Understanding the Old Testament (Ethel M. Wood Lecture, London).
Editor: *Archaeology and Old Testament Study* (Oxford).
'Some Observations on the Hebrew Word רַעֲנָן', *Hebräische Wort-forschung* (Festschrift für Walter Baumgartner) (eds. B. Hart-mann *et al.*) (*VTS*, xvi), 387–97.
'A Note on the Hebrew Text of Isaiah 41 : 27', *JTS*, N.S. xviii, 127 f.
Review: *The Land of the Bible: A Historical Geography* (Y. Aharoni), *JC*, 31 March, p. 26.
Review: *Amorites and Canaanites* (K. M. Kenyon), *JTS*, N.S. xviii, 163 f.

1968

'A Consideration of Isaiah 53 in the Light of Recent Textual and Philological Study', *Ephemerides Theologicae Lovanienses*, xliv, 79–86.
'A Note on דְּרָכִים in Isaiah 49: 9b', *JTS*, N.S. xix, 203 f.
'Some Further Remarks on Unusual Ways of Expressing the Super-lative in Hebrew', *VT*, xviii, 120–4.
'A Note on זְרַמְתָּם שֵׁנָה יִהְיוּ in Psalm 90: 5', *ibid.* pp. 267 f.

To appear

'Jesaia', *BH* (4th ed.)
'"A Drop of a Bucket?". Some Observations on the Hebrew Text of Isaiah 40: 15', *In Memoriam Paul Kahle* (eds. M. Black and G. Fohrer) (*BZAW*, ciii), 194–201.

14 June 1968

INDEX OF REFERENCES

APOCRYPHA

QUMRAN WRITINGS

Index of References